HITLER'S
LOST STATE

Tim Heath
For my grandmother, Kath, with fond memories which now seem so long ago.

Michela Cocolin
In liebevoller Erinnerung an meine Mutti, Elke, und Omi, Luise, die am 30.01.1945 die Heimat verlassen mussten.

In loving memory of my mother, Elke, and grandmother, Luise, who had to leave their homeland on 30.01.1945.

HITLER'S LOST STATE

THE FALL OF PRUSSIA AND THE WILHELM GUSTLOFF TRAGEDY

TIM HEATH AND MICHELA COCOLIN

Pen & Sword
MILITARY

AN IMPRINT OF PEN & SWORD BOOKS LTD.
YORKSHIRE – PHILADELPHIA

First published in Great Britain in 2020 by
PEN AND SWORD MILITARY
An imprint of
Pen & Sword Books Ltd
Yorkshire – Philadelphia

Copyright © Tim Heath and Michela Cocolin, 2020

ISBN 978 1 52675 610 7

The right of Tim Heath and Michela Cocolin to be identified as Authors of this work has been asserted by them in accordance with the Copyright, Designs and Patents Act 1988.

A CIP catalogue record for this book is available from the British Library.

All rights reserved. No part of this book may be reproduced or transmitted in any form or by any means, electronic or mechanical including photocopying, recording or by any information storage and retrieval system, without permission from the Publisher in writing.

Typeset in Times New Roman 11.5/14 by
SJmagic DESIGN SERVICES, India.
Printed and bound in the UK by TJ Books Ltd.

Pen & Sword Books Limited incorporates the imprints of Atlas, Archaeology, Aviation, Discovery, Family History, Fiction, History, Maritime, Military, Military Classics, Politics, Select, Transport, True Crime, Air World, Frontline Publishing, Leo Cooper, Remember When, Seaforth Publishing, The Praetorian Press, Wharncliffe Local History, Wharncliffe Transport, Wharncliffe True Crime and White Owl.

For a complete list of Pen & Sword titles please contact
PEN & SWORD BOOKS LIMITED
47 Church Street, Barnsley, South Yorkshire, S70 2AS, England
E-mail: enquiries@pen-and-sword.co.uk
Website: www.pen-and-sword.co.uk

Or

PEN AND SWORD BOOKS
1950 Lawrence Rd, Havertown, PA 19083, USA
E-mail: Uspen-and-sword@casematepublishers.com
Website: www.penandswordbooks.com

Contents

Introduction vi

Chapter 1	Prussia: Birth of a European Power 1
Chapter 2	The First World War 12
Chapter 3	1918–1933: The Descent into Madness 29
Chapter 4	Black Aurora 38
Chapter 5	By a Cursed Hand 54
Chapter 6	The Minority Nightmare 67
Chapter 7	Resisting Evil 88
Chapter 8	Blood and Fire 107
Chapter 9	Harbour of Hope 124
Chapter 10	The Cruellest Night 136
Chapter 11	A Tale of Two Lost Cities 152
Chapter 12	Nemesis at Potsdam 167

Afterword 176

Acknowledgements 178

Bibliography 179

Introduction

It was in August 2018 when I received an email via Claire Hopkins, my Commissioning Editor at Pen & Sword Books, that the synopsis for *Hitler's Lost State* had been approved. I was busy adding the final narratives to my fifth book, *Hitler's Housewives*. For a while I had thought about co-writing a book, but the idea somehow never materialised. My co-author, Michela, had made contact with me through the *Hitler's Girls – Doves Amongst Eagles* social media page. From the conversations that followed, including some fascinating revelations regarding Michela's Italian/German ancestry, it instantly occurred to me that here was an individual who I could comfortably work with in the co-authorship sense.

Initially, Michela offered me the freedom of her entire family archive to formulate a book. It was then that I suggested she co-author the project with me. This would be my sixth foray into the dark spheres of both the Second World War and the Third Reich, and it would be Michela's first. I had every confidence that between us we could produce a work charting a useful portion of the history of East and West Prussia, utilising, as much as possible, previously unpublished material from those who witnessed the events. Neither of us were under any illusion as to the substantial nature of the project we were about to undertake. It was with the title *Hitler's Lost State*, which was penned by Michela, that we began to formulate the book. The subtitle, *The Fall of Prussia and the Wilhelm Gustloff Tragedy*, may appear somewhat long-winded and a little at odds with the main title, but many historians will understand the inexorable link that the two historical facets possess.

The German colonies of East and West Prussia, especially during the Third Reich era, appear largely forgotten by military historians since the end of the Second World War. Viewed largely as an agricultural utopia and pseudo universe within the Nazi state, it is often the view that both

Introduction

East and West Prussia had remained relatively untouched by war. Yet all of the violence, prejudice and murder, combined with the political/social interferences that one commonly associates with National Socialism, were present and active throughout the state's existence.

The close proximity of their enemies in the east meant that the very survival of East and West Prussia depended totally on a Nazi victory, particularly in the war being fought against Germany's ideological enemy of Soviet Russia. As Germany's military fortunes began to falter in the campaign against Russia in the east, it soon became clear that both East and West Prussia would inevitably fall to a hated enemy.

The cruise ship *Wilhelm Gustloff*, which was launched by Adolf Hitler himself on 5 May 1937, had originally been intended to be named the Führer. Constructed at a cost of twenty-five million Reichsmarks for the *Deutscher Arbeitsfront* (DAF/German Labour Front) and used by its subsidiary organisation, the *Kraft Durch Freude* (KDF/Strength through Joy), she had a relatively unremarkable career until her requisitioning by the German *Kriegsmarine* (Navy) in 1939. It was the *Wilhelm Gustloff* that transported home the victorious German military personnel of the Condor Legion, which had aided Fascist dictator General Franco secure victory in Spain. From there the *Wilhelm Gustloff* served as a hospital ship and floating barracks for the German military.

From the moment Nazi Germany began to lose its grip on its conquered territories in the East, the fates of East and West Prussia, along with the *Wilhelm Gustloff*, were sealed. Under Operation Hannibal the *Wilhelm Gustloff* was one of the ships sent to help the evacuation of German troops and civilians from areas such as Courland, East Prussia and Danzig, West Prussia. Many Germans had already witnessed the brutality of the Red Army during the massacres at Nemmersdorf and Metgethen. Many committed suicide in order to avoid such brutality.

At 9.16pm on 30 January 1945 the Russian submarine S-13 fired three torpedoes into the *Wilhelm Gustloff*, which was packed with 10,582 passengers. Just sixty minutes after the torpedoes had struck her, the ship sank beneath the dark, icy waters of the Baltic Sea. Some 9,343 passengers – around 5,000 of them children – perished in some of the most harrowing scenes ever recorded in a maritime disaster, yet the *Wilhelm Gustloff* remains a name unknown to a great many. Both Michela and I are hoping this book will add some balance to the events in East and West Prussia and their links with the greatest disaster in maritime history.

Michela's heart is particularly close to the tragedy. As her then five-year-old mother, Elke Gerns, and forty-one-year-old grandmother, Luise Gerns, fled Danzig from the approaching Red Army, with columns of terrified German refugees trying to board a train heading for the port of Gotenhafen (Gdynia), they became separated. In the chaos that reigned on the platform, somebody had helped the little girl onto the train, but the mother was stuck behind the hordes of people pushing to get on board. The young mother frantically cried out for her little daughter, trying to alert the conductor. Thankfully, just as the doors were shut ready for departure, a passenger, realising what had happened, managed to lower the carriage window and swiftly passed the child back to the mother. The incident, which may have ultimately saved their lives, delayed their arrival at Gotenhafen where hundreds of thousands of refugees had been flocking for days, hoping to get onto the ship that would take them to safety. By the morning of 30 January 1945 the *Wilhelm Gustloff* was full; in fact, overcrowded with more than five times her capacity. Despite having obtained passes for the *Gustloff*, they were assigned to a different ship of the *Gustloff Geleit* (escort). Had Michela's mother and grandmother not become separated at the train station there could have been a very different outcome to their ordeal.

This is, therefore, a project which has become very close to myself and Michela in terms of the scale of the tragedy brought about by war.

Chapter 1

Prussia: Birth of a European Power

During its relatively brief existence as a state within Europe, Prussia was subject to a volatile and complex history. Having been involved in conflicts with her neighbours since the 1600s, it is easy for Prussia to be construed as a warlike nation. She has also been blamed for planting the seeds of the two great conflicts of the twentieth century. Though this is subject to much debate by historians today, it has to be said that Prussia was once a powerful state that wielded much influence within the old Europe, reaching its zenith in the eighteenth and nineteenth centuries. It would not be possible in the context of this volume to document any detailed history of Prussia, but hopefully the following text will suffice in setting out a basic understanding.

Many have asked the question 'What is a Prussian?' Today the term 'Prussian' no longer relates to any specific ethnic group of people within the former state. It has often been the mistaken opinion that the peoples of Prussia were merely a hybrid race of Russians and Germans, but this is, of course, not the case. There were those who were referred to as 'old Prussians', referring to a race of Baltic people who were related to the modern Latvians and Lithuanians. However, they were little more than small tribal communities residing along the coastlines. These communities practiced paganism, often referred to as the 'Religion of the Peasantry'. During and after the Middle Ages the term pagan was used to describe any non-Abrahamic or unfamiliar religious practice. There was also a general consensus of opinion that the practitioners of paganism possessed a belief in false gods and they were viewed as little more than heathens by the Holy Roman Empire. A full-scale invasion of Prussia and the Baltic region was carried out by the Teutonic Order in 1217, resulting in a victory for the crusaders. The Christianisation and Germanisation of the Prussian people thus began to be instituted.

The Teutonic Order's interest in Prussia goes back to Konrad I of Masovia who gave the Teutonic Order an opportunity to set up its own stronghold within Europe. Konrad I was involved in fighting his own expansionist wars in the adjacent pagan territory of the Prussians. His military endeavours in the region were producing little in the way of results. Frustrated by the Prussian presence, which threatened the security of his own residence of Plock Castle, he enlisted the services of the knights of the Teutonic Order. They agreed to Konrad's request, on condition that the territory around the frontier town of Kulm be gifted as recompense.

After almost fifty years of brutal warfare the Teutonic Order was successful in defeating Prussia and effectively ruled the state under charters issued by the Pope and Holy Roman Empire. The implications of this were complex and in turn created a power struggle on the Baltic frontier between various European and Eurasian factions, including the Lithuanians, Russians, Livonians (comprising Estonia and Latvia), Sweden, Catholic Poland and even the Golden Horde Mongols and Tatars.

The Teutonic Order bore close similarities to the Crusader orders such as the formidable Knights Templar and Hospitallers. It was controlled by the High Masters within the upper echelons of its administrative power. These were accompanied by representatives of the administrative provinces along with five other senior officers within the order whose titles ranged from treasurer and supreme marshal to supreme draper. The Teutonic Order was subject to very stringent disciplinary measures along with monastic vows. Only after these vows were given was a member of the order permitted to marry.

The demise of the Teutonic Order came about with the death of Ulrich von Jungingen in the Battle of Grunwald, which was fought on 15 July 1410. As a result of this defeat most of the leadership of the order were hunted down and killed, with many others being taken prisoner. The Teutonic Order would never recover their former status. The financial burdens created by war reparations caused internal conflicts within the order and an economic downturn in the lands under their control. The Battle of Grunwald undoubtedly shifted the balance of power within Central and Eastern Europe and marked the rise of the Polish-Lithuanian Union as the dominant political and military force in the region.

After Prussia's incorporation into the Holy Roman Empire large numbers of settlers of Germanic origin began to arrive in the region.

Prussia: Birth of a European Power

Those who termed themselves as 'old Prussians' thrived in the rural parts of the region up until the eighteenth century when the dwindling population became assimilated into Germany and Lithuania.

From the demise of the Holy Roman Empire a number of German republics, kingdoms and empires were spawned, the two largest being the Austrian Empire in the south and the kingdom of Prussia in the north, both of which were mainly made up of German-speaking peoples.

The Prussian military's reputation as one of the most effective fighting forces in Europe is no historical exaggeration. Though initially only a supporting element in many of the early military campaigns, by the time of the Silesian wars of the eighteenth century she had developed a significantly more independent role.

It has to be said that under Frederick William I (1713–1740) the Prussian army was moulded into a professional force not unlike that of a modern-day army. Frederick understood that any large army required strong, skilled and competent leadership if it were to be effective in battle, and in 1716 he instituted the first Prussian military cadet school. At the time of its creation the cadet school was only open to candidates belonging to the Prussian aristocracy, then, in 1733, a conscription system was introduced. This system divided Prussia into small regions comprising approximately 5,000 households each, with every available able-bodied male member of each household becoming a potential army recruit. This meant that Prussia would soon possess the fourth largest army in Europe.

No army, however large, would have been effective without strategy and discipline. Three key factors were introduced during Frederick's rule. The first one was an iron ramrod for the Prussian army's standard muzzle-loading weapon. Experience had proved that the previous wooden ramrods were woefully inadequate under battle conditions as they tended to break, which in turn had an adverse effect on firepower for an infantryman. The second factor was that each rifleman of Frederick's army was relentlessly drilled to fire six shots per minute. Such a rate of fire with the muzzle-loading rifle of the day was impossible. Even the most skilled of riflemen could not hope to achieve this rate under the stresses of battle. Yet it did ensure that in battle Prussian riflemen would fire a greater volume of musket balls than their enemy. The third factor was the marching technique known as the military goosestep, which was found to be highly advantageous on the battlefield of the eighteenth and nineteenth centuries. Adopted in the 1740s, the goosestep style of marching ensured a higher degree of cohesion in battle. It was also beneficial to officers and commanders in the field as it enabled a higher degree of tactical control over their forces. Individually these three key components may not appear to possess any great relevance, but combined they would serve the Prussian army well.

The introduction of a cavalry arm into the Prussian military was also to prove a vital factor in its success. The Prussian cavalry regarded themselves as an elite force, which indeed they were. They acted as a form of shock force and these highly efficient mounted soldiers struck fear into their enemies. The mere thought of a Prussian cavalry charge bearing down on you, the thunderous noise of this sabre-wielding mass scything anything down in its path, would often be enough for many an enemy soldier to question his own bravery. The Prussian cavalrymen wore the insignia of the *totenkopf* or 'death's head', an ominous precursor of things to come.

Upon Frederick the Great's (1740–1786) succession of Frederick William I, Prussia had at its disposal a well-equipped, well-trained and motivated army. The aristocracy were not only loyal but also accustomed to service and an efficient administration was in place. Prussia also possessed a large enough economy that no form of taxation or need for loans were required should a war suddenly become inevitable. Frederick the Great also insisted that he personally command his army in battle. He was without doubt one of the greatest military leaders in history and would achieve an almost mythical status in Nazi Third Reich histories. There is no doubt that Prussia's success as a nation could not have come to pass without either William Frederick I or Frederick the Great.

Prussia's army was not always successful in its military campaigns, however. It suffered a catastrophic defeat at the hands of Napoleon I of France in the Battle of Jena-Auerstedt, which was fought on 14 October 1806 on the plateau west of the river Saale in what is modern-day Germany. The Prussians under Frederick William III suffered a decisive defeat, with 38,000 dead, wounded and captured. This resulted in the subjugation of the Kingdom of Prussia to Napoleon until the War of the Sixth Coalition, which lasted from March 1813 to May 1814, drove the French out.

By 1860 the Kingdom of Prussia was extensive, covering almost all of northern Germany and including Brandenburg, Hannover and

Schleswig-Holstein. Yet it was not a continuity of the old Prussian nation in the east. Any connection to the old Baltic Prussians was purely in name only.

Created by the Congress of Vienna in 1815, the German Confederation was an association of thirty-nine German-speaking states in Central Europe instituted with a view towards coordinating the individual economies of the separate German-speaking countries and to serve as a replacement for the former Holy Roman Empire, which had been dissolved in 1806. In the minds of many, the German Confederation plan was a good idea, but it was weakened by the rivalries between the Kingdom of Prussia and the Austrian Empire, the two leading powers within the confederation, as well as numerous other quarrels between member countries over their own political and economic issues.

In 1848 revolutions orchestrated by liberals and nationalists made an attempt to create a unified German state with a progressively liberal constitution under the Frankfurt Convention. The ruling body, the Confederate Diet, was dissolved on 12 July 1848, but reinstituted in 1850 after attempts at replacing it had failed.

Tension continued to build between the Austrian Empire and the Kingdom of Prussia until the outbreak of what became known as the Austro-Prussian War. This relatively brief conflict lasted for just one month and twelve days, from 14 June till 26 July 1866 (hence it also being referred to as the Seven Weeks War). In Germany it is known simply as the German War. Both sides were aided by allies within the confederation. Interestingly, Prussia had allied with the Kingdom of Italy thus linking this conflict to the Third Independence War of Italian Unification.

The end result of the Austro-Prussian War was a victory for Prussia and Italy, which for Prussia meant that it became the dominant power over the other German states. Prussian casualties are quoted at 28,793 total losses: of these 4,454 were deaths as a result of the actual fighting, 6,427 were due to disease, 16,217 wounded, 785 listed as missing and 910 captured. The consequences of the war were an obvious power shift among the German states away from Austria towards Prussian hegemony, and an impetus towards the unification of all of the northern German states in a *Kleindeutsches Reich* or 'Lesser Germany'; in other words Germany without Austria. It brought about the abolition of the German Confederation, ushering in its partial replacement by a North German

Confederation. This North German Confederation excluded Austria as well as other southern German states. The conflict also brought about the Italian annexation of the Austrian province of Venetia. A number of southern German states remained independent for a while until they too joined the North German Confederation, which was then renamed and proclaimed the German Empire of 1871. Germany was now unified, with the Prussian king as *kaiser* (emperor) following her victory over the French emperor, Napoleon III, in the Franco-Prussian War of 1870.

The Franco-Prussian War (19 July 1870 to 28 January 1871) was primarily the result of Prussian ambitions to extend German unification, along with the French paranoia over the shift in the balance of power in Europe if Prussia were to prevail. The French declaration of war was issued on 16 July 1870 and fighting began some three days later when French forces invaded German territory.

Some historians are of the opinion that Prussian chancellor Otto von Bismarck provoked the French to respond militarily in order to draw the independent German southern states into the alliance with the North German Confederation. Bismarck may well have exploited the situation to his own advantage. He must surely have recognised the potential for new German alliances to be made from this war with the French.

The German coalition mobilised its forces far more swiftly than the French had expected. The Germans rapidly invaded north-eastern France, fully exploiting their superior numbers, training, leadership and firepower. The Germans were particularly adept at utilising the modern technology of the day. The rail networks proved invaluable for transporting troops, weapons and artillery rapidly to wherever they were required. The end result was a decisive for the Prussian/German forces. They won a series of battles in eastern France culminating in the Siege of Metz and the Battle of Sedan, the latter taking place on 1–2 September 1870 and bringing about the capture of Emperor Napoleon III. The French suffered major casualities; some 17,000 troops were either killed or wounded in the battle with a further 21,000 captured. By the next day, 2 September, French Emperor Napoleon III ordered the white flag of surrender to be run up. The emperor then offered his own surrender. The deployment of Prussian military forces towards the Franco-Prussian war amounted to 1,494,412 men. Total casualties were listed at 144,642: 44,700 were killed, 89,732 wounded and 10,129 listed as missing or captured. The French had deployed 2,000,740 men and suffered 756,285 casualties: 138,871 were killed, 143,000 wounded and 474,414 were captured or interned. It also has to be noted that it is estimated that 250,000 civilians were killed as a result of the fighting.

Despite Napoleon's surrender, a defiant Government of National Defence declared a Third French Republic in Paris on 4 September, which dragged the war out unnecessarily for another five months. The German forces engaged and defeated the so-called new French armies in northern France following the Siege of Paris. The capital fell on 28 January 1871. This was followed by a revolutionary uprising called the Paris Commune, which seized power in the city and held it for two months until it was brutally suppressed by the regular French army at the end of May 1871.

The German states proclaimed their union as the German Empire under Prussian King Wilhelm I, finally uniting Germany as a one nation-state. The Treaty of Frankfurt of 10 May 1871 established the frontier between the French Third Republic and the German Empire. It also handed Germany most of Alsace and portions of Lorraine. French nationals in the Alsace-Lorraine region were given until 1 October 1872 to retain their French nationality and emigrate or remain in the region and become German citizens. The French were ordered to pay a war indemnity of some five billion francs, to be paid in full within five years.

Not only did the Franco-Prussian War bring about an end to French hegemony in continental Europe but it would also have ramifications for the French whose Second Empire had been crushed so decisively and skilfully by the Prussians and their coalition of German states. Even to this day it is a memory that evokes mixed emotions in the French people. For the Prussian/Germans the 2 September became *Sedantag* (Day of Sedan) and was celebrated every year until 1919, though the kaiser himself refused to declare the day as an official public holiday.

Kaiser Wilhelm II has become synonymous with Prussian/German history. Born on 27 January 1859 in Kronprinzenpalais, Berlin, in the kingdom of Prussia, Friedrich Wilhelm Viktor Albert was the eldest grandchild of Britain's Queen Victoria. Wilhelm II was the last German emperor and king of Prussia. He was related to many monarchs and princes of Europe, most notable of those being King George V of Britain and Emperor Nicholas II of Russia. Upon acceding the throne in 1888 he dismissed the chancellor Otto von Bismarck in 1890. Wilhelm II was also responsible for launching Germany on a bellicose 'New Course' in foreign affairs, which culminated in his support for Austria-Hungary in the July 1914 crisis that led to the outbreak of the First World War.

Wilhelm was often described as possessing a bombastic and impetuous attitude. This was a personality trait that would lead to many damaging personal blunders. He had a habit of making tactless pronouncements on sensitive topics without the consultation of his ministers, the most damaging of which was an interview which he granted to the *Daily Telegraph* in 1908, in the course of which he made wild statements along with remarks that would prove diplomatically counterproductive, not only for himself but also for Germany. Using the interview to promote his beliefs and ideas on Anglo-German friendship, his emotional outbursts ended up alienating not only the British but also the French, Russian and Japanese governments. Included in his interview were derogatory remarks on the attitude of Britain towards the Germans. He also implied that Germany cared little for the British, that the French and Russians had made attempts to incite Germany to intervene in the Second Boer War, and that the German naval build-up was targeted towards the Japanese and not Britain. Perhaps his most infamous comment during the interview was, 'You English are mad, mad, mad as March hares.' This quote alone had serious repercussions and certainly did not endear him to the German people, who called for his abdication. It is a sad irony of history that his abdication was not forced through. Had it been, the course of world history as we now know it may well have been very different.

In the wake of his disastrous *Daily Telegraph* piece Wilhelm was forced to keep a low profile on the political stage, though he would later exact his revenge on the chancellor, Prince Bulow, who he personally blamed for the *Daily Telegraph* fiasco. Wilhelm forced Bulow's resignation on the pretext that he failed to edit the newspaper transcript prior to its publication in Germany. Wilhelm was of the opinion that Bulow had abandoned him to face public scorn as a result of this misdemeanour. A once highly self-confident Wilhelm II soon drifted into severe depression, something that would blight his life thereafter. Much of the influence he once possessed in domestic and foreign policy was now lost. Personally ill-equipped to steer German foreign policy along a rational course, he was now subjugated and often partially encouraged by a German foreign policy elite that was, in a sense, responsible for many of the unorthodox decisions that Wilhelm made during his reign as king and emperor of Germany and Prussia.

It can be said that the First World War resulted, at least in part, from the arms race that existed between British and German empires from the last decade of the nineteenth century until the outbreak of hostilities in 1914. This arms race began with a plan by Admiral Alfred von Tirpitz in 1897 to create what was termed a 'fleet in being' to force the British into making diplomatic concessions. Tirpitz did not expect Imperial Germany to defeat the Royal Navy, but with the support of Wilhelm II, he had free rein in the passing of a series of new laws to building an increasing number of large warships. With the launch of the Royal Navy's HMS *Dreadnought* in 1906 Tirpitz was prompted to increase the construction rate of German warships.

Some British observers felt uneasy at the German naval expansion taking place, yet there were no real concerns until Germany's naval bill of 1908. The British public, along with political opposition, demanded that the Liberal government match the Germans, which resulted in the funding and construction of extra dreadnoughts in 1910.

Maintaining Europe's largest army and second largest navy took an enormous toll on Germany's finances. Chancellor Theobald von Bethmann-Hollweg introduced a policy of détente with Britain to alleviate the fiscal strain, thus focusing on the rivalry with France. Under Bethmann-Holweg, particularly from 1912 onwards, Germany abandoned the dreadnought arms race and instead focused on a commerce raiding naval strategy which would be carried out with submarines, or U-Boats as they became known. This latter strategy would prove most effective by the outbreak of the First World War and would be one of the primary naval strategies employed by Hitler in the Second World War.

It has been argued that Kaiser Wilhelm II did not actively seek war with the British or any of his European neighbours, and that he even made attempts to prevent his generals from mobilising the German army in the summer of 1914. Either way, his swaggering militaristic nature, his speeches and his ill-advised newspaper interviews had all cemented the universal opinion that Kaiser Wilhelm II was indeed a warlord in the making. Whether or not he was the puppet whose strings were being pulled by his military generals is now quite irrelevant: he could have used his influence to avoid Germany heading down the path to war.

Although many factors were responsible for bringing about war in 1914, the trigger for conflict is seen as the assassination of Archduke Franz Ferdinand and his wife. The archduke's wife, Sophie, Duchess of Hohenberg, was said to have been concerned for her husband's safety prior to their fateful trip to Sarajevo. It was for this reason that the duchess was accompanying her husband that day the 28 June 1914.

The Archduke Ferdinand was heir presumptive to the Austro-Hungarian throne. The assassin, Gavrilo Princip, was one of a group of six (five Serbs and one Bosnian) coordinated by Danilo Ilic, a Bosnia Serb and member of the Black Hand secret society. From a political point of view, the theory behind the assassination was to break off Austria-Hungary's southern Slavic provinces so they could be incorporated into Yugoslavia.

On that fateful day in Sarajevo security had been light. Local military commander General Michael von Appel had forwarded proposals to have troops line the intended route of the archduke's car. His concerns were dismissed on the belief that this would offend the loyal citizenry. In effect, protection for the visiting party lay in the hands of the Sarajevo police and only sixty officers were available for duty on that summer Sunday morning. The archduke's motorcade passed the first two assassins who both failed to act. Further along the route Illic had placed Nedeljko Cabrinovic, who stood on the opposite side of the street near the Miljacka river. Cabrinovic was armed with a single explosive device. At 10.10am, as the archduke's car drove past, Cabrinovic seized his chance and hurled the bomb which bounced off the folded-down back cover of the car and fell into the street. The bomb exploded beneath the car behind, putting it out of action and wounding sixteen to twenty people. Had it not been for the slight delay in the timed detonator the archduke and his wife would have undoubtedly been killed instantly in the explosion. Cabrinovic immediately swallowed a cyanide pill in an attempt at suicide before hurling himself into the river, but his suicide attempt failed as the pill he had swallowed only induced vomiting. The water that Cabrinovic fell into was also only some 13cm deep due to the hot dry summer. Cabrinovic was dragged from the river by police only to be set upon by an angry crowd. He was severely beaten before being taken away into police custody.

The archduke was visibly shaken by the attempt on his life. Arriving at the town hall for a scheduled reception, he interrupted a prepared speech of welcome by Mayor Fehim Curcic to protest: 'Mr Mayor, I came here on a visit and I am greeted by bombs. It is outrageous.' Duchess Sophie was seen whispering in her husband's ear, after which the archduke said 'now you may speak'. At 10.45am the archduke and his wife climbed back into their car with the intention of visiting the wounded bomb victims at the hospital instead of their planned programme. However, following the failure of the earlier assassination attempts, Princip decided to try to assassinate the archduke on his return journey. He took up position by a nearby food shop called Schillers Delicatessen near the Latin Bridge. At this point the archduke's motorcade turned off the Apel Quay, mistakenly following the original route which would have taken them to the National Museum. Governor Potiorek, who was in the second car with the imperial couple, shouted out to the driver to reverse and take the quay road to the hospital. The driver stopped close to where Princip was standing and the assassin seized his chance, stepping forward and firing two shots from a distance of 4ft with a 9mm calibre FN pistol. The first shot hit the archduke in the jugular vein and the second hit Duchess Sophie in the abdomen.

Princip was immediately arrested, later confiding that his intention had been to kill Governor Potiorek rather than Sophie. Both the archduke and duchess remained upright in their seats as they were driven to the governor's residence for treatment, but both died shortly after their arrival at the governor's home. The archduke's last words to his wife were 'Sophie, Sophie, don't die, live for our children.'

The assassination of Archduke Ferdinand and his wife caused shock and widespread outrage. After a series of events, Austria-Hungary declared war on Serbia, and Germany, as an ally of Austria-Hungary, soon followed suit. The seeds for one of the bloodiest wars in human history were planted in the wake of the assassination. It was a war of horrific proportions that would see the deaths of hundreds of thousands of men in a single day. It was a war that Gavrilo Princip, who fired those fatal shots on that summer's day in Sarajevo, would later feel wholly responsible for, later remarking, 'Had I known that my actions would lead to the deaths of so many people I would never have done it.'

The First World War would begin on 28 July 1914. Many were optimistic that it would be a short conflict and be over by Christmas that same year. Germany was confident of a rapid victory. Nobody could have imagined the sheer scale of the slaughter that awaited so many in the following four long years of war in Europe.

Chapter 2

The First World War

The series of events that followed the assassination of the Archduke Ferdinand and his wife in Sarajevo on 28 June 1914 set in motion a chain reaction to tragedy. The first country to declare war in 1914 was Austria-Hungary. Having issued an ultimatum to Serbia, which was effectively ignored, a declaration of war was announced on 28 July. As Austria-Hungary was a close ally of Germany it meant that German intervention was inevitable and war was declared in the name of the German Empire in support of her allies against Serbia.

The war would be fought on eastern and western fronts yet German territory remained relatively free from widespread enemy incursions, apart from a brief period in 1914 when East Prussia was invaded. From August to September 1914 Russian forces had been embattled in East Prussia. In 1914 the Russians had boasted that they could mobilise a peacetime army numbering some two million men. Russian Minister of War, A.V. Sukhomlinov, had already devised 'Plan 19', a series of detailed instructions for the launch of a Russian offensive into East Prussia in the event of a war with Germany. Its purpose was primarily to relieve pressure on Russia's ally, France, in the West.

Russia's armed forces at the time were not as badly equipped as contemporaries have suggested, yet their war effort in East Prussia was consistently hindered by faulty and inadequate communications and rivalries and jealousies amongst its officer corps, as well as poor planning and staff work. Russia's problems were further compounded by the decision to launch an additional offensive into Austrian Galicia, which meant that they would be dividing their forces between the northern and southern theatres. At the outbreak of war the tsar appointed Grand Duke Nicholas as commander-in-chief of the Russian armies, with General Yanushkevich as his chief of staff. Neither had any knowledge of the war plans that Sukhomlinov had drawn up. They were merely figureheads, with much of the military planning, such as it was, being organised by the Quartermaster General, General Danilov. General Yakov Zhilinkski was appointed commander of the front against Germany but was not on favourable terms with his army commanders and was frequently out of touch with developments on his front. Despite the Russians having superior manpower over the Germans, they had made the tactical error of spreading their forces too thinly over a wide area of the battlefront.

In response to desperate pleas from the French for a Russian advance into Germany to draw German forces away from the Western Front, Zhilinski ordered an offensive into East Prussia on 17 August. The Russian 1st Army, under the command of General Pavel Rennenkampf, with three corps, was to advance towards Königsberg, and the 2nd Army, led by General Aleksandr Samsonov, was to attack the Germans from the south-west. This division of his forces at the outset was due to the obstacle presented by the Masurian Lakes. Zhilinski, however, hoped that the two armies would soon join up on the coast at Königsberg. Rennenkampf advanced cautiously into East Prussia as a cat might when stalking a bird. The German 8th Army, under the command of General Max von Prittwitz, attempted to stem the advance at Gumbinnen on 20 August, but was brushed aside. Prittwitz appeared to lose his nerve and ordered his forces to retreat to the lower Vistula. As a result he was subsequently replaced by General Paul von Hindenburg and General Erich Ludendorff, who arrived at the 8th Army HQ at Marienburg on 23 August. Ludendorff adopted plans drawn up by the head of the operations department, Colonel Max Hoffmann, for a German counter-offensive in the south.

Samsonov's poorly provisioned force of 200,000 men had, meanwhile, moved slowly across the frontier in the direction of Allenstein. It would appear that Samsonov made little effort to maintain communication with Rennenkampfs army, which, by 26 August, had resumed its advance towards Königsberg. Ludendorf, who had heard of the Russian intentions from uncyphered wireless communications, decided to deal with Samsonov's army first. Utilising his superior railway network, Ludendorff concentrated the bulk of his resources against the Russian 2nd Army on the twenty-sixth Samsonov's forces were strung out along a sixty-mile-long front, and the German army tore into the exposed Russian forces near Tannenberg. By 30 Samsonov's army had been categorically defeated by the Germans and the Russian general felt he had no other option than to commit suicide. Fearing the retribution that was inevitably to come, he put a pistol in his mouth and squeezed the trigger.

Rennekampf, who had halted his advance, did little to aid Samsonov. His army were in fortified positions between the sea and the Masurian Lakes. Ludendorff, whose forces soon arrived at this front after defeating Samsonov, was able to exploit a Russian weak spot at the Loetzen Pass. The German breakthrough on the 9–10 September resulted in the collapse of Rennekampf's army, which, having already suffered 125,000 casualties, retreated in a state of complete disorder to the Nieman River with the Germans in close pursuit.

The Battle of Tannenberg, fought between 26 and 30 August 1914, was a fierce affair which resulted in the near complete annihilation of the Russian 2nd Army. A series of 'mop up' battles, including the First Battle of the Masurian Lakes, followed Tanneburg, wiping out most of the Russian 1st Army as well.

Tannenberg/Masurian Lakes was a brilliant German victory. East Prussia had been cleared of the Russian enemy in just a few days. However, a German advance into Russia was repulsed and in the ensuing battle the Germans lost 10,000 men, with the outcome of the battle proving inconclusive for both sides. It was a morale-sapping moment for the Germans who had suffered no serious setbacks militarily up until this point.

German NCO Karl Ludwig Wehrhaffen wrote his observations down in a small leather-bound diary his sister had given him before he left for the battlefront some six months earlier. In it he wrote a somewhat cryptic poetic note regarding the failed incursion into Russian territory:

> A fox might with all his stealth and cunningness sneak into a chicken pen and take all of the birds before it might be discovered, leaving behind only a trail of blood and feathers, by which time the guns and dogs which might pursue him would be nothing more than a distant hum, incapable of presenting anything of a threat to him. I feel we have been foxes caught in the gaze of the enemy's oil lamp. Their land is their chicken shed and we have been caught and bloodied. We are for the moment a beast now licking its wounds before anticipating the next move. History has taught us that

Napoleon amongst others had failed to capture this land. I hope this was the last of this land that I see. We as the foxes play a dangerous game!

Ludendorff's attention was distracted by the difficulties of his Austrian ally in Galicia. Conrad had decided to embark upon an offensive in this theatre, rather than remaining on the defensive along the San River, which is what the Germans had desired. Towards the end of August, three Austrian armies advanced from north-east Galicia in the direction of Warsaw and Brest-Litovsk.

Conrad planned to surround the Vistula fortress and occupy Russian Poland. Initially his advance proved successful, but the Austrian right flank ran into a Russian offensive in eastern Galicia and broke up before fleeing southwards. By 3 September General Alexei Brusilov's 8th Army had captured the Galician capial of Lemberg (Lviv). Conrad's left flank was in turn defeated at Rava Russka on 10 September.

By 11 September the Austrian armies were in full retreat on all fronts and were crossing the San. The Russians captured the Austrian fortress of Jaroslav and besieged Przemsyl, which was garrisoned by 150,000 Austrians. By mid-September Brusilov had driven the Austrians out of the Bukovina, reaching the Carpathian passes that guarded the plains of Hungary. During these battles the Austrians had 400,000 men killed, wounded or taken prisoner, while the Russians lost 250,000 men.

Ludendorff, in response to Conrad's appeals, was forced to send German reinforcements to assist his ally. In the latter part of September the German 9th Army was despatched from East Prussia to Breslau. Ludendorff had planned a new Austro-German offensive into Poland with the objective of capturing Warsaw. This offensive opened on 28 September, but the Russian high command had rather prudently withdrawn its forces from West Poland to the Vistula, in the hope of mounting a new counter-offensive.

Early in October the Austrians launched a counter attack in Galicia, driving the Russians beyond the San and relieving Przemysl on the 9 October. By the 12 October the German 9th Army had advanced rapidly and was around seven miles from Warsaw. In the south of this front, heavy fighting on the Vistula resulted in a Russian repulse, although the Russians managed to hold the area around Ivangorod. Conrad sent Austrian reinforcements to Ivangorod but these were defeated.

On 18 October the Russians launched a counter-offensive in Galicia, which forced the Austrians to retire from the San and retreat to Krakow. As a result Ludendorff ordered the 9th Army, in danger of being cut off, to abandon its efforts to take Warsaw.

The Russians did not pursue the retreating 9th Army with much effort; as a result this gave both Hindenburg and Ludendorff time to prepare a new offensive in north Poland. They requested that General Erich von Falkenhayn, the German Chief of Staff, send them reinforcements from the Western Front, but he refused to do so until December. Falkenhayn had more confidence in the staying power of the Russian armies than his Eastern Commanders. He was also convinced that a decisive defeat could be executed on the Entente's armies on the Yser River. Ludendorff concentrated General August von Mackensen's 9th Army at Thorn (Torun) in the north. He planned a southwards thrust to smash the Russian flank at Lodz, enabling the Germans to move to the north of Poland to capture Warsaw.

The German advance began on 11 November. The Russians were caught off guard and Mackensen broke through the Russian 2nd Army covering Lodz, forcing it to retreat into the city where its destruction was threatened by the encircling German armies. The Russian high command ordered Rennenkampf's 1st Army from the north to relieve the 2nd Army. From 18–25 November fierce fighting ensued and the 50,000-strong German 9th Army was trapped by the arrival in its rear of the Russian 5th Army from the south. The Germans escaped to the north. Heavy fighting continued for a month, when the arrival of reinforcements from the Western Front enabled the Germans to capture Lodz on 6 December and to advance around thirty miles. Strong Russian entrenchments, however, stopped the Germans from mounting any further progress until July 1915.

Walter Tullus, a twenty-three-year-old Corporal in the German army, wrote at the time:

> The Russian is a most hardy and stubborn of enemies. We give them no ground as they do not us. Men are cut to pieces as they rush forward across the ground between opposing lines. The deathly clatter of machine-guns, how their bullets tear off pieces of flesh and the bodies perform a morbid dance before they fall as if ragdolls to the ground.

The First World War

Every soldier fears the thunder that is artillery. Some shells are fused to explode in the sky above whilst others as they make contact with the ground. You can hear the shrapnel splinters whine as they are propelled outwards from the core of the explosion. If one of these splinters hits you it can tear off your arms, your legs and even your head. I watched a man hit by a shell splinter. The piece of red-hot steel passed clean through his chest and exited through his back, striking a man standing several yards behind him. It still retained sufficient velocity to inflict a second injury. Its second victim was more fortunate, suffering an arm injury which required just a bandage.

To take ground in this place is costly so we dig in and we dig deep and we wait. A snatch patrol went out a few nights ago. Their objective was to try and capture a Russian for intelligence purposes. They crawled out across the death zone of corpses and rotting flesh in the pitch darkness of night. They managed to capture a lone Russian, but he struggled violently as he was being dragged back towards our line. The Russian was punched hard in the face in the hope of rendering him unconscious. He continued to fight and, afraid his comrades might hear him cry out, they had no choice but to stab him to death. They stabbed him in the head to ensure a quick death and left his body where it was. The snatch patrol was severely reprimanded for not trying hard enough. No one really wants to volunteer for these tasks now.

Accounts such as the one described above were to become commonplace wherever the stalemate of entrenched warfare prevailed. Weather conditions also posed a great threat to both German and Russian forces in December 1914. The freezing weather brought with it the dreaded snow and ice and the scourge of trench foot became a real problem, occurring with varying degrees of severity. Keeping feet, socks and footwear dry was imperative in avoiding trench foot, but this was impossible in the prevailing conditions. Some of the worst cases were documented by medical staff behind the lines. One soldier complained that he could no longer feel his feet in his boots. His trench had filled with winter rain and when the freezing weather came snow and ice only added to the misery. The soldier's boots had to be cut from his feet by the medical staff and as his boots were removed they were horrified to find that most of the skin had literally rotted off the bones of his toes. Subsequently both feet had to be amputated at the ankles to prevent potentially life-threatening infection spreading further up his limbs.

There was considerable activity on the Carpathian front in January 1915, but neither side made much in the way of territorial gains. Here, Ludendorff, Hindenburg and Conrad agreed that a new offensive should be launched north of the Carpathians, between the Vistula and the San, in order to relieve the Russian pressure on Krakow, and remove the threat to Hungary. The Russian high command also ordered a new offensive in March 1915, with the intention of breaking through into the Hungarian plains, but the German offensive wrecked these plans. Mackensen's 9th Army of eight divisions, drawn largely from the Western Front, was to spearhead the assault, which was launched on 2 May at Gorlica-Tarnow. After a shattering German artillery bombardment, the Russian defences crumbled, and by the end of May the Russians had fallen back in confusion to the San and Dniestr rivers. The despatch of Russian reinforcements to this theatre was hindered by a German advance in the north through Kurland towards the Dvina River, with the objective of seizing Riga. By June the Russians had been pushed out of Galicia, apart from a small area in the east, which they held until 1917. Austro-German forces recaptured Lemberg on the twenty-second and Mackensen took Lublin and Kholm on 31 July. Warsaw fell on 4 August.

As the Russian forces made their retreat, they adopted a scorched earth policy, destroying anything that might be considered useful to the enemy. Even water sources were doused with gasoline or oil to deny the enemy fresh supplies. Much of the material considered useful was destroyed by burning, or in the case of buildings or structures, blown up with explosives. On 25 August, after bitter fighting, the Russians abandoned Brest-Litovsk, and with most of Russian Poland now under German control, Falkenhayn decided to halt further operations, his forces having advanced into Belorussia and captured Kovno in Lithuania on 17 August. In the face of these disasters, Nicholas II dismissed the Grand Duke Nicholas on 1 September, taking over personal command of the Russian armies and appointing as his chief of staff the weak, inept General Mikhail Alexeiev. This did not prevent the Austrians from capturing Lutsk at the end of

September, or the Germans from taking Vilna in the Baltic on 9 September, although this was the limit of the German advance on this front.

There was little further activity in the East between October 1915 and March 1916. As a result of these tremendous battles, Russia, whose forces heavily outnumbered those of her adversaries, had lost Poland and, between May and December 1915, had suffered losses of two million men, one million of whom became prisoners of war. The Russian army, although severely shaken, was far from being a broken force. In December 1915 Russian high command promised the Entente that they would launch a major offensive in the East in June 1916. Throughout the winter the Russians had managed to mobilise two million men, making successful efforts to increase armaments production in order to re-equip their armies.

The morale of the Russian army was undermined by its defeat at the hands of the German army at the Battle of Lake Naroch, east of Vilna, in March 1916, where it suffered losses of 100,000 men. The Russian high command, however, persisted with its plans for a summer campaign, which became even more urgent when the Italians appealed for Russian assistance in May after Conrad had launched his Trentino offensive. The energetic, capable commander of the Russian armies of the South-Western Army Group, General Alexei Brasilov, prepared for an assault by four armies along a 300-mile front in his sector. The objective was to take back Lutsk and Lemberg in Galicia and then advance into Bukovina, in the hope of encouraging Romania to join the Entente.

Brasilov began his offensive on 4 June and, at least initially, it proved a success. On 6 June the Austro-Hungarian armies at Lutsk collapsed and the Russians once again threatened Galicia. The Russian 7th Army entered Bukovina, reaching the Carpathians and the Romanian frontier by the end of June. Only the German centre at Tarnopol held. The Austro-Hungarian army was completely demoralised as a result of these Russian victories. On 2 July the Russian general, Evert, who commanded the Central Army Group, launched an attack towards Vilna, but his forces were beaten back, taking heavy casualties near Baranovichi. Brusilov continued his offensive in Galicia until the end of September, but was unable to exploit his initial successes when Ludendorff sent German reinforcements to bolster Austria's forces in Galicia. Between June and September fifteen German divisions were transferred to the East from the Western Front. Russia's offensives cost her a further one million casualties. As a result her army never recovered from the hefty sacrifices it had endured.

In 1917 the political and social climate in Russia had deteriorated to the point where a revolution in Petrograd led to the abdication of Tsar Nicholas II on 12 March, along with the establishment of a provisional government. The Entente had hoped that the new regime might inspire the Russian armies to prosecute the war more ruthlessly. This was indeed a vain hope as war weariness and severe lack of morale had infiltrated through the rank and file of the Russian military. The provisional government, however, could see no alternative other than to remain committed to the continuation of the war. Many army units were at the point of mutiny. Indiscipline and desertion were rife throughout the ranks and there was a growing opposition to any further bloodletting for the sake of the Entente. Inflation, along with widespread economic chaos, added to the mounting dissatisfaction against the war. The Russian Minister of War, Aleksandr Kerensky, appointed Brusilov as commander-in-chief of the Russian armies in an attempt to inspire troops with anti-German zeal. Brusilov managed to scrape together around 200,000 men for an offensive against the Austrians in Galicia, which opened up on 1 July. The Russians advanced into Galicia but were met by an Austro-German counter-offensive on 19 July, which forced them back across the frontier.

The internal political situation in Russia deteriorated even further when the Bolsheviks attempted an uprising in Petrograd in July. The uprising was crushed by Kerensky, who, for a brief period, was a virtual dictator. Kerensky appointed General Lavr Kornilov as commander-in-chief, but the latter attempted a coup d'état, which was foiled by Kerensky. In August, Ludendorff ordered a German offensive towards Riga, and although the Russians put up spirited resistance at first, the Germans broke through, threatening Riga and Petrograd. The Russian army disintegrated, and on 7 November (or 25 October using the old calendar) the Bolsheviks seized power in Petrograd, forcing Kerensky to flee from the Russian capital. The Bolsheviks signed an armistice with the Central Powers, and on 3 March 1918 the Germans and their allies exacted huge territorial gains from Russia at the Treaty of Brest-Litovsk.

The Russian departure from the First World War enabled Ludendorff to shift German forces from the East to the Western Front to reinforce his offensive there in March 1918. This came close to destroying the Entente armies. The Entente powers might protest at the perfidy of their former ally, but they had long since written off Russia as an effective military force in the East, despite the colossal sacrifices the Russians had made since the start of the war. The effectiveness of the Russian army had been severely blunted by the political and social chaos that erupted in Russia, the ineptitude, particularly among the officer corps, and the scant regard for the confidentiality of in-field communications, many of which were not encoded. The Russian soldiers, however, were never short on bravery, and the appallingly high casualty rates suffered by the Russian army are testimony to this fact.

During 1915, 1916 and 1917 Germany and the Allied powers were bleeding each other to death on the Western Front in France. Names such as Ypres, Verdun, the Somme and Passchendaele are now synonymous with the wholesale slaughter that would become the hallmark of the First World War. By February 1916 over 5,800,000 soldiers had been assembled on the Western Front. They were transported to the battlefronts by an endless stream of trains to the railheads, but once at the battlefront the problem of mobility soon became apparent as men, animals and machinery all fell victim to the siege warfare conditions that prevailed on the Western Front. Much of the ground resembled a lunar landscape having been torn apart by artillery fire, and when the rains came, shell craters and trenches filled with water. Artillery guns in particular were prone to sinking into the deep, strength-sapping mud. Having to fight in these awful conditions was a like living hell.

It was clear to the Allies that nothing other than the total defeat of the German army on the Western Front could secure victory, but 1915 had been a frustrating year for the Allies. This was blamed on the disconnected fashion in which the Allies up to that point had been conducting the war. It was clear to all that the solution to achieving victory and defeating the Germans lay in coordinated simultaneous actions as opposed to individual ones. And so 1916 was the year the Allies would attempt to bring forth an end to the war by combining their superior strength to bear all at once on their German enemy. The Germans, however, stole the initiative from the Allies. Falkenhayn concluded:

> The stress upon the French has almost reached breaking point. If we succeeded in opening the eyes of the French people to the fact that, in a military sense, they have nothing more to hope for, that breaking point would be reached.

> Within our reach behind the French sector of the Western Front there are objectives for the retention of which the French General Staff would be compelled to throw in every man they have. If they do so, the forces of France will bleed to death as there can be no question of a voluntary withdrawal whether we reach our goal or not.

Falkenhayn's decision to adopt the strategy of 'bleeding to death' would mark the beginning of the war of attrition, and the place he chose for this to begin was Verdun. The German blow fell on 21 February, taking the French high command completely by surprise. One of the reasons for this was largely due to the poor quality of the French intelligence. Verdun was to prove disastrous for the Allies and added a whole new dimension to the horrors of the First World War. This was the moment that the Germans fully exploited their artillery, subjecting the French defenders of Verdun to a devastating maelstrom of shell fire. During the course of the battle 1,000 shells fell to every square metre of ground. The Germans fielded a vast array of artillery, from lightweight 77-mm calibre field guns up to the heavy calibre mortars and naval guns of 420-mm calibre. The French described the German artillery assault as a hell beyond any description. A French Sergeant named Vincent Petau recorded his observations of the battle:

> We were forced to cower like rats trapped within a barrel. It seemed that a shell was landing on every single piece of ground around us. The noise I can only describe as being like a thousand thunderstorms rolled into one. I saw men driven to the point of insanity by the German bombardment. I was forced to drag one fellow back by the scruff of his greatcoat as he attempted to flee. He had been standing with his hands over his ears and I could see he was going to go crazy at some point. We had to restrain him with all our efforts. Had we not done so he would have climbed up and out of the trench to almost certain destruction in a rain of razor-sharp steel fragments. Was I afraid? Yes, I was terrified to the point where my inner thinking made me question my own loyalty. Your mind attempts to convince you that all of the wrong actions under such conditions are the right ones.

In the aftermath Verdun was a virtual wasteland: no woods, no fields, no roads, just shell craters, many of which were by now filled with putrid water. Many wounded men from both sides fell into these water-filled craters and, unable to escape, they drowned.

It was not until July that British pressure on the Somme caused the Germans to abandon their Verdun offensive. Through the summer and autumn the French went on the counter-attack, finally recapturing most of the territory they had lost. The losses on both sides totalled 976,000 men in ten months of fighting. The Germans had suffered almost as much as the French. At the close of the sixth month, Falkenhayn was replaced as chief of staff by Field Marshal Paul von Hindenburg, with General Erich Ludendorff as First Quartermaster General.

As the First World War dragged on, the British Expeditionary Force (BEF) had increased its strength to fifty-six divisions (one and a half million men). There was pressure on the British commander, Field Marshal Douglas Haig, to relieve the burden of Verdun. Haig was aware that his army, comprised largely of volunteers who had responded to Lord Kitchener's call in 1914–1915, was still unprepared for battle, and would have preferred to wait until August to commit this force, but on French insistence he gave in to the pressure and agreed that the Allied attack on the Somme should commence on 1 July 1916, day 132 of the Battle of Verdun. This would become a date etched into the British memory as much as the attack on Pearl Harbour would be etched into the memory of the Second World War.

The British opened the Battle of the Somme with a massive artillery bombardment. It was hoped that the bombardment would accomplish two major things: firstly, it was hoped that it would have a softening-up effect on the Germans; secondly, it was hoped that the maze of barbed wire entanglements strung out before the German lines would be destroyed, allowing the Allies to storm through to the enemy trenches. But the British had no idea how well prepared the Germans were. They had dug deep fortifications and trenches, and within the safety of these trenches the Germans simply waited out the intense Allied bombardment. The Allies were convinced that nothing could have survived such intense fire and so confidence was very high as the artillery fire dwindled and the Allied soldiers prepared to go 'over the top'. All along the Somme battlefront soldiers prepared for the whistle signal, bayonets fixed at the ready. As the whistles sounded the men clambered out from their trenches and began to advance towards the German lines. The Germans climbed out from their deep subterranean defences and busily set up their machine guns. German infantry and machine-gun crews began to fire on the advancing British soldiers who were cut to pieces in a hail of fire. The barbed wire entanglements were still largely intact despite the ferocity of the artillery bombardment. Men trying to fight their way through soon became snagged up and were easy prey for the German gunners. With German artillery pouring in support fire, the Somme became one of the worst bloodbaths in British military history. At the close of that fateful on 1 July 1916, some 57,000 British soldiers were killed or wounded.

Despite the catastrophe of the Somme, the British army would go no to inflict a major defeat on the Germans a few months later. It was the first step towards grinding down the enemy and ultimately bringing about the collapse of the German army. In September 1916 came the much-needed fully coordinated attack of the Russian army, Italians, French and British, who had assumed the lead role on the Western Front. It was also on 15 September that a new weapon was to receive its baptism of fire for the first time. Forty-nine British Mark I tanks made their debut in the hope that the new weapon might prove a tactical success for the Allies. In the event, the tanks were unable to give any decisive advantage. The technology, although relatively advanced at the time, was still in its infancy and would only come into its own in future wars. As 1916 came to a close, the Allies could see that victory was now in sight. Germany had admitted casualty statistics of some 1,400,000 men. Ludendorff had effectively been fought to a standstill and admitted to being worn out.

As 1917 heralded the fourth year of the First World War, there was much hope for the Allies that Germany could soon be brought to heel and that the fight in the dog was beginning to fade. The whole dynamic of the First World War was changing. The French army was much rested and restored in the wake of its tribulations of the past year and could now boast powerful reserves at its disposal. America joining the Allies in the war against Germany in 1917 meant there was also a steady flow of US troops and equipment entering the theatre. The British, though, were suffering manpower issues, a fact compounded by the political bickering back home.

At this stage of the war the Germans were relying more and more on artillery. A good example of the German use of both light- and heavy-calibre mortars and guns was at Picardy on 21 March, where the Germans fielded 6,473 guns backed up by 3,352 trench mortars of varying calibres. Fortunately, the British 3rd Army in the north had suffered less heavily and was able to hold its ground on vital positions. Poor tactical management on part of the Germans meant that any success their huge bombardment had achieved was not properly exploited.

As the First World War neared its climax, many of Germany's allies had fallen away, and much of her once-mighty army was now reduced almost to the level of a militia. The Germans fought with great bravery but could offer no answer to the Allied advance. The last great Allied offensive of the First World War began in the Argonne Forest region. This French/American attack was successful, but also very costly in lives due to the American lack of experience.

On 1 October, German soldier Holger Schildt, who was twenty-four years of age, was sitting in a trench four miles outside the Argonne Forest when one of his troop came running towards him in a state of immense excitement.

> "It's over, it's over! This war is over," he was shouting. I asked him, "What are you going on about?" Then he explained he had heard the news of an armistice and that this came direct from the Reichstag. Hindenburg had told a Council of War that an armistice must be reached to prevent a catastrophe. Then more of our men appeared, all excitedly shouting the same thing that the war is over. Many of them were rightly excited at the possibility we had survived and that we could now go home. I don't think many of them really thought about the Germany we would be going back home to though. It wouldn't be the same, and it became a festering sore of discontent, unemployment, hyperinflation and borderline starvation. It became a country where bread was worth more than gold and coal worth more than gold and bread together. If you married and had young children, chances were they wouldn't survive the hard times, particularly in the winters. While the others celebrated the ending of the war the only thing I could think of was "Oh my god, things are going to get very bad now."

Holger Schildt's words, written in a page of his journal over 100 years ago, are painfully prophetic. The now faded pencil screams out a warning to a future generation of people and politicians alike, many of whom would remain ignorant to the consequences of Germany's defeat. Germany would be rightfully punished for her part in creating one of the greatest tragedies of the early twentieth century, yet she too would become one of that century's greatest tragedies herself. The years that followed 1918 would spawn a greater terror than any other that had previously been witnessed.

Prussian militarism and Kaiser Wilhelm II became the focus of hatred and ridicule in the wake of the 1918 armistice. Wilhelm was forced to abdicate in 1918, whereupon Germany became a republic. The majority of West Prussia and the former Prussian province of Posen, territories annexed by Prussia during the eighteenth-century partitioning of Poland, were ceded to the Second Polish Republic as set out within the terms of the Treaty of Versailles. East Prussia effectively became an enclave, separated from mainland Germany. Germany herself was ordered to pay substantial reparations as she was viewed as the root cause of a war that had cost the lives of over thirty-seven million people. It was one of the deadliest conflicts in the relatively short history of our human race.

There was also the question of war crimes that had been perpetrated by the kaiser's army throughout the course of the First World War. These, of course, gave weight to the argument that Germany was an aggressive race prepared to turn to barbarism in her pursuit of power. When Germany invaded neutral Belgium on 4 August 1914 the German forces advanced toward their first major objective of the campaign, the ring of fortifications around Liege. It was from this period that the first acts of German brutality were catalogued. As the Germans advanced on the ring of forts around Liege, they came under shell fire from the guns. In retaliation for the shelling, German troops rounded up the inhabitants of surrounding villages. Random victims were selected for execution and then shot, and any still alive after the shootings were stabbed with bayonets to finish them off. By the 8 August nearly 850 civilians would be dead, including women and children.

Many theories have been posited to explain the conduct of the German forces during their advance on the forts around Liege. The German rank and file genuinely felt that the civilian population were attacking them.

This rather delusional view was sometimes countered by individual commanding officers, sometimes not. The Belgian men of military age were suspected of sniping against the German troops, thus the majority of victims were men of such age. There was also the belief that the German troops were resentful of the Belgians for enjoying civilian lives that the German troops themselves had so recently been torn away from. Apart from the killing of civilians, the local populace was often terrorised into cheering the German troops, while local dignitaries were often publicly humiliated, mistreated and sometimes killed. However, this was just the beginning of reports of the violence that would be splashed across the newspapers of countries around the world highlighting what became known as 'Hun Barbarism'.

Some of the worst massacres of civilians in Belgian territory took place between 18 and 28 August in places such as Aarschot, Andenne, Tamines, Dinant, Louvain, and the Belgian Ardennes region. As the German armies continued their advance, the violence appeared to cease, yet incidents of war crime continued to occur. In September dozens of civilians were killed in East Flanders as the invading German troops skirmished with Belgian military forces. Some weeks later, when the German army attacked the defenders at Diksmuide in West Flanders, mass killings occurred in the area. Between 19 and 21 October, 161 civilians were recorded as having been shot outright or killed as a result of having been used as human shields by the Germans. As the invaded territories of Belgium and northern France fell under German military occupation, the mass killings of civilians ceased. The war was now one of stalemate. Some 906 victims of 'Hun Barbarity' were recorded in France, while in Belgium the figure was considerably higher at 5,521 victims. This shift in the momentum of the war did not mean the end of violence in the German-occupied territories, however. During the four long years of German occupation there were numerous individual executions and killings. In the second half of the war some 2,500 Belgian men died as a result of the general conditions, malnutrition or ill treatment in forced labour camps that were in operation by the German military.

Following the defeat of Germany in 1918 the world was determined that she should never again be a threat, either to her neighbours or world peace. It was hoped the Treaty of Versailles would prevent any future German aggressive aspirations in Europe. While many military historians and economists have argued that the Treaty of Versailles was not unduly harsh in its context, there are those who counter that it alone was the single most significant factor in the causes of the Second World War. Germany ended the war without the destruction of her country's infrastructure; her towns and cities remained unscathed in comparison to Belgium and France, where many towns, cities and villages had been the front lines of the fighting. The political and social chaos, combined with steadily increasing economic collapse, left many Germans feeling that they had been betrayed by their own government. This attitude was particularly prevalent among the embittered German soldiers returning home from the war.

Soldiers like twenty-three-year-old Ernst Faber who lost his right leg and part of his right hand in a shell attack. Faber wrote after returning home to his family in 1918: 'What have I returned to? I cannot find work as no one wishes to take on and pay a cripple to do a job that would take a fitter man or a woman half the time. It would have been easier to have died in France than return home alive. I am in constant pain and if I cannot make a living I will be forced to beg for charity on the city streets. This is no way for a soldier to end his days.' Another wrote: 'There has to be hope. Even Christ was resurrected from his misery. There are some hard times ahead. We feel abandoned by the very government we fought for. They left the sinking ship as rats. We can only hope that from the ashes a new phoenix will rise.'

The new phoenix would indeed materialise out of the discontent and chaos of 1918 and Versailles, bringing forth a terror greater than any previous known to the world. This terror would exploit both the fears and hopes of the people of Germany. The road to power of the Nazi Party would be paved in corpses and leave much of Europe a funeral pyre. Under its charismatic leader, Adolf Hitler, a former corporal in the kaiser's army, just fifteen years after the end of the First World War Germany would have an established new order under the Third Reich.

Chapter 3

The Descent into Madness

The First World War had been so catastrophic in terms of loss of life that it was proclaimed to be 'The War to End All Wars'. Such words provided a fitting epitaph to all those who had fallen and they reflected the emotions of people the world over. The naivety with which world leaders talked of peace became lost amidst the loud demands for Germany to be punished. Germany was now a nation on the gallows surrounded by a world eager to place the noose around her neck in recompense for the death and suffering it had caused. Many viewed her in much the same way as a terminally sick animal needing to be killed off quickly and humanely and the implementation of the Treaty of Versailles was seen by many Germans at the time as the deadly poison administered to carry out that humane killing.

Versailles brought about the slow economic strangulation of Germany, and was worsened by the depression that hit many nations, particularly in the early 1930s. It was right that Germany should face retribution for her part in the First World War, but with hindsight it could be argued that the war reparations imposed upon her were unduly severe. This complex issue has been the subject of much debate among historians ever since. When one considers the total loss of life during the First World War (thirty-seven million) against the financial reparations imposed upon Germany as a leading instigator of the war (132 billion gold marks), the figures speak for themselves. Jewish student Martha Ohlins remarked of the situation:

> Germany was not the kind of dog that took kindly to the leash. Restraint or subservience has never been the trait of the German race. In this sense Germany could have been construed as being "warlike", thus it should have been handled in a slightly different manner, erring on the side

of caution, as one might with an animal prone to biting. Of course, with the current state of affairs the victorious Allies felt that the steps which they had taken were the best course of action towards neutralising any future threat from Germany. Instead it proved to be a catalyst, the opposite of the original intention. It put Germany on course for yet more trouble. I was born in Germany and my father was an economist who saw the writing on the wall in 1930. He made the decision that we should move. That decision, made by a loving father, also German-born, probably saved our lives.

Prussia after 1918 was established into the Free State of Prussia. This came about as a consequence of the 1918 German Revolution, which effectively abolished any of Germany's imperial connections. In its place the Weimar Republic evolved. This was a direct successor to the Kingdom of Prussia, but featured a democratic republican government as opposed to the totalitarian rule under Kaiser Wilhelm II. Prussia remained the dominant state of Germany, comprising sixty-five percent of the country's territory and population. However, East Prussia was separated from West Prussia by a division known as the Polish or Danzig corridor, the purpose of which was to give Poland access to the Baltic Sea. Danzig itself was a '*Freie Stadt*' or Free City, independent from both Germany and Poland.

Unemployment in Germany became a major concern in the aftermath of the First World War. It was a steady descent into chaos which affected not only Germany as a whole but also the Free State of Prussia. The autumn of 1929 witnessed the Wall Street Crash, which would have severe consequences all over the world. High unemployment led to dreadful poverty, forcing many men in particular to take drastic action in order to feed their families. Matilda Kuhn spoke of her family who lived at that time in the city of Königsberg in East Prussia:

> My father had served in a Siege Battery during the First World War in Belgium. His unit had wrought much destruction there. When he returned home, far from being greeted a hero, he found it difficult to support his family. He worked along with my mother repairing shoes and clothing. As the situation with the German economy

worsened, even this work died out. People began to do such repairs themselves rather than spend money for others to do it for them. My father got together with friends he had served alongside in the army and they went out and robbed the rich houses in and around Königsberg. They stole anything they could carry away and trade for food or other goods. I know he was not proud of what he did, but he had to do something in those dark times. He only stopped going out with the other men after one of them was shot while running away from a house they had just left. Luckily the man was not badly hurt, but it served as a warning. After that my mother forbade him to continue with the enterprise. My father even went out begging on the street. He would wear the medals he had been awarded for his service and hope that some kind soul would give him some money.

In parts of rural East Prussia the populace fared little better, as Ernst Giestl recalled from his grandfather's writings of the time:

> My grandfather would go out at night and take the odd chicken, goose or duck from one of the local farms in the area. One night he went out with his three brothers and they discovered a goat in a small pen. The goat was quickly dispatched with a single blow from a razor-sharp weapon. My grandfather said the head of the animal came clean off and fell to the floor. They gave the animal no time to make any noise that might have alerted the landowners. After the goat was beheaded my grandfather's brother let go of the animal only to watch in astonishment as it got up and ran off into the darkness headless. They gave chase, diving on top of the animal. It twitched for a minute or so before lying still. They laughed about it later when they were carving the beast up between themselves. They also trapped rabbits and shot birds in the countryside and stole vegetables where they could. The landowners became aware of these activities; they had guns and would shoot you if they caught you in the act of stealing animals or vegetables from their land. These were, of course, desperate measures carried out by

men desperate to feed their families. Things such as cheese, rye bread and eggs became luxury items, unaffordable to many working-class families as hyper-inflation took hold. People used to say, "Why didn't you use money to pay for what you needed?" The problem was that our currency became worthless overnight. People would have wheelbarrow-loads of banknotes which were worthless. In fact, many people began to use banknotes as fuel for their fires. This may be difficult to believe but it was true.

East Prussia had always been rich in agricultural heritage. Many large farms grew sugar beets, turnips and potatoes in large volume. Many men from the cities, particularly those who did not wish to work in the coal mines or other industries, had the opportunity to work on the farms. The work back then was virtually all manual labour. The pay was not high, and the hours were long. Hermann Rastief recalled his grandfather, who, having returned from the war, found himself unemployed and unable to find work.

> My grandfather was Johann Polhmann and he was born and raised a true East Prussian in Allenstein. He had been an infantryman in the kaiser's army during the Great War. When he returned home, I remember him saying what a mess the country was now in and that we would inevitably suffer from some hard times as we were the losers. With no skills to his name he drifted into farm labour work. Even for that he had to literally plead to be given a chance. He learned how to drive horses in the fields and would be out from first light in the morning until it was dark at night. There were many women working with him and this is where he met my grandmother. That aside, he had few happy memories of the farming work.
>
> All the crops back then had to be picked or pulled by hand. He had a painful back due to it all and his hands became like the claws of a bird, the skin like hard leather over his bones. When the winter came bringing heavy snowfall he would be up with the others even if he were sick, picking out in the fields. The pay was just enough to

survive but still not enough. The people who owned the land did give the workers a share of the crops, like turnips and potatoes. They even received a chicken at Christmas which was special for a poor family from the working classes. The job crippled him eventually. His hands went first. All those years of working in the heat and then the freezing cold had brought on arthritis. In the end he could no longer work and instead his family had to go out and work to earn money.

He recalled that most days they ate vegetable stews with the occasional rabbit thrown in, and bread of course. The rabbits would be poached from the very land they were working on. Most of the men would go out at night and hunt rabbits either with guns or traps. If the landowner found out or caught you, he would cancel your employment, lodgings, everything, and then you would be in trouble. You see, if you worked on the farms back then you often had a small cottage allocated to you. My grandfather's was in a terrace. There was a single coal fire in the tiny kitchen and there was no other heating, or running water. Water came from a pump in the communal yard.

There were rats, mice and insects to contend with. I remember him telling me once that he and the other men had made a small barrel of liquor from some apples they had collected. The cover of the barrel had been left off one night and a rat had fallen in and drowned. Rather than tip it away one of the men said, "It'll be fine. The alcohol will break it all down and it will add to the flavour!" My grandfather also said that my grandmother despised the mice that infested the cottage, particularly in the wintertime. If you were quick enough you could kill them with a stick. My grandmother said there used to be a mouse that would venture out cautiously from a hole beside the fireplace. She started to leave a few crumbs for the mouse to encourage it to come out. After doing this for some weeks she had gained the trust of the mouse. One evening the mouse came out and began to nibble the crumbs my grandmother left for it when – bang! – she killed it with one of her slippers. The remains of the mouse were then tossed onto the fire.

In the summer a cat was permitted and was shared between the group of workers' cottages. My grandmother would sit out the backyard on summer days and watch the cat drag a rat back. She would watch fascinated as the cat and rat would duel to the death out on the grass beneath the apple tree. Then she would complain later when the corpse of the rat was deposited on her doorstep with its throat ripped out. So, in all they had a hard existence, typical of many Germans of their day.

Change could only ever have come through politics, yet at that time the working men had no real voice. Many political parties attempted to attract the support of German workers, but many failed. There were far too many political parties and organisations leading into the late 1920s. People like my grandparents were in a sense detached from Germany, yet they felt her pain. It couldn't have gone on like that. People needed work, and most importantly people needed to be able to feed themselves and their families. Many suffered a downslide into poverty and many disgruntled ex-soldiers felt the government were all to blame for it.

Nobody in my family would speak of Versailles. They hated it and they hated the French in particular. They viewed the French as the main executors of their misery and poverty. Many ex-German soldiers vowed that vengeance would fall upon the French and the English one day. It was strange that in the future my father, encouraged by my grandfather, went to listen to a new politician with radical new ideas. He was a former corporal of the kaiser's army and he had won awards for his bravery. He had formed the political group which called themselves the German Workers Party [DAP]. This party initially consisted of just a few hundred supporters, but soon gathered momentum. They said this new charismatic leader hailed from Austria and his name was Adolf Hitler.

On Thursday, 4 September 1930 Adolf Hitler, leader of the NSDAP (National Socialist German Workers Party), gave his first speech on Prussian territory in the city of Königsberg. An audience of some

16,000 people turned out to listen to what Herr Hitler had to say. By the time he had finished his speech most of those present were convinced he was the man who could restore Germany to greatness. That's not to say that Hitler did not have his critics in East Prussia, as Elizabeth Steiner recalls:

> My father worked in the coal mines of Königsberg. He was just the kind of ordinary worker that Herr Hitler was desperate to gain the support of. My father went to listen to Hitler with hundreds of miners from the east. They all listened intently to the rhetoric and some of it appealed to them while some of it did not. My father came home with mixed feelings on Herr Hitler. He felt that while the NSDAP and Hitler cared about German workers, especially Prussian ones, he felt that the NSDAP had other agendas which they were not being ultimately clear on. My father and his friends argued over whether Hitler was being genuine or not. My father told us, "I smell a rat and whenever I smell a rat, I am usually correct."

The Nazis were certainly not a new entity in the lives of East Prussians in 1930. Erich Koch had been the voice of the East Prussian Nazi Party from 1928 when he became *Gauleiter* of the province. Koch was characterised by his efforts to collectivise agriculture in the region, and was known for being a ruthless individual who would silence his critics both within and outside of the NSDAP. Koch's ideas for large-scale industrialisation made him an unpopular figure, in what had always traditionally been an agricultural community. However, his publicly funded and highly successful emergency relief programmes focusing on agricultural land improvement and road construction meant that many East Prussians, including the peasantry, hailed the 'Erich Koch Plan [for East Prussia]' as something of a miracle. By 16 August 1933 the 'Erich Koch Plan' allegedly ended the scourge of unemployment in East Prussia.

With an individual such as Koch, however, there would more than likely have been an ulterior motive. Koch would later receive a detailed population inventory sent to him by Theodor Schieder. Koch was eager to know the political, social and ethnic demographics of the territories annexed to East Prussia. The information the reports contained would prove useful in later Nazi policies of extermination and settlement, as well as providing the basis for the segregation of Jewish and Slavic spouses from ethnic Germans on the *Deutsche Volksliste* (German People's List). The *Deutsche Volksliste* was a Nazi Party institution, the purpose of which was to classify the inhabitants of German-occupied territory into categories of desirability according to the criteria set out by chief of the SS, Heinrich Himmler.

Roberta Irmfjeld's father was a serving senior police officer who came under the jurisdiction of Erich Koch. Roberta recalls:

> Koch specifically asked for records on all criminal convictions in the area. The documents contained the names, addresses and case files on all those convicted of crimes in the area. The documents my father had to hand over concerned all manner of offences: political activism, assault, murder, theft and robbery, vagrancy and crimes of a sexual nature. My father told me that he did not like Koch at all, and that the files that he had to hand over were later given to the Gestapo. Any offender named in the files, depending on their loyalties of course, would have been in great danger. My father also said that when the paperwork was returned, he was not in receipt of the originals but retyped copies. Crimes involving German nationals had all been deleted. It had to be ascertained that the Gestapo used the information gathered from these files to assist them in making of a series of arrests in the area. Things became very sinister in what had been a largely peaceful agricultural state. Herr Koch was one of the leading figures in Nazi oppression in the region, though he receives little attention from modern historians for this.

There were a great many Prussians who viewed Adolf Hitler and the Nazi Party as offering them liberation; a path towards unity with Germany once again. Many were of the view that East Prussia was much like a naughty child that had been banished to some dark corner. East Prussians felt forgotten and abandoned throughout the years after 1918, and this fact was ripe for exploitation. Roberta Irmfjeld's perspective was shared by thousands of East Prussians at the time:

The Descent into Madness

Despair in the social sense becomes like a disease, it affects the populace which then awaits a cure for all of its ills. When Hitler appeared on the political scene with the NSDAP, they were viewed as the only logical political solution under the circumstances. In that context, we were all victims of the circumstances. People forget East Prussia suffered terribly too in the years following 1918, where Prussia had been parted from Germany. It had been parted in much the same way a diseased organ might be cut from a body. That said, my father was not all that sure of Hitler and I recall him saying to my mother, "Hitler is undoubtedly a man of immense personality and strength, and he possesses an enormous charisma. I feel he is perfectly genuine, yet there is something cold, distressing about him."

An American news reporter recalled Hitler's visit to Königsberg in March 1938: 'There was the usual press frenzy as everyone wanted to interview Herr Hitler. It was impossible to get near the man most of the time. The sheer adoration displayed towards the man makes you feel you are in the presence of some god-like individual.' Hitler's speech given to the people of Königsberg formed part of his 1938 German parliamentary election campaign. In it he told the people of Königsberg, 'In an age which it is self-evident that all the peoples of the earth are accorded the right of self-determination, one has denied this right of self-determination to the members of a great civilized *volk* [people] and robbed them of it.'

Clearly, in this part of his speech Hitler was referring to East Prussia, and the desire to have Prussia reinstated as part of a new German Reich. Hitler spoke with passion about the national community and how 'blood binds more firmly than business.'

The Hitler allure had proved spellbinding and the NSDAP won a total of 44,964,005 votes in Germany. In Austria a total of 4,471,618 votes were won and in the Sudetenland 2,497,604 votes were won. Due to the outbreak of the Second World War, which would be orchestrated by Hitler in September 1939, there would be no further elections in Germany. With Hitler and the NSDAP in total control of Germany, war was inevitable. Prussia would later be clawed back from Poland, but its soil would once again be stained red with blood.

Chapter 4

Black Aurora

From 1919 to 1932 Prussia was governed by a coalition of the Social Democrats, Catholic Centre and German Democrats. From 1921 to 1925 coalition governments had included the German People's Party. Unlike in other states of the German Reich, majority rule by democratic parties in Prussia was never endangered. That said, in East Prussia and some industrial areas the National Socialist German Workers Party of Adolf Hitler had gained greater influence and popular support, particularly from the lower and middle classes of society.

Otto Braun, a Social Democrat from East Prussia, served as Prussian minister-president in an almost continuous capacity from 1920 to 1932. Braun was a capable leader who had introduced several of what can best be described as 'trend-setting' reforms together with his minister of the interior, Carl Severing. For example, a Prussian minister-president could only be removed from office if there was a positive majority for a potential successor. It was a concept that became known as the constructive vote of no confidence. It was largely due to this political policy that the centre-left coalition was able to stay in office because neither the far left nor the far right could possibly put together a majority.

All of this would change on 20 July 1932 in the wake of the *Preußenschlag* (Prussian Coup). Reich chancellor Franz von Papen persuaded President Hindenburg to remove the elected Prussian state government under Otto Braun on the pretext that it had lost control of public order. This was triggered by Altona Bloody Sunday, a shootout between the SA (*Sturmabteilung*), SS (*Schutzstaffel*), the police and KPD Communist Party supporters. The violent confrontation on 17 July 1932 left eighteen people dead. After this emergency decree orchestrated by von Papen, the Reich chancellor appointed himself Reich commissioner for Prussia, thus taking control of the government.

This made it easier for Adolf Hitler and the Nazi Party to assume power over Prussia in the following year.

The quid pro quo of Hitler's appointment as chancellor of Germany on 30 January 1933 was von Papen's formal appointment as minister-president of Prussia, in addition to his role as vice-chancellor of the Reich. At the same time, in a little-noticed appointment, Hitler's most senior lieutenant, Hermann Göring, was allocated the role of state interior minister.

Four weeks later, on 27 February 1933, Hitler would seize his chance to gain absolute power in Germany and show that violence and intimidation would sweep aside any opposition that lay in his path to glory. This was the day that the Reichstag was set ablaze. Under Hitler's insistence, President von Hindenburg issued the Reichstag Fire Decree, which effectively curtailed civil liberties in the country. Six days after the Reichstag fire, on 5 March, the election strengthened the position of the NSDAP, although they failed to achieve an absolute majority. But with their coalition partner, the German National People's Party, Hitler now commanded a slim majority in the Reichstag.

Hermann Göring would figure prominently in this election as he was in command of the largest police force in the country. Under Göring's direction, his police intimidated the other political parties. It was not uncommon to witness mass street brawls where violence would be directed towards the Communists and Social Democrats in particular. The only political groups free to campaign on the streets were the NSDAP and the Nationalists.

The new Reichstag was opened in the Garrison Church of Potsdam on 21 March 1933 in the presence of President von Hindenburg. The president was by this time a shadow of his former self, a sad, diminished old man who appeared disinterested in the world around him, yet whose propaganda value was still of use to the Nazis. This 'marriage of old Prussia with young Germany' was celebrated in order to win over the Prussian monarchists and induce them to vote for the Enabling Act, which proved crucial. Once passed, on 23 March 1933, it legally granted Adolf Hitler the dictatorial powers he had so yearned for.

The Nazis acted quickly to consolidate their power base in Prussia. In April 1933 Franz von Papen was away on a visit to the Vatican in Italy. In his absence Göring was appointed to take his place. This was a tactical move by Hitler, allowing him to take power decisively as he now had the whole apparatus of the Prussian government, including the police, at his disposal. By 1934 almost all Prussian ministries had been absorbed into the corresponding Reich ministries. Like Germany itself, Prussia was now firmly in the grip of the tentacles of Hitler's National Socialism. The romantic notion of historical Prussia in a marriage with the young Nazi Germany would be a short-lived one. This would be a marriage consummated in blood and would change Prussia forever from its peaceful image as an agricultural backwater.

On 30 November 1933 an organisation that would become synonymous with the terror of National Socialism was born in Prussia. This organisation would become known as the Gestapo, or *Geheime Staatspolizei*, the Secret State Police. It was created by Hermann Göring in an attempt to combine all of the existing security police agencies of Prussia into a single unit. By 1936 the Gestapo had become a national agency as opposed to a Prussian state agency and was considered a sister organisation to the SS *Sicherheitsdienst* (SD or Security Service) under Heinrich Himmler (who, in 1936, had been appointed Chief of German Police). From 27 September 1939 the Gestapo was administered by the *Reichssichherheitshauptamt* (RSHA or Reich Main Security Office). The Gestapo would also play a key role in the Nazi plan to exterminate the Jewish population of Europe.

It was after the successful German invasion of Poland, which would mark the beginning of the Second World War, that Orphelia Maschmann joined her family on a journey to a place she had never even heard of before in East Prussia. Orphelia was the youngest of three children of Friedrich and Anna Maschmann. The family were proud of their Prussian heritage, which had spanned several generations up to the First World War. Orphelia explained that after 1918, for several reasons, it became difficult for Germans living in Prussia, particularly East Prussia, even though there were more Germans there than any other nationality at the time. Orphelia's family were forced to move to Germany, where it was hoped fresh opportunities might present themselves.

> My grandparents and parents always told me stories about the old days in Prussia. They used to say what a marvellous kingdom it was, and that it was a traditional German heartland that should always belong to Germany by right. They told

me that after the defeat of 1918 it became unbearable to live in East Prussia. They said the Polish were not sympathetic to Germans after the First World War. German families who had always lived there suddenly found themselves in very difficult situations. I was told Polish businesses would refuse to employ Germans. Some families moved to the bigger cities in the hope of finding a better way of life, but mostly they found tougher times, not easier ones.

My father and mother had always been Nationalists, so National Socialism was a natural political choice for them. My father joined the NSDAP and I recall how proud he was of his membership card. He worked as a regular member of the police in Brandenburg where we lived. I know that he went quite high up in the police and also had powerful friends there. He would rub shoulders with some important Nazis. My father's transition into the State Secret Police was down to two main reasons: a) he was considered not fit enough to join the military; and b) the regular police soon came under the auspices of the State Secret police, or Gestapo as they were called.

My father's loyalty was without question and I remember him coming back from a meeting somewhere and he was very excited. He told us we were going to return to Prussia where we belonged. With hindsight I think he had scores to settle back there. He was almost crying with elation at the thought of going back, as if he were somehow restoring pride to the family name. My father's skills in administration were exemplary, and I believe he was chosen for these rather than sentimentality.

The journey to Friedland, which was to the south of Königsberg, was long but not unpleasant. The first part was by boat. Once there, we were greeted by a group of gentlemen in suits. All of them wore golden party badges [NSDAP membership badges]. When my father showed us to a big, black car, I asked him who the men were. He grumbled that I always asked too many questions, then he smiled and said they were work colleagues with whom he had made some arrangements. He had some papers in his hand, which he folded and placed in his inside coat pocket. We then got into the car and I recall how cold the red leather seats were. They sent a chill through my body as we settled down for the drive to Friedland. As we drove, a dense fog shrouded much of the scenery in a silvery veil. It was not quite evening, but it was getting dark. Our journey took us through a primeval-looking countryside of hills, mountains and forests. I sat up on the car seat so that I could look over my mother's shoulder and see the road ahead. The dull yellow light of the car's headlamps did not seem strong enough for my father to be able to see, but he was a good driver. With my child's imagination in overdrive, I imagined all manner of beasts of ancient folklore running across the road in front of our car, leaping out from the dark woods that lined the roadside and momentarily stopping to look at us before dashing off into the darkness on the other side. My father said that goblins and wolves lived in these woods and that I should never go there alone. I had believed his tales of wolves, witches and goblins, but if it were monsters I was looking for, then clearly I should have been looking closer to home.

After what seemed a long time, and with me becoming slightly restless, we drove up a long, bumpy driveway to a large house. As we pulled up outside, the front door of the house opened and a rather large, smart, yet jovial-mannered man came out to greet us. My father told me that this was Mr Freilehrer, who would be teaching us at our new home. I came to know him as 'the man with the glass eye'. He used to go to the houses of children receiving home tuition and he gave the three of us the best possible education. The other girls where we lived used to make derogatory remarks about Mr Freilehrer. They would say, "His glass eye that he wears was probably specially made by Lalique or maybe even Murano." They would giggle about this, much as bitchy young rich girls would do about anything considered different to themselves. Mr Freilehrer's glass eye was one he had to wear after being wounded in the eye during the First World War. You could tell it was not real as it did not move with his other one.

After a brief meeting with the man who would oversee our education, we drove off again, a short distance down a lane where a group of men stood outside another large house. My father told us, "This is it. This is our new home." I couldn't believe it; it looked wonderful. Our fatigue from the long journey seemed to evaporate in an instant as we yelled, "Can we go inside and see. Oh please, father, please!" Father replied, "Just all calm down and we will all go inside in just a moment." We jumped out the car. The men waiting outside shook hands with father and he handed them the papers he had inside his coat pocket. I recall father saying how nice the property looked from outside and he asked them how long it had been standing empty and things like that.

The house had a huge, heavy wooden front door and when it was opened inside was everything we had imagined; all completely furnished and very lavish. I say it was a big house. It was not a mansion and only had four bedrooms, but the other rooms were huge, and at that time it was the biggest house I had ever lived in. There was a great big sitting room with a large open fire, which had already been lit for us in anticipation of our arrival. After all, it was winter and it was chilly outside. Our mother showed us to our rooms. The beds were all made, and my mother said to us, "It is getting late now, you need to go to sleep and you can explore in the morning." We were hungry, so mother made us some sandwiches and gave us a glass of milk each while we sat at a long table in the dining room. After our little snack we went up to our rooms and changed into our night clothes. Mother came in and checked we were all tucked in properly, and kissed each of us on the forehead and wished us goodnight. I recall lying awake for a while, my eyes staring around the room, a mixture of both excitement and fear. I imagined an old house like this could have ghosts, and hoped they would not come and make their presence known to me. I heard one of my sisters getting up in the night and mother taking her to the toilet.

When I woke next, light was flooding in through the windows and I could hear the birds singing outside. I was eager to begin exploring; not only the house but the garden outside too. I ran downstairs in my nightgown and mother was making breakfast for us. My father was in the room he used as a study. Whenever he was in there, we were told we were not to disturb him under any circumstances. Only mother was permitted to go in while he was working. I never actually saw the inside of that room until a year or so later; it was often locked and out of bounds to us. Father just told us the room contained valuable documents and we were not allowed in, and besides, he needed peace and quiet while he was working at home. We sat at the table and ate breakfast and father joined us shortly after. It was hard to take in, where we had lived before and where we were now. I wondered how all of this could be; I just didn't get it at the time.

After breakfast, father said to me, "You can come with me, I am going to see someone today." I thought this was great and ran upstairs to change. Father shouted up that it was cold outside and I must wear boots and a coat and put a hat on. The car did not have any heating and the short drive was not exactly pleasant. I was glad to get out and stamp my feet to regain my circulation. The house we had pulled up outside had a big garden with an ornamental pond at the front. As I got out the car, I made immediate eye contact with a large German shepherd dog, which was assuming a squatting position, preparing to defecate, and did not seem concerned at our intrusion at that instant. Our timing had been impeccable and we stood watching the dog defecate. We did not feel it was a good idea to open the gate and enter the garden with the dog there. Almost on cue the front door of the house opened and a man walked up the path to us, saying "welcome, I am Hans and it's great to meet you". The greeting was directed more at father than at me and before we took another step Hans looked over at the dog and shouted *"bleiben* [stay]". The dog assumed a sitting position, with a disgruntled growl.

We went into the house and sat down in the living room. Hans asked if I would like to play with his daughter, and so I said "yes please". Hans called out, "Klara, Klara, come down here a minute please." I heard footsteps coming down the stairs and then a tall girl with brown hair entered the room. She looked at me and smiled and held out her hand, saying, "Come with me. I'll show you around. My name is Klara. What's yours?" Klara showed me around their house and her bedroom and then we went outside into the back garden; a long stretch of grass bordered by a wood. We both walked towards the wood and chatted. Klara said that my father would be working closely with her father. I asked Klara, 'But what will they be doing?" She replied, "It's police work here: Reich security. You know there are still Jews hiding here and they must be found. My father says there are traitors within every society and his job is to seek them out." After that she said, "Come on, it's cold, we must go back in the house now." She took me by the hand and we ran back to the house where her mother made us each a hot drink.

The next morning Mr Freilehrer arrived to give us our first session of home tuition. Mother had woken us early and ensured we were smart and ready. Far from the jovial man he first appeared, Freilehrer read out his rules to us: "You shall not speak until spoken to. You shall sit upright in your chairs at all times and before we begin a lesson you shall salute our Führer, Adolf Hitler." He then explained how this should be done properly, by standing to attention and thrusting out one's arm and shouting "Heil Hitler". Our first lesson was titled "racial geography" and was written by Freilehrer himself. It was a preliminary to understanding how sub-human elements and activity had polluted not only German territory through the ages but also the world. It portrayed the Jews as our greatest racial enemy and stated it was every true German's duty to ensure that once Jews had been eradicated from German society —especially here in Prussia – they should never again be allowed to thrive in the way that they had done over the centuries.

Freilehrer concluded that Prussia belonged to Germany, not Poland or anyone else, and was now again a part of the greater German Reich, as it should be. Prussia had been restored to its rightful people again by the divine hand of Adolf Hitler, saviour of the German race. At the close of the lesson the "Heil Hitler" was also to be given as a mark of respect. Freilehrer then smiled and said, "You have all worked very well today, your parents will be happy." Mr Freilehrer agreed to supply our parents with a weekly written report on our progress. We were told that our parents were investing good money into our education, for which we should all be very thankful.

In addition to our home tuition we joined the League of German Maidens. This was expected of every German girl. I would meet with Klara Wyborny [Hans's daughter] and we would go to the twice-weekly meetings. One meeting was on a Wednesday and the other was on Saturday afternoon, and this was known as sports afternoon. On Wednesdays we learned political theory, gave readings, and learned how to do first aid and sewing, and things. In the summer we went to summer camp. We went swimming in the rivers and lakes and learned to use maps and a compass. We sang and marched, and we felt pretty proud of being Prussian Germans by blood. We all felt different and maybe thought we were better than the German girls of Berlin, for example. Our father was proud to be working with the Gestapo as one of their officers carrying out vital Reich duties. I never really asked him about it and neither did my sisters.

It was Klara Wyborny who told me exactly what was happening in Friedland at the time. We were both fourteen both believed that Jews and other traitors were the reason for Germany's downfall in 1918. It was then Klara said, "The house you call home once belonged to Jews, and it was confiscated from them after the invasion of Poland. The previous owners were marched out of the house at gunpoint by our soldiers. It served them all right as Prussia is ours, not theirs, Prussia does not belong to Jews or Poles."

Klara then went on to explain that my father, along with her father, Hans, had been working through an extensive list of names that Klara's father had compiled. The list was several pages long and the people on it were suspected of being non-sympathetic to the National Socialists. Klara then went on to say, "All suspects on the list are investigated, and any found to be guilty of crimes against the state are rounded up, along with their families, and sent to Germany for forced labour. Orphelia, your father helps to process these people. My father says he is good at his work and is a good friend."

So that's what my father was doing for the most part in Friedland, and he was paid well for doing it. I later discovered that in some cases accusations had been fabricated and my father went along with these fabrications, but for what reason I don't know. Maybe he had heard things he didn't like about these people. I did hear that my father took bribes early on. Someone said he let a Jewish family slip through the net for a fee. I don't know if that is true, I have never been able to find out much about his activities during that short time in Prussia. My father is dead now, so I can't ask him any questions. My mother is also dead, though I don't think either would have been willing to talk about it to strangers. It was all part of an era that I would later refer to as the Black Aurora.

We will hear further memoirs from Orphelia Maschmann later in this work. Alexandria Busch, a resident of Königsberg, recalls:

My first year of full-time education had been under the old Prussian regime, so when the Hitler government gained control it all changed. The whole thesis reflected the pride one should have in nationalism. Hitler, of course, was considered the one who had freed Prussia from its Versailles-imposed Weimar slavery. My father was a miner, just a working-class man who worked very hard to keep his family. We were not a big family, only my father, mother, me and my older sister, Becki. Both our parents were hard-line patriots. They welcomed the National Socialists and were eager to experience the changes they would bring with them. My father did not like having to work down in the Königsberg mines, but the mines were vital to the German industry back then. The coal fuelled the production of arms and other weapons, so in that sense they were of huge importance. My father used to say, "They should make the wealthy go down into the mines, let them learn what hard work it is, and what facing death every day is like." Both our parents were scathing of the "wealthy parasites" who had been party to Prussian Germany's downfall. Goaded by the Nazi mobs, they too blamed Jews for their hardships. Not just Jews but the old political elite as they called it. My father said, "All this will change soon. These people who have prospered through our hard labours will learn that finally German patience has run out."

When people talk about the persecution of minority races, this certainly occurred in Prussia. For example, Prussia had always been traditionally agricultural, and gypsies had always been present and were often welcomed by farming communities. Gypsy people were of a rustic breed and no strangers to hard, physical work. Many were decent hard workers who kept themselves to themselves in many respects. Their presence in Prussia largely vanished during the great war of 1914–1918, but then they seemed to trickle back in the years after the war. When the Nazis made clear their intentions in Prussia from 1933, the gypsy people stayed away, though they soon found themselves hunted down quite ruthlessly in the peripheral territories. The excuse given for the persecution of gypsy people in school was that they were thieves and vagabonds, unfit to be a part of German society. It was also said that gypsy people operated as an independent society, with a non-conforming way of life, and with their own cultures and beliefs. This was an ethos permitted to flourish under the old Weimar society, but would not be tolerated in Hitler's new Germany. In fact it was deemed an offence. They also blamed the gypsy people for the spread of disease, which, of course, was untrue. Gypsies were blamed for some of the major flu outbreaks of the early twentieth century, as well as other diseases. It was convenient to blame a group of people who could easily be made scapegoats for the ills of the world.

This same thing was applied to anything Jewish. A Jew was an enemy; a rat. There could be no compassion towards them. They had to be destroyed: men, women and children, all of them. I learned most of this when the Nazi education was introduced. They wasted no time at all. We went from cultivating vegetables and crops to that of evil, hatred and destruction. My parents hadn't always been Nazis; they were made into Nazis by the old German system. Society was looking to blame someone or something for their problems. The Weimar government was the obvious choice. People only became Nazis in Prussia because they felt their heritage and traditions had been diminished due to the partitioning from Germany as a whole. Prussian society wanted to be reunited with the fatherland; it was the rightful way. Only the Poles who lived amongst us were fearful of a Prussian reunification with the fatherland. And Jews, of course.

I remember walking home from school one day in the winter of 1948. There was a commotion outside one of the big houses near my school. One of my friends said, "Hey, what's going on here? Let's stop and see." So the four of us stood there watching as the SS broke down the front door of this house. There were two Gestapo agents, both armed, and one was at the side of the house, the other man was at the back with some of the SS. We knew they were Gestapo as they wore long, black leather coats and those trilby-style hats. We watched the SS go into the house after knocking down the door. It was quiet for a few seconds then there were shots from inside the house. Instinctively, we jumped over the wall into someone's garden. Peering over the top, we watched as a body was dragged out by the SS. They threw it down onto the ground and went back into the house. There was some shouting and we could just about make out the words "tell me, where, where". One of my friends, Dana, said, "Shit, they are looking for someone in there. Someone is in big trouble." The SS came out with four people, their rifles pointing into their backs. A lorry pulled up and the people were ordered to get in the back. Once they had climbed into the back of the vehicle, the dead body was thrown in, and we could hear sobbing noises. Then some of the SS jumped in the back with them and the lorry drove off at speed. The Gestapo then went into the house. As they were doing this we climbed back over the wall. The youngest of my friends was a girl named Ursula. She said, "I don't like this. Let's go home." We hurried past the house and there was a streak of blood on the ground outside where the body had been dragged.

The strange thing was it was becoming common to see people being beaten up in the streets, or dragged out of their houses and thrown into the backs of cars or other vehicles. We learned this is what happened if you didn't conform or follow the rules and do as you were told. I was later told the drama we had been witnesses to was down to people trying to hide political activists in their home. The man who was shot was wanted by the authorities and had been in hiding. The fate of the family who had been hiding the man is unknown to me, but it is very likely they would have been sent to one of the camps. The way to survive was to just behave, conform, and do as you were told. When I arrived home, I told my parents what we had seen. They replied, "Good. That's one less group of traitors living in our midst."

We were under the Third Reich: an iron society. In school we once had a visit from SS chief Heinrich Himmler. He spent the day with us, partaking in all our activities. Before home time we had an assembly where he addressed us, telling us, "Prussian youth. If you are not cruel, unbending in your loyalty to the Führer, not ruthless in every single endeavour, the iron-rich soils of these lands long disputed over the centuries of their existence will only serve as the ceiling of your tomb." It was an eloquent speech, and we understood what it was saying to us. Before Himmler left, he was happy to shake our hands and sign autographs like a celebrity. When he left it felt as if a ghost had left the room. A chilled air had somehow followed him out of the door from which he came. I'd shaken his hand not moments ago, and my hand was now cold and clammy. We all went home and said, "We spent the day with Himmler. How many young people in Prussia could boast of that honour?"

By the twentieth century Königsberg had one of the largest Jewish communities in the German Reich. In 1750 Frederick II of Prussia issued an edict which classified Jews in Prussia into several categories. The main division was between so called "tolerated Jews" (*geduldete Juden*), who were permitted to remain in Prussia, and "not tolerated Jews", who were required to leave Prussia upon reaching adulthood. There were also "protected Jews" (*schutz-Juden*), whose numbers were initially limited to 203 families in all of Brandenburg-Prussia, who could reside in a city but had their right of mobility removed. The "tolerated Jews" fared the worst. They were unable to purchase houses or land or engage in any commercial activities. They were generally not permitted to live in the cities unless they were clients or in the employment of "protected Jews".

Over the course of the nineteenth century these restrictions became somewhat relaxed, but persecution was always present, as it was in most areas of Germany. It is a sad irony that many of Königsberg's Jews served in the kaiser's army during the First World War. By 1917 there were 820 Königsberg Jews in the Prussian army, including eighty volunteers. They included fifteen recipients of the decoration of the Iron Cross First Class, and 102 recipients of the decoration of the Iron Cross Second Class. These military decorations were held in very high esteem and were not awarded lightly.

By the 1920s and 1930s the Jewish population of Königsberg was in decline. This was due to the rise in antisemitism, combined with the general persecution of Jews in the city. By the time the Nazi Party had taken control through the 1933 *Machtergreifung* there were only 3,500 living in the city. As a consequence of the anti-Jewish legislation enforced by Erich Koch, many of Königsberg's Jews realised that they had few options other than to emigrate to either the United States or Great Britain. Many of those who emigrated did so out of fear of what was to come.

Michael Rössner, a Königsberg Jew who was eight when his parents decided it was no longer safe to remain in Königsberg, wrote:

> My father talked of a great terror that would swallow Europe. He was convinced that Hitler and the Nazis would remain a threat to the entire world until they were destroyed. We were some of the lucky ones. We had many relatives in the United States of America, and that is where we went. My mother and father packed everything into crates. The only things that were left behind in our old home were three sofas that we couldn't take with us. One of my most vivid recollections of that time was my mother and father closing the front door of our old home for the last time. They both stood consoling one another. My mother was crying and wiping her eyes with a white handkerchief. It was a damp, cold, grey morning in winter when we left the house. We looked back at it before we got into the car. The now-empty house looked like a corpse, the bare windows resembling darkened eyes that would remain closed by fear of the world around them. Many of us sensed that something dreadful would come if we did not leave. We would try to convince the others [Jews] to follow us. They thought it would all be alright once things had settled down. Nobody imagined that within such a short period there would be no escape, and that killing factories would be built with the specific intention of wiping us – as a race of people, of human beings – out of this world and out of history.

Kristallnacht, or 'Night of Broken Glass' was the name given to the wave of violence, murder and destruction that broke out across Germany in November 1938. The victims were of course the Jewish population, along with their homes, businesses, synagogues, hospitals and schools. The exact figure of how many Jews died as a result of this incident is still unclear. Early reports estimated that ninety-one Jews were murdered during the attacks. Modern-day historians believe the death toll was considerably higher, as deaths from post-arrest maltreatment and the subsequent wave of suicides that occurred afterwards were not taken into consideration.

Black Aurora

By May 1939 there were only 1,585 Jews in residence in the city of Königsberg. Emigration was now prohibited and those Jews who remained or who had gone into hiding were actively and aggressively hunted down. Prominent Königsberg Jews who chose suicide as opposed to incarceration, slave labour or death at the hands of the Nazis were Paul Stettiner, Felix Japha and his wife, Lotte Gottschalk, and Alfred Gottschalk. The leader of the Jewish community, Hugo Falkenheim, was smuggled to safety. By 1942 many of the Königsberg Jews had been shipped to concentration camps. These included Theresienstadt in Nazi-occupied Czechoslovakia, Kaiserwald in occupied Latvia, and camps in Minsk in the occupied Byelorussian Soviet Socialist Republic. Very few of the Königsberg Jews would survive the Holocaust, and the exact number of victims remains unknown.

Chapter 5

By a Cursed Hand

When we think of the greatest maritime disaster in history, the RMS *Titanic* springs to mind. The British passenger liner was on her way to New York from Southampton when she collided with an iceberg and sank in the North Atlantic Ocean on 14 April 1912. An estimated 2,224 passengers and crew were on board; more than 1,500 died. The *Wilhelm Gustloff* tragedy was six times greater than the Titanic in terms of loss of life, yet, more than seventy years after that fateful night of 30 January 1945, only few people outside of Germany have heard about it. According to German survivor and archivist Heinz Schön, 9,343 people died in the sinking of the *Wilhelm Gustloff*; some 5,000 of them were children and babies.

The *Wilhelm Gustloff* was nothing like any other cruise ship of her era. She was the ultimate Nazi dream ship, built to take German workmen on the holiday of a lifetime. On 30 January 1945 she was the last refuge for thousands of refugees when she was hit by Russian torpedoes and sank.

The *Wilhelm Gustloff* story begins with the *Kraft durch Freude* (KdF) or Strength Through Joy organisation instituted by the Nazis in 1933. Although the *Wilhelm Gustloff* would only enjoy a brief flirtation with the KdF, it is worth explaining a little about the proposed role of the organisation, of which the ship was to be a part. The KdF was the state-operated leisure organisation of the Third Reich, forming part of the *Deutsche Arbeitsfront* (DAF), or German Labour Front, set up primarily to promote the advantages of National Socialism to the German people.

Upon the Nazis' seizure of power they sequestered the trade unions. German workers were then required to join the DAF. It occurred to many German workers that there was little to gain from joining the DAF, so a sweetener had to be devised as an incentive and this is where both the DAF and the KdF in combination proved so valuable. DAF membership meant that the average German worker could enjoy all the benefits that the KdF were offering, such as movies, keep-fit clubs, hiking, sporting activities, concerts, holidays and cruises. Large ships like the *Wilhelm Gustloff* and her sister ship, the *Robert Ley*, as well as several other ships, were built specifically for KdF cruises. A low-price cruise to some exotic destination would have been the source of great joy to any working-class German family. The working man himself would return happy and refreshed from his experience, thereby increasing his productivity, hence the 'Strength Through Joy' motto. Borrowing from the Italian Fascist *Dopolavoro* (After Work), but extending its influence into the workplace, the KdF soon developed into one of the largest Nazi organisations and the largest tourism and leisure operator of the 1930s. The KdF was also a clever attempt at bridging class divisions in the way that it made middle-class leisure activities available to the masses in Germany, thus breaking down the exclusivity barriers that Hitler believed should not be permitted to exist in his brand of National Socialist society.

The cruise ships became extremely popular within the KdF as few working-class Germans could have previously afforded to take a holiday at sea. The allocation of cabins on the ships was carried out on a drawing of lots basis, therefore eliminating the social status stigma that existed in many other societies at the time. All the passenger cabins were of the same size and specification, to further enhance the ethos of being ships without social classes. Adolf Hitler had larger private cabins available to him on board the *Wilhelm Gustloff* and *Robert Ley*, but he never used them.

When it began, the Strength Through Joy programme was viewed as a revolutionary concept that was readily embraced by the German people. It had a beneficial effect on the economy as it stimulated the tourism industry, which had been ailing throughout the 1920s. It was clear the programme would be a great success, and by 1934 over two million German citizens had participated in its activities. The varied range of leisure activities available included concerts, plays, libraries, day trips, and extended holiday breaks. There were also film screenings, keep-fit clubs, hiking and all manner of sporting pursuits. It was hoped that those who were not convinced National Socialists upon entering the KdF leisure programme would leave with a more supportive attitude. It was upon this foundation, of a nation looking after its own regardless of social stature, that the cruise ship *Wilhelm Gustloff* was conceived.

Plans were laid down on 1 August 1936, with the Blohm & Voss company overseeing the building of the vessel. The specification for the cruise ship was set out as follows:

> Builder: Blohm & Voss
> Owner: DAF (German Labour Front)
> Operator: Hamburg Sud
> Port of Registry: Hamburg, Germany
> Cost: 25 million Reichsmark
> Yard Number: 511
> Laid Down: 1 August 1936
> Launched: 5 May 1937 (by Adolf Hitler)
> Acquired: 15 March 1938
> Identification: Radio ID-DJVZ
> Class and type: Cruise ship
> Tonnage: 25,484 (Gross Register Tonnage)
> Length: 684ft 1in
> Beam: 77ft 5in
> Height: 183ft 9in
> Draught: 21ft 4in
> Number of decks: 5
> Propulsion: 4x8 cylinder MAN diesel engines with 2x4 bladed propellers giving 9,500 horsepower
> Speed: 17.8mph
> Range: 12,000 nautical miles
> Passenger capacity: 1,465 in 489 cabins
> Crew: In peacetime as cruise ship – 417. After 1939, 20 officers and 145 enlisted (naval)
> Armament: In peacetime no weapons were fitted to the *Wilhelm Gustloff*. After 1939 the ship was fitted with the following armament primarily for defence against aerial attack – 3x105mm (4.1in) anti-aircraft guns and 8x20mm (0.79in) anti-aircraft cannons.
> Fate: Requisitioned into the *Kriegsmarine* at the outbreak of the Second World War in September 1939.

By the time the *Wilhelm Gustloff* was completed, it was clear that she was a fine cruise ship and the KdF was rightly proud to receive her.

She was originally going to be named the *Adolf Hitler*, but following the assassination by a Croatian Jewish student in February 1936 of Wilhelm Gustloff, founder of the Swiss NSDAP, Hitler decided to name the ship after the murdered leader of the Nazi Party organisation for German citizens abroad. On 5 May 1937 the *Wilhelm Gustloff* was launched in the presence of the Führer himself, though she would not embark on her maiden voyage until the following year, on 24 March 1938. During the seventeen months of her brief peacetime service, the ship had run some fifty cruises and had transported some 65,000 holidaymakers. However, despite the romantic notions associated with the KdF organisation and its intentions, it was not possible to simply book a voyage on the movement's flagship. Those who travelled on the ship had to be selected by the Nazi Party. The ship was also requisitioned for public-orientated missions. For example, on 10 April 1938 the *Gustloff* was used as a polling station for German and Austrian nationals living in England to forward their votes on the annexation of Austria. In May 1939 the *Gustloff* and other cruise ships of the KdF fleet were ordered to transport back home the victorious German soldiers who had been fighting with the Condor Legion in the Spanish Civil War.

Orphelia Maschmann has memories of the KdF and how it benefited the new German society of the time in Prussia.

> I recall the cruise ships they used, but the name *Wilhelm Gustloff* never really meant anything to me personally, and I never even heard about it until a while after the Second World War had ended. We never went on any KdF cruises as my father's activities with his work in Prussia meant he had many wealthy Nazi contacts who owned homes in some of the most beautiful and exclusive resorts in Europe. We did go out on the sea on several occasions with the Kuthner family. They had a large cruiser boat that could sleep up to twelve people comfortably. We would go out on the sea on coastal cruises. My father didn't like crowds and didn't want to go out on the KdF cruise ships. I know that sounds like he was acting like a snob, but I understood what he meant. It was beautiful in the good weather. We would cruise up and down the coastline, with me and the Kuthner girls sitting at the

front of the boat with our bare legs dangling over the side. We would find somewhere to anchor up and spend the night. One of the memories I have is of lying outside on the front deck of the boat in the warm summer air, staring at the cobalt heavens, seeing all the stars uninterrupted by lights. Sometimes we even saw shooting stars and the Kuther girls would say "quickly, close your eyes and make a wish". My wish was that all of this would never end, and that I could have remained in that moment as a child forever. It was like leaving a fairytale behind every time we had to return to land and head back home to the house.

Through my father's other contacts we were able to secure weekend stays at castles too. Father would go out on shooting parties with the people he worked with while we played in the castle grounds. Neuschwanstein Castle, which is in south-west Bavaria, was one of the places we stayed. That was a place where art looted by our forces during the Second World War was kept. It was very secluded and an ideal place to hide things. While there I virtually had the run of the place, and as there were other children there, we played all kinds of games like hide and seek and war games. There was one we played in which I played the part of the princess, only instead of being rescued from dragons I had to be rescued from bad Jews. Some rooms in the castle were locked and had notices warning "Keep out". We didn't try to go in and we didn't ask any questions, though now I know why these rooms were locked.

Malbork Castle, in what was once Danzig in Prussia, was another place where we had a weekend stay. It was very nice there, but when I went it was winter and very cold. My father and his friends went out to hunt boar and woodland fowl. My mother took me to the huge old library with its roaring fire and rows and rows of books. She carefully selected a book for me to read and I would spend most of the day and evening reading by the fire as it was too cold to go out and play. We were given hot drinks at bedtime and tucked up under heavy thick blankets in ancient bedrooms with suits of armour standing in them. The suits of armour used to frighten me and the other girls who shared the bed with me. They would say things like, "I just saw it move. Look, its hand has moved, it wasn't like that a few minutes ago." In the end we hid our heads under the blankets and would squeal as we put our cold feet on one another. It was such fun. In the morning there would be a wonderful breakfast. It was always sad to leave, but I enjoyed those wonderful holidays. We didn't have to use the KdF facilities like most people had to. I understood the reason why we were getting these privileges. My father was important. He was a Nazi – he wore the party badge on his coat – he worked hard and was rewarded for his work in this way. It was perfect, really, and I was not going to complain even if his work had meant condemning a few hundred or a few thousand Jews to hard labour back in Germany. It was a good life and I never questioned any of it until much, much later on in my life.

Alexandria Busch, a Königsberg miner's daughter, recalls how the Strength Through Joy programme benefited her family, even though their use of the facilities was somewhat limited.

Were these KdF holidays actually holidays in the sense that we perhaps today view as a holiday? No, I would say they were not. With hindsight they were little more than state-controlled environments; an exercise in bringing everyone into the jolly folds of National Socialism. Everything about them was centred around control, and each excursion was pre-planned. You still had no real freedom. You still had to listen to the rhetoric, and you still had to do physical exercise and abide by the regimen. I think the only part I can say that actually felt like we were on a holiday was when we disembarked the boat and spent time on a beach somewhere. My parents were loving all of it. It was a stick and carrot that was irresistible to us at the time. We were pure-bred Prussians, working class, and my father, being a hard-working miner, was just the kind of man that Hitler felt should be his most ardent supporter.

The mining families – many of them friends of ours as we were a tight-knit community back then – were given priority for the cruise ship experiences. I remember a trip on one of the big boats, I think it was the *Robert Ley*. I recall the excitement of walking up the gangway onto this huge white ship. It seemed to shine in the sunlight and was welcoming at the same time. We were allocated a cabin and once we had unpacked the few bags we had with us, we went up onto the deck. I remember looking out over the deck rail as we slowly pulled out of the port. This huge boat had to be towed out of the harbour before its engines started for the trip out into the ocean. You couldn't hear the engines when they started; it was just a gentle vibration you felt. I looked over the rail at the sea with the breeze in my hair and I took a deep breath and closed my eyes for a second. It felt nice to be away from the city; the houses and the smoke and the perpetual dirt. Mother and father stood looking out onto the horizon. They embraced, and they felt happy, which made me feel happy. We were all happy.

Of course, obligations were never far away. The next day I was encouraged – or more or less told – that I should join the other girls on board for physical exercise routines to develop our wellbeing and maintain health. The influence of the BDM was felt even on board the ship. It wasn't that I disliked it, I just wanted a break from it, that's all, but it was not allowed even here. So I put on my black shorts, white sports vest and joined the other girls in a very large gymnasium inside the ship. It was not too bad as I bumped into a few girls that I knew and made friends with many I didn't know. We all said we would keep in touch after the trip.

We ended up in the Mediterranean and the scenery made me gasp as we approached the land. We were permitted a short time on the Sicilian coast to go and explore. My parents took me to a beach and we threw down towels and just lay in the sun. We spent some time swimming in the beautiful, crystal-clear water. It was a thousand miles away from the dirty, pea-coloured waters of the harbour in

Königsberg, which had been my first introduction to the sea. Here there were no massive industrial cranes perching like steel vultures all around you. There was no acrid industrial smoke and no noise. It was a joy in every sense of the word. Here we were, a working-class family enjoying a break that, just a few years previously, we could never have dreamed of. It was all too short, but we made the most of it.

Of course, when the war broke out these cruises had to stop. We then had to use the popular German resorts back home, which was not a problem. We had many good times at the Havel Lakes, for example, until the war even began to interfere with these holiday breaks. The KdF cruises and associated holidays could only continue for as long as things were going well for Germany. The moment things started to go badly meant the end of these things. We had to face reality and prepare for total war. In the BDM we continued with the summer camps, which we went on every year through each summer, but these were far from holidays; they were strict, regimented and ideological, and parents were not allowed to accompany their children. It was considered strictly Hitler Youth business.

Claudette Bauer's family had a long tradition of farming in the East Prussian countryside. As part of a large farming and agricultural community, their personal reward could only ever be gained through their own hard labours. When Hitler came to power the Bauer family imagined that huge changes would take place in all areas of Prussia, and that somehow a different dynamic would come into force. Claudette explained that when her family applied for a place on one of the KdF cruise ships, their application was sidelined in favour of the city families:

> I can remember being around livestock ever since I had learned to walk. My parents often took me down into the fields and animal paddocks with them for the whole day, even in the wintertime. I had to learn all of the skills as soon as I was old enough. I was one of four children, there were two boys and two girls. When I was seven years old, I was taught how to milk the few goats we kept. I was not allowed

to milk the cattle as they would kick you if you didn't do it properly. A kick in the head from one of those cows could easily have killed an adult let alone a child. As I grew older I did more and more work and learned more farming skills. None of us were ever allowed to sit around daydreaming or even read books. We had to help with the work, which began early in the morning and finished sometimes late at night. We went to school too on top of all of this.

Father applied for a holiday on one of the cruise ships. We all needed some of this 'Strength Through Joy', as we worked very hard all year round and felt we deserved it. He was astonished when he received a letter informing him and mother that, as we were a farming family living in a rural area, we had access to the beautiful countryside, lakes and woodlands and that in itself was strength through joy. It was explained that the city dwellers, who had few of these luxuries on their doorstep, would be a priority for the cruises on the KdF boats. It seemed everyone wanted to go on cruise boats like the *Wilhelm Gustloff* or *Robert Ley* and so there was a long waiting list; so long that it would be years before we would get our chance.

It annoyed my parents very much, but they understood the hardships of the people who lived in Königsberg among the industry and its pollution. People who lived in the cities were more prone to health problems than those out in the countryside, and we generally ate better than they did, so in one way we already had our own brand of 'Strength Through Joy' and didn't need the holidays. We did go to seaside towns, usually just for a weekend as we could not leave the farm for very long even though people were there to run it in our absence. My father never trusted his own labourers and he was suspicious that they might not do much work while he was away.

One resort we went to frequently is in modern-day Poland. It was named Cammin in Pommern [Kamien Pomoroski as it is pronounced in Polish]. We enjoyed family breaks there, especially swimming in the bay. The summers there were never really hot like more exotic places, but they were warm enough. We did all the usual things kids did back then like playing on the beach and building sandcastles. We went searching through the rock pools for crabs and fish that had become trapped by the last tide. Even seaweed was a novelty to us. We would chase one another with handfuls of this slimy, green yuk and throw it at each other. My brothers would always try and throw it at me and my sister, being bigger and stronger than us. It wasn't fair. My eldest brother, Willi, was the worst. He would chase you, get you on the sand and pin you down, then dangle the seaweed he had in his hands over our faces. These weekends were very brief, and few and far between, but they enabled us to let off some steam before going back home.

As I grew older I worked more with the goats than any of our other animals. I loved the goats as they were playful and mischievous. I recall my father once having to repair some wire fencing and put in some new posts in the goats' enclosure. He made the age-old error of turning his back and bending down in front of one of the large male goats we named Billie. Before I could even shout a warning, Billie had charged forward and I watched in slow motion as Billie's head crashed against my father's backside. The butt sent him sprawling face down onto the ground. I jumped down off the fence and ran over to see if my father was alright. He stood up cursing, using language I had never heard him use before. He told me not to say anything to mother about this. I tried to keep a serious face, but I started laughing. My father started laughing too, in fact, we were both in hysterics. Even over dinner that evening we kept laughing, and mother and the others kept asking "what is it with you two, what is so funny?" My father never told them. He just said it was a private matter between himself and his eldest daughter. In future, though, he never again turned his back on any of the goats, not even the baby ones, and always gave Billie healthy respect.

So really this was our 'Strength Through Joy'. We worked very hard indeed, yet we did have some fun times. We had all the joy we needed right here, so why bother going on a crowded boat full of complete strangers? That was our logic. Many families who should have gone on those boats didn't get the chance anyway due to the outbreak of the war. Once the war began the cruises stopped and the ships were taken over by the German navy for military use. In fact, the one and only time I ever went aboard a ship was during the evacuations from Prussia at the end of the war.

Although not directly connected with Prussia, Prora was perhaps the greatest failure of the Nazi Strength Through Joy programme. Originally intended as one of the showcase developments, it would have been – had it commenced operation – one of the first truly modern holiday resorts. Yet its construction mirrored the monotony of many post-war Eastern bloc buildings, possessing an arresting lack of sentimentality, colour and detail, especially when compared to the architecture of the old Weimar Republic. It was in every sense a machine aesthetic designed along the lines of Nazi ideology. Despite this, the design won a Grand Prix award at the 1937 Paris World Exposition. The six-storey complex consisted of 10,000 rooms, all with a view of the Baltic Sea, stretching over an area of 4.5km. Had it been completed, it would have been something of Nazi utopia, boasting many recreational facilities ranging from swimming and tennis to bowling, along with other general fitness disciplines such as gymnastics, running and cycling. The resort was designed in such a way that it could, in the event of war, be turned over for military use with the principle idea of the complex being used as hospital. As war was foremost in Hitler's mind, German society would never make use of the Prora resort. From the outbreak of war in September of 1939 building and construction work slowly fizzled out and the project was never completed. During the course of the Allied bombing campaign many residents of Hamburg sought refuge in one of the housing blocks of the resort complex. In later years female *Luftwaffe* auxiliaries were billeted there along with refugees from eastern Germany.

With the outbreak of war in 1939, the *Wilhelm Gustloff* was withdrawn from the KdF and requisitioned for use in the German *Kriegsmarine*. One of her first operations for the navy was to transport German service personnel of the victorious Condor Legion back to Germany during the summer of 1939. For those on board the liner it would have felt like they were on a KdF vacation, had it not been for the constant yelling of NCOs and officers reminding the men that they were still in military service and therefore obliged to maintain weapons and complete drill parades on a daily basis. The *Wilhelm Gustloff* brought the soldiers home to a rapturous welcome.

Ellie Mitzelbruck was six years old when her mother took her to welcome her father back home from the Spanish campaign in May 1939. She recalled:

> My father had been in the artillery as a field observer with a howitzer gun crew. We made the short journey from our home to Hamburg to await the arrival of the ship. I don't really recall taking much notice of anything as there were so many distractions, bands playing and large crowds of people. When the ship came into view there was a loud roar from the crowd, many people, including children, were waving those little triangular hand flags, red, white and black with the swastika in the middle. They were like miniature versions of our national flag of the time. The flags were handed out to all those present and photographers were there, most likely for propaganda purposes. I remember the huge white ship coming in almost silently. For such a huge ship it made so little noise. There was so much noise from the crowds of people we would not have heard anything anyway, I don't think. When the ship docked it seemed an age before my father came off with his comrades from his unit. I remember shouting at the top of my voice "daddy, daddy". We all embraced and then father came home with us. As we left the harbour at Hamburg I looked back at the big white ship. There was no sense of foreboding or that anything bad would ever happen to the ship, but then I was just a child at the time. All of this was just an adventure, nothing more really.

Following the return of the Condor Legion the *Wilhelm Gustloff* was pressed into use as a hospital ship from September 1939 to November 1940. Her official designation during this period was *Lazarettshiff* D (hospital ship D). From 20 November 1940, the medical equipment aboard the ship was removed, and it was repainted from its hospital ship colours of white with a green stripe to the standard naval grey. Due to the British naval blockade of the German coastline, the ship was put to use as a floating barracks for approximately one thousand U-Boat crew trainees of the 2nd Submarine Training Division (2 *Unterseeboot-Lehrdivision*) in the Free City of Danzig port of Gotenhafen, which today is Gdynia and forms, together with Sopot and Gdańsk, the so called 'Tricity' in modern-day Poland. The ship remained in this role as a floating barracks for virtually the remainder of the Second World War.

In January 1945 the *Wilhelm Gustloff* would be called up to take part in Operation Hannibal, the evacuation of German civilians, military personnel and refugees from East Prussia, Courland and the Polish Corridor to the West. The speed and aggressiveness of the advance of the Soviet Red Army filled those waiting to be evacuated with terror. The terrible irony of all of this was that even greater terror lay ahead.

Chapter 6

The Minority Nightmare

Before the Second World War Europe was home to ten million Jews. They belonged to a faith that had existed for 3000 years. At sunset each Friday, religious Jews observed the start of the Sabbath, a day set aside for prayer and rest. Judaism, the Jewish faith, gave the world the Bible and the idea of one strict but just God.

Originally from the Middle East, Jews were scattered by migration and foreign conquest. They settled as a minority in many European countries alongside people who did not share their faith. Encountering hostility from some of their neighbours, Jews were forced to flee from country to country. Around the ninth century the majority, known as Ashkenazi Jews, eventually settled in Poland, where their skills were welcomed. There they developed a distinguished culture and their own language, Yiddish.

Over the centuries Christians were taught to mistrust and despise Jewish people as a matter of faith. Yet Jesus Christ, whose life and teachings Christianity had celebrated for over a thousand years, was born a Jew and died a Jew. The Christian Church blamed the Jews unjustly for killing Christ.

From medieval times onwards Jews were often attacked and killed by Christian believers or forced to convert to Christianity. In an age of superstition, Jews were accused of the most bizarre and diabolical crimes. They were said to kidnap Christian children and use their blood for religious rituals. In Christian mythology the Jews were the embodiment of the devil. Christians singled out Jews for persecution, forcing them to wear special clothing, restricting them to certain trades and professions and confining them to special districts called ghettos.

With the coming of modern political ideas nearly all these anti-Jewish restrictions disappeared. By the twentieth century most Jews still retained their traditional ways, though in appearance and way of life many Jews were indistinguishable from the rest of society. They had successfully made their way out of the ghettos and into the modern world.

Jews made their mark in industry, in the arts and in the sciences. Among them was Albert Einstein, one of the twentieth century's most brilliant minds. Throughout Germany and the rest of Western Europe they became more accepted and enjoyed greater prosperity, but a hatred of Jews persisted. For modern racists, religion was no longer an issue. They believed that Jews were members of a dangerous and inferior race. These antisemites blamed Jews for everything that was wrong in society, depicting them as revolutionary fanatics or blood-sucking capitalists whose aim was world domination.

Adolph Hitler described Jews as a disease that had to be wiped out. He believed in a struggle for survival between the German nation and the Jewish race, a struggle in which there could be only one victor. Like Jews, other groups of people found themselves outcasts due to reasons of political, social, cultural or sexual orientation.

Before Hitler's rise to power in 1933 few Jewish families living in Germany, Austria and Czechoslovakia foresaw how much their lives were about to change. Children could not possibly imagine that their childhood would be taken away from them. Anni Taubmann from Breslau was eight years old when Hitler came to power. She remembers: 'My mother always tried to give us a birthday party, she baked a cake and we invited a few school friends. That year the table was set for eight children including myself. Nobody came, not a single child came to this birthday party. That was the first terrible blow to me. I know it sounds trivial, but for a child it was the first sort of understanding that you are left out, that there is something different about you.'

For Jewish children life under Hitler became increasingly threatening and isolating. While the Nazis stripped their parents of their jobs and citizenships, the children were gradually barred from schools, theatres, parks and swimming pools. Jack Helmann from Hesse was walking to school one day when six or seven boys came up to him. They called him 'Jew bastard', attacked him and threw him through a glass window. He was badly cut and needed to go to hospital for stitching. After that he didn't go to school anymore and constantly felt threatened.

As Hitler strengthened his control, he began looking for opportunities to extend Germany's power beyond its borders. In March 1938 German troops entered Austria and without firing a single shot annexed the country. Nazi authorities took just weeks to implement the anti-Jewish laws that had taken Hitler five years to put in place in Germany. Jewish families started to look at ways to get out of Germany and Austria. But how easy was it to leave? Anni Taubman recalls:

> First of all you had to have a sponsor in the country you were going to, who would promise that you wouldn't become a burden on the government. You would need to get a visa from the state department or government to allow you in. Then you would need to get an exit permit from the Nazis. All these things had to happen within a limited time frame and you would need to collect them all together before they expired. Possible destinations were Argentina, Uruguay, Paraguay, Venezuela, Cuba, the Dominican Republic and Shanghai. I remember going with my father to the American consulate. There was a queue all around the block, up the stairs, along the corridor, in the office, around the desk. Everyone wanted to go to America. This was late summer 1938. I got to America in early May 1951.

Soon after the annexation of Austria, Hitler demanded the annexation of Sudetenland in Czechoslovakia. The region was home to over three million ethnic Germans and Hitler insisted that it should become part of the Reich. With international agreement, in October 1938 Sudetenland was added to Germany territory. Less than half year later Hitler would destroy the Czech state, but for now he continued to persecute the Jews.

Things escalated further following the assassination on 7 November of a German diplomat, Ernst vom Rath, by Hershel Grynszpan, a seventeen-year-old Polish Jew living in Paris. On 9 and 10 November 1938 the Nazis orchestrated a vicious programme called *Krisiallnacht* – the 'night of broken glass' – during which Jewish homes, hospitals, schools and shops were attacked with sledgehammers and ransacked. Over 200 Synagogues were destroyed throughout Germany, Austria, Sudetenland and, on 12 and 13 November, also in the free city of Danzig. Over 700,000 businesses were either destroyed or damaged, their merchandise dumped on the street or looted completely.

At least ninety-one people were killed during the attacks, around 300,000 were arrested and incarcerated in ghettos to be later deported to concentration camps. *Kristallnacht* was followed by additional economic and political persecution of Jews. It is often viewed by historians as a key event in Germany's broader racial policy programme and the beginning of the Final Solution and the Holocaust.

By the end of 1938 it became clear that Jews were increasingly in danger. More and more wanted to desperately leave and some were relying on relatives abroad for help, with employment or to look after their children with the promise that they would soon follow. Although most countries condemned Hitler's attacks on the Jews, Britain was the only one willing to relax its immigration control, though only for children, who would not threaten British jobs or public funds. Days after *Kristallnacht*, Anglo-Jewish leaders met with Prime Minister Chamberlain and urged him to let Christian as well as Jewish unaccompanied children up to the age of seventeen into the country.

A concrete rescue plan, the Kindertransport, to be funded by private and religious organisations, was drawn up eight days later and approved by the House of Commons. Over 10,000 children, mainly Jewish, from Germany, Poland, Austria, Czechoslovakia and the free city of Danzig, arrived in the United Kingdom in the nine months that followed. They were placed in foster homes, hostels, schools and farms. The Refugee Children Movement (RCM) was formed, with representatives in Germany and Austria. In Germany, a network of organisers was established with volunteers working round the clock with the RCM to compile priority lists of those most in danger: teenagers in concentration camps or threatened with arrest; children in Jewish orphanages; children whose parents were too poor to maintain them or had been deported to concentration camps. Since the Nazis' policy was to get rid of all Jews, they did not oppose the departure of children, providing that they were not taking any valuables with them. They could only take one small suitcase and no more than ten Reichsmarks. Each child was issued with a tag to wear round their neck with a number on one side and the child's name on the other.

The first transport was organised by Florence Nankivell, who spent a week in Berlin, hassled by Nazi police, organising the children. The train left Berlin on 1 December 1938 and the children arrived in Harwich by boat on 2 December 1938 with 196 children on board. The majority of refugees travelled by train and boat, arriving at the port of Dover before continuing to London by train. A sculpture by Israeli artist Frank Meisler called *Kindertransport – the Arrival* was erected outside Liverpool Street Station in central London in 2006. The outbreak of war put a stop to the Kindertransport, with the last shipment of seventy-four children leaving on the passenger-freighter SS *Bodegraven* from the Netherlands on 14 May 1940.

Some children in the Kindertransport went through severe trauma. Many younger children could not understand what it meant to be away from their families for a few months, they could not speak the language of the host family, nor could the hosts speak German or Czech. In British schools refugee children were often seen as 'enemy Germans' rather than 'Jewish refugees' and treated badly by fellow pupils as a result. The younger they were, the more unforgiving they were of their parents. Older children had a better understanding of what was happening and were more willing to accept the situation.

In 1940 the British Government ordered the internment of all male refugees aged sixteen to seventy from enemy countries. Around 1,000 children from the Kindertransport, who by then had turned eighteen, were kept in internment camps, often on the Isle of Man. Around 400 were transported overseas to Canada or Australia, others were offered to do war work or to enter the Army Auxiliary Pioneer Corps. Some of them joined elite formations such as the Special Forces, where their language skills were put to good use during the D-Day landings in France, and later as the Allies progressed into Germany.

Parents suffered greatly too, not knowing where their children were going, who would look after them and if or how they would find them again. Any correspondence that had been established between the children and their parents soon stopped after the outbreak of war, or when the parents were deported to concentration camps. And after the war ended there were many problems as agencies were flooded with requests from children seeking to find their parents or any surviving members of their families.

There are many, many accounts of children from the Kindertransport; some happy stories of survival and reunions, other sad or even tragic stories of loss and abuse. Most children never saw their parents again, while others had not only found their parents still alive but had acquired another set of 'parents' as well. Others still had forgotten their native language.

People wanted to carry on where they left off but that was, of course, impossible for the vast majority. As one former Kindertransport child put it: 'To be a refugee is the most horrible feeling because you lose your family, you lose your home. You are also without an identity. Suddenly you are a nothing. You are just reliant of people's good nature, help and understanding.'

By early 1939 the Nazis had closed most of Germany's borders and many countries had imposed quotas limiting the number of Jewish refugees they would allow in. Yet attempts to reach other countries, especially by ship, were still being made. On May 13 1939, for example, more than 900 Jews fled Germany aboard a luxury cruise liner, the SS *St Louis*, hoping to reach Cuba and then travel to the US.

Cuba was seen as a temporary transit port to America and officials at the Cuban Embassy in Berlin were offering visas for about $200–300 each (£1,900–3,100 at today's prices). Under order from the ship's captain, Gustav Schroeder, the waiters and crew members treated the passengers politely, in stark contrast to the hostility Jewish families were facing in Germany under the Nazis. On board the SS *St Louis*, traditional Friday night prayers were allowed to be held, during which the captain gave permission for the portrait of Adolf Hitler hanging in the main dining room to be taken down.

Sadly, once they reached Havana it quickly became clear that they were not going to dock. For the next seven days Captain Schroeder tried in vain to persuade the Cuban authorities to allow them in. In fact, the Cubans had already decided to revoke all but a handful of visas for fear of being inundated with more refugees in the near future.

After steering the ship towards the Florida coast and being refused the right to dock by the US authorities, despite direct appeals to President Roosevelt, Captain Schroeder had no option but to return the giant liner back towards Europe. However, the refugees didn't have to go back to Germany. Instead, Belgium, France, Holland and the UK agreed to take them. On June 17 1939 the liner docked at the Belgian port of Antwerp, more than a month after leaving Hamburg.

In early 1939 some 3,500 Jews were recorded as living in the city of Danzig, Prussia. In March 1939 the first transports to Palestine departed. At the outbreak of war 1,700 mostly elderly Jews remained in the city in defiance of the growing threat from the Nazis.

The Minority Nightmare

Around 140 Jewish children had already been evacuated to England by the Kindertransport throughout 1938–1939.

The Danzig *Kristallnacht* of 12–14 November 1938 mirrored the antisemitic riots taking place in Berlin and other cities around Germany. The synagogues in Knagfuhr, Mattenbuden and Zoppot were destroyed. The only one to survive the violence was the Great Synagogue, which was only saved due to Jewish war veterans standing guard outside.

Many of the older Jewish population in Danzig were initially of the opinion that the Nazis, while problematic, would not pose too serious a threat to them. Many did not want to leave their homes, businesses and possessions behind, and defiance of the Nazis was commonplace. Olga Bachmann, now well into her nineties, recalls her family's struggle to decide whether to stay in Danzig or leave with many of the others:

> Such decisions were not easy. It was our home, our livelihood and where we belonged. The thought of having to leave everything behind and go somewhere that was not only culturally different, but where you felt that you didn't belong, was very sad. I know my family sat down and argued over staying or leaving for many hours at a time. The arguments were based on feelings of the time. Some of our people felt a sense of dread; that something evil was emanating from within Europe. The horror stories of the hatred vented towards Jews in Germany frightened my family greatly. They decided they did not wish to gamble with our lives. We should go, and we could always return when things calmed down or when Hitler was gone. Looking back, we made the right decision, didn't we? Had we stayed I don't think I would be here to tell you this now. The Nazis would have killed us all. They despised us. In all my life I have never felt such hate before or since the Nazis.

In the wake of the German invasion of Poland in 1939 by *Wehrmacht* and SS *Heimwehr* 'Danzig' forces, followed by the German annexation of Danzig Free City, around 130 Jews were held in a 'ghetto' in a building on Milchkannengasse street (today's Ulica Stagewna). Another group was imprisoned, along with the city's Poles, at the Victoriaschule, which was an old gymnasium building. Here, beatings and torture were carried out on a daily basis, and many of those held in the building died as a result. There were also camps set up to hold Jews and Poles at Westerplatte and Ohra (modern-day Orunia). Jews from Zoppot were herded into the forest at Piasnica and massacred. The last group of Jews able to flee for Palestine departed in August 1940. It is a sad irony that many of those fleeing Nazi oppression would then face the *Patria* disaster, which occurred in the port of Haifa. Some 267 Jews lost their lives because of a bureaucratic bungle on the part of the British.

On 1 September 1939 the first shots of the Second World War were fired by German troops at Westerplatte and at the Polish post office in Danzig (created in 1920 under the Treaty of Versailles and considered extraterritorial Polish property). The *Heimwehr* 'Danzig' took part in the attacks under German army command, together with special units of Danzig police. At that time fifty-six people were in the post office complex, including the caretaker, his wife and ten-year-old daughter, Erwina. Polish defenders managed to repel the first attack. The commander of the Polish defense, Konrad Guderski, died in the second attack from the blast of his own grenade, which stopped the Germans from entering the building. Further attacks followed as the day unfolded. Frustrated by the Poles' refusal to surrender, the commander of the Danzig police units, Willi Bethke, requested a rail car full of gasoline, which the Danzig fire department then pumped into the basement of the building and ignited by hand grenade. Three people were burned alive. The first people to leave the building, Director Dr Jan Michon, carrying a white flag, and commander Jozef Masik, were shot by the Germans. The rest of the Poles were allowed to surrender and leave the burning building while German forces captured it. Sixteen wounded prisoners were sent to the Gestapo hospital, six of them later died from their injuries, including ten-year-old Erwina. All those who survived the post office attack were apprehended and an immediate trial was organised. The trial – which was a mockery – sentenced the men to death on the accusation they were bandits. Since none of the accused was of military affiliation, they were denied the rights given to combatants by the Geneva Convention. All but four of the fifty-four defenders who were able to escape the building during the surrender were either killed or executed afterwards. They had held out for fifteen hours. The reinforcements never came as they were occupied fighting the *Wehrmacht* invasion in the Tuchola Forest.

The Minority Nightmare

A similar fate awaited eleven Polish railway workers south of the city after they foiled a German attempt to use an armoured train. They were tried and executed, together with their immediate families, on 5 October and buried in a mass grave at the cemetery of Danzig-Saspe (Zaspa).

Gisela Teschke remembers:

> I remember that day only too clearly. I was six years old. It was early in the morning and still dark when my father put on his police uniform and left for work, unaware of what gruesome event lay in store for him. I went to take his place in my parent's bed, jumping up and down, when my mother told me to be quiet as Adolf Hitler was about to make a speech. I'll never forget the crackling of the static and the announcer introducing the Führer, then that awful, raspy voice I heard for the first time as he said, "People of Danzig, rejoice, you are now German." And with that, we suddenly heard heavy artillery being fired. My mother quickly jumped out of bed, just as scared as I was. We dressed quickly and listened in horror. That very moment I never wanted any part of Hitler ever again.
>
> Anxiously we waited for my father to return. I still see him, distraught, exhausted and covered in dust. He told us that he had to go to the Polish post office, where Poles had refused to surrender. There was an exchange of fire and the whole building set alight from the outside. Those inside perished in agony. Others who had surrendered were shot. The carnage of the Polish people had begun.

As well as Jews, another group that has suffered historical prejudice are the gypsy peoples of Europe. This goes as far back as the thirteenth century. The Romani gypsy people of Eastern and Central Europe were (and still are) viewed with much suspicion and fear by established communities. The Romani people were nomadic, travelling the countryside with their horse-drawn caravans and forming their own separate communities. They lived by their own set of rules, customs and traditions, and lived largely off the land. Romani children grew up learning the skills of their elders until they reached an age to marry. Their marriages were often arranged; a bride or bridegroom would be either from within the particular Romani tribe or from another. Romani girls and boys were raised under the rule that they were forbidden to marry an 'outsider' (one from outside the Romani community) and though there were cases of young Romanis eloping to marry outsiders, such occurrences were very rare.

The fear and suspicion with which many viewed the Romani people resulted from them being labelled 'wizards', being able to predict the unknown and having no permanent professional affiliation. Many Romani worked as musicians and craftsmen often making things from wood, cloth or any other materials they could procure and then sell on. They were known for making good luck charms and not all were greeted with hostility. Orphelia Maschmann recalls:

> My parents once told me about a woman they knew who had been trying for a baby for some time without any luck. When the Romani people came by one afternoon they convinced her to buy some charms from them that would make her fertile. The strange thing was that they knew nothing about the woman or her apparent infertility. One of the elderly Romani women told her to place the charms beneath her pillow before attempting union with her husband. The old woman kissed the charms and handed them to the young woman. The Romani people then set off with their horses and carts and she never saw them again. She followed the old woman's advice and within a month of receiving the charms she fell pregnant. When she later told her family about the charms, they told her she would have to destroy the baby, because it would be born a devil as it was conceived through witchcraft and sorcery, not through nature as God had intended. I don't know what happened to this woman or her child. My parents refused to tell me anymore about it other than I should have nothing to do with Jews or Romani peoples or anyone who was not a pure-blood German.

The above tale is typical of the mistrust vented toward the Romani people. They suffered prejudice everywhere they went, and they had to be prepared to meet fire with fire.

The Minority Nightmare

When Hitler came to power and the tentacles of National Socialism began to spread throughout Europe, attacks upon Romani communities increased.

Prussia was no exception and it was not uncommon for bands of men to go out at night specifically with the intention of raiding Romani camp sites. In many of the skirmishes that resulted, the attackers came off far worse than the Romanis. Many Romani males were proficient bare-knuckle fighters who could look after themselves and their families. The real problems began with the arrival of Hitler's Third Reich. The Romanis would now be faced with armed soldiers as opposed to men and their fists. Many Romanis were reported to the Gestapo who then acted with ruthless efficiency. Thousands were rounded up and subjected to sterilisation, murdered or sent to the concentration camps. Others were forced to flee into Russia, where they met further hostility. The Romani were a community in very real danger of being ethnically cleansed from Europe with the outbreak of the Second World War.

On 26 November 1935 Hitler added a supplementary decree to the Nuremberg Laws, classifying gypsies as 'enemies of the race-based state', just as Jews were under the Third Reich. Historians estimate that between a quarter and half of the one million-plus Romani present in Europe at the time were killed by the Nazis and their collaborators.

Perhaps a more tragic element was the fact that many Romani children rounded up in Prussia and the Eastern territories were sent to Auschwitz where they were to be used in horrific medical experiments. These so-called medical experiments often included surgery with no anaesthetic, dissection, and the administering of various toxins into the victims. Much of this work was carried out by the infamous 'Angel of Death', Dr Josef Mengele.

Born in Bavaria in 1911, Mengele was a *Schutzstaffel* (SS) officer and physician. Before the war he had received various doctorates in medicine and anthropology and had been actively involved in research. Mengele joined the Nazi party in 1937 and the SS in 1938, but was not initially involved in Hitler's 'euthanasia' programme. Starting in spring 1939, this was aimed to eliminate what the Nazis considered 'life unworthy of life': i.e., those individuals who, they believed, represented a genetic and a financial burden on German society and the state because of severe psychiatric, neurological or physical disabilities. The programme's functionaries called their secret enterprise T4. This codename came from the street address of the programme's coordinating office in Berlin, Tiergartenstrasse 4.

Led by Philipp Bouhler, the director of Hitler's private chancellery, and Nazi physician Karl Brandt, the programme was based on a decree which required all physicians, nurses and midwifes to report newborn babies and children under the age of three who showed signs of severe mental or physical disability. From October 1939 public health authorities began to encourage parents of children with disabilities to admit them to one of a number of specially designed pediatric clinics throughout Germany and Austria. In reality, the clinics were children's killing wards, run by specially recruited staff who would murder the young patients by lethal overdoses of medication or by starvation. As the programme widened, youths up to the age of seventeen were admitted to such clinics.

Although the programme was at first confined to Germany and the annexed territories of Austria, Alsace-Lorraine, Bohemia and Moravia, it soon spread to the Eastern territories of Prussia and the Soviet Union, making institutionalised patients who were considered 'unworthy of life' the target of SS officers and police forces. In areas of Pomerania, West Prussia and occupied Poland, SS and police units murdered some 30,000 patients by the autumn of 1941 in order to accommodate ethnic German settlers transferred from the Baltic and other areas. Many more thousands of disabled people were also murdered in mass shootings and gas vans in occupied Soviet territories. Hospitals emptied by these killings were often used as barracks or turned into euthanasia centres.

In many ways, the euthanasia programme represented a rehearsal for Nazi Germany's subsequent genocidal policies. Following the Wannsee Conference, held at an SS guesthouse near Berlin in January 1942, and chaired by Reinhard Heydrich and attended by fifteen senior officers of the Nazi Party and the German government, over eleven million Jews would fall victims of the 'Final Solution'. This figure represents approximately ninety per cent of the Jewish population of Poland and two thirds of the Jewish population of Europe. Planners of the Final Solution used the gas chambers and crematoria designed for the T4 campaign to murder Jews in German-occupied Europe. Staff from the euthanasia programme were then transferred during Operation Reinhard to killing centres such as Belzec, Sobibor and Treblinka.

The Minority Nightmare

At the beginning of the Second World War Mengele was assigned as battalion medical officer then transferred to the Nazi concentration camps in 1943. When he arrived at Auschwitz he saw the opportunity to conduct genetic research on human subjects. Mengele had a fascination for Romani children, particularly sets of twins. The following account was recorded by Vera Alexander, a Jewish inmate at Auschwitz who was tasked with looking after fifty sets of Romani twins:

> I remember one set of twins in particular: Guido and Ina aged about four. One day Mengele took them away. When they returned, they were in a terrible state. They had been sewn together, back to back like Siamese twins. Their wounds soon became infected and began to ooze thick, green-and-yellow pus. The twins screamed out in agony day and night. I remember their parents well. The mother's name was Stella, and she managed to get some morphine and they used this to euthanize the twins in order to end their terrible suffering.

How many of Prussia's Romani people had their lives snuffed out in this manner will never be known. Dr Josef Mengele was a monster who typified the Nazi terror. The disgusting human experiments carried out in his name and often by his own hand went unpunished after the war and Mengele went on to live a very comfortable life in South America after fleeing a war-ravaged Europe. This led one Romani elder to remark of Mengele, 'There will be no peace for him in heaven. He did not receive punishment for his crimes in this world, but in the next one he will.'

Claudette Bauer recalls the Romani people she encountered in her rural area, near Rastenburg:

> The Romani people would often pass through the villages. They would set up camp near the woods or in the fields and the women would usually come into the villages to sell their wares. They sold things like wooden clothing pegs, scarves, cloth, wooden carvings and lucky charms. I wouldn't say the Romani people were always welcomed, but not everyone was hostile towards them. The men were refused service at the local inn and told to leave, while the women would walk

about with small baskets of flowers and other things under their arms. They would go from house to house knocking on doors. Sometimes someone would answer and buy things from them, other times they would be told to go away.

Some of the farming communities felt a kind of bond with these people. The Romanis were a hardy people and lived outdoors all the year round in sun, wind, rain and snow. Sometimes the men would come looking for extra work to earn some money and my father always obliged. They were hard-working men who asked for little in return other than somewhere to camp for a few days, though in some areas we heard there were problems of livestock being killed and taken. Goats and chickens would disappear overnight and eggs were stolen. Many of the farming communities began to feel anger towards the Romani for the bad deeds of a few.

I remember seeing them in one of our fields; three, sometimes four, wooden caravan-type dwellings that were beautifully decorated with little windows and curtains. The horses that pulled the carts would wander around eating the grass. I used to see the Romani people washing themselves in the stream nearby. The women washed the children and then the men washed. Any dirty clothing was then washed and hung out on a line between the carts to dry. They had a pot suspended over a fire, usually with a stew cooking away inside. They put rabbits in the stew as these were plentiful on the land. Rabbits were a pest as they ate crops so we didn't mind the Romani people snaring them and eating them. In some ways the Romani seemed to be living an idyllic lifestyle, one I could quite easily have chosen to live myself had circumstances been different.

The irrational fears that some Prussian Germans had about the Romani were set deep in German folklore. Children were told by their parents that the Romani would kidnap them, that they possessed magic powers to turn themselves into animals, and that they could predict the future and so on. So, many children in the region were afraid of gypsies. When Hitler came to power everything changed. It was no longer safe for Romani people to travel around the new Third Reich. The authorities were very cruel to these people. They would arrest them and burn their caravans and confiscate their horses. The horses would be handed over to local farmers as a goodwill gesture. Many farmers benefited from this arrangement, but we didn't.

Many Romanis perished in the camps in the East. It is a shameful episode in our country's history. I always looked upon Prussia as a place where outdoors people worked together for the good of the land, but the Nazis forced us to comply with their ideals and their rules of the land. This was all for the greater German Reich, they would say to us. First the Jews, then the Romani, then anyone who didn't agree with them, then who next? "Will they ever run out of enemies?" I used to think to myself. My father just used to say, "Keep your thoughts to yourself, do your work and say nothing." There were things the Nazis introduced that were greatly useful to us on the farms, but some of their policies, no matter how young you were, you sensed were somehow not right.

The Nazis believed that Gypsy people were a non-Aryan inferior race that had genetically inherited criminal traits. This theory was reinforced by the research of the eugenics scientist Dr Robert Ritter. As a result of Dr Ritter's work, many gypsies were rounded up and forcibly sterilised to prevent them from producing children.

As the war progressed, gypsy people who had been placed in fixed camps that allowed some degree of freedom were then subjected to the kinds of restrictions placed upon Jews. Many were initially marked for deportation to areas in Poland, then it was decided that the entire Romani population should be sterilised, until eventually the theory of extermination became the favourable option in the eyes of the Nazi authorities. Due to the overly complex bureaucratic nature of the way in which the Third Reich functioned, it is no surprise that all of these methods were employed at one stage to deal with what SS Chief, Heinrich Himmler, referred to as the 'Gypsy Nuisance'.

The SS *Einsatzgruppen* (Task Forces) were also dispatched to murder gypsy people in their thousands. Many gypsies were rounded up and sometimes hundreds at a time were killed in mass shootings that went on day after day. Many men, women and young children were forced to dig their own mass graves prior to their execution. The murderers carried out their duty in a thorough manner, often bayoneting the bodies to ensure they were all dead. Afterwards, the execution pits were filled and a tank drove over the ground to ensure it was compacted enough to ensure that if anyone was still alive they would remain buried. Orphelia Maschmann recalls:

> It wasn't just Jews and gypsies who were viewed as a threat to the bloodline of Germany. Homosexuals, lesbians and Jehovah's Witnesses, and any non-conformists were all considered dangerous to the new Germany. I was aware of these things from school. They taught us that Jews, gypsies, sexual deviants and those politically active against the state had no place in the new Germany and they would have to be destroyed like cockroaches. People were terrified of being informed against. At school there were certain kids who wouldn't sit by me. They were terrified I'd tell my father something about them and they would be taken away. Of course, this was an irrational fear. I had no idea at the time of just how much power my father wielded when I was a child. You could be walking home from school and meet a man and think "oh, he is very effeminate, or like a girl perhaps". If you mentioned this to your parents or a teacher who was a loyal Nazi they would pass on the information to the authorities and often the Gestapo would follow up on any concerns. People were killed as easily as this, through small talk and opinions, without any clear proven foundation. People vanished never to be seen again and it was very sinister for the victims' families as they were often told nothing.
>
> Homosexuals were tolerated in the Nazi elite, it seems, yet on the lower rungs of the social ladder they were classed as deviants and criminals. There were thousands of homosexual males in the Hitler Youth, yet these men were protected. Lesbians were universally despised because the woman is supposed to be the bearer of children, isn't, she. I recall my father mentioning the word 'sapphism' once and

saying that a woman who goes with another woman was the biggest waste of a resource ever and should be euthanized out of her misery. Yet I know for a fact that there were girls having relationships with girls in the BDM. If you heard of anything going on you were obliged to report it to the Hitler Youth authority for that area. If caught, I could imagine the trouble it would have caused those involved. After the war I heard of girls in the BDM leadership who were involved in affairs with girls under their charge.

As a rule, homosexuals and lesbians were sent to the camps, and many thousands died there. My friend Klara Wyborny once told me that her father had investigated and arrested two men who were thought to be homosexual. The two men were taken away and never seen again, their fate remaining unknown to her. Yet she was very proud of her father's work on that occasion. She told me, "The mere thought of two men is disgusting, is it not? The things they do are likely to cause disease and not an appropriate manner in which German males should behave. It is abnormal and I think it is right they are rid from our society." I didn't really understand much about sex at that time, but I had the feeling that Klara knew much more than many girls did. She described in detail what homosexual men did with one another and I was shocked, yet slightly amused at the same time. My reaction was typical of many a child.

Matilda Kuhn recalled the paranoia that was felt in Third Reich Prussia regarding Jews and other groups the Nazis classed an 'undesirable' social element':

In the Nazi schools they taught you that gypsies, Jews, Homosexuals and Lesbians were a polluting element in the Nazi biomechanism. They [the teachers] would never actually utter the word "homosexual" or "lesbian". They would refer to them as being "deviant" or spreaders of disease of a moral and physical nature. Jews, of course, were the most hated and we had been convinced that they were the root cause of Germany's problems. My parents were of the same opinion, that the Jews had all the wealth in the city, could dine in the fine restaurants and wear the best clothes and jewels, while we were effectively the dogs awaiting their scraps. I vividly recall how the teachers said that extermination of the undesirables was a righteous course and every society had an obligation to rid itself of such parasites. We should not only despise the Jew in our midst but also the deviants, whether religious, cultural or sexual.

Our teacher had a particular hatred towards Jehovah's Witnesses. He was a catholic and he referred to them as the "devil's offspring". I'd seen Jews around our city but had never encountered any gypsy people as they frequented the rural countryside and never the cities. As for Jehovah's Witnesses, I never knew anyone who followed this faith and I knew nothing about it other than they did not recognise Christmas, Easter, birthdays or any other holidays they considered to be of pagan origin. As a child I thought such a religious practice was crazy. To not celebrate Christmas especially was unheard of amongst Germans. We loved Christmas and anything that went against this would be met with violence for sure. I remember my mother talking about these people calling at our door offering us "salvation". What possible salvation could they have given us, it was a joke, and when I heard they people were being hunted down and arrested, I was happy to hear of it. I didn't like them at all, and I didn't want to know anything more about them or their religion. For us at that time the only thing that could save Germany was Hitler. I'm sorry if this makes me sound a hateful person, but if many of us were honest, we'd all hold up our hands and say the same as it was the truth at that time.

The mentally ill and those considered seriously physically impaired were also selected for elimination from Prussia's new Nazi society. The mentally ill were often subjected to what can only be best described as medical torture. It is known that mentally ill patients throughout East and West Prussia were transferred to the district known as Soldau in East Prussia. In 1940 a specialist military unit were tasked with the killing of some 1,500 mentally ill patients. They were murdered over an eighteen-day period. This was just a small part of a very large Nazi operation to rid areas of East and West Prussia of anyone perceived to have been unfit by Nazi ideology. After committing the murders, the unit carrying out the killings would then report back to their headquarters in Berlin with the words 'the patients have been successfully evacuated'.

Former nurse Hilde Hermann, who contributed material to the book *Hitler's Housewives: German Women on the Home Front* (Pen & Sword Books Ltd) was perhaps best qualified to address the subject of the treatment of the mentally ill and physically impaired in Nazi German society. Hilde recalled:

> The murder of psychiatric patients in the Third Reich amounted to yet another act of genocide. When Hitler came to absolute power mental institutions automatically came under the exclusive control of the Nazi state. They were terrified of the thought of mentally ill people being born in Germany. People like Heinrich Himmler [Chief of the SS] were obsessed with the theories of race and eugenics. This obsession soon spread into the medical profession in Nazi Germany. Families with mental illness or psychopathy in their bloodlines were subject to immediate sterilization, even if they themselves had no mental impairment or disability. The mere thought of hereditarily diseased offspring was enough. The Nazi physicians carried out numerous experiments on the mentally ill in an effort to determine the effects of mental illness through family generations. It was no different in Prussia. It was the same for all German-occupied territory. As most of the severely mentally ill were already in secure institutions, when the Nazi doctors arrived and dismissed the old doctors who cared for these people, death was just a matter of time. The things the Nazi doctors did to these people are beyond description. I have no joy whatsoever in telling you.
>
> After the war, I carried out my own research into this area to try and find some peace for myself. I learned that all over the Reich the mentally ill were detained in their institutions and subjected to all manner of experiments in

the name of genetic science. Most of the severely mentally ill patients [...] had to be either subdued or straightjacketed prior to experiments being carried out on them [...] some were hit over the head with batons before being placed on operating tables where leather restraints held them still, others were injected with drugs to sedate them. Some had their brains removed without any anaesthetic for analysis and comparison. Other bodily organs were of no interest. It was just the brains that were examined carefully. These were placed in large glass jars, as I had witnessed with my own eyes. Each container was labelled and given its own unique reference number. Patients were also injected with various substances to see how they reacted. The substances were anything from narcotics and pharmaceutical drugs to poisons of various types. I know rat poison was injected into some to see how and when death would occur. Also powdered glass was injected into the arms and even hearts of the patients. Live dissection for the purpose of organ removal was commonplace and the patient would die in agony from the procedure. They were also subjected to extremes of temperature, I heard of one man being put inside a freezer room naked. They dropped the temperature right down as far as they could to see the patient's reaction. Then they would carry out the experiment using extremes of heat. In a medical context it was all pretty pointless. What could one learn from carrying out such acts?

It is clear that the mentally ill were often murdered in the name of Nazi science. The testimony given by Hilde Hermann should provide ample proof of what happened to Germany's psychiatric patients in the Third Reich. It is believed the death toll among psychiatric patients under Hitler's brief reign of Nazi Germany stands at around 275,000.

Those unlucky to have been born in Germany with any severe physical impediment would almost certainly be selected for compulsory sterilization or 'medical execution'.

The term 'medical execution' seems appropriate in this context as many of the Nazi doctors – especially those operating under the auspices of the SS – were executioners in every sense.

The Minority Nightmare

Since the end of the Second World War there have been countless tales of German couples with physically disabled children who were then persuaded to hand them over to doctors at so-called 'special clinics' for examination and treatment, never to see their children again. Often their deaths were recorded as being caused by contracting measles, chickenpox or influenza from another patient. The parents of the children were then often subjected to sterilisation to prevent the risk of them ever having physically impaired children in the future. Such was the fear of physical and mental impairment within the gene pool of the Third Reich that many of those who had the moral duty to treat and care for these human beings preferred murder instead.

The genocide of the mentally and physically impaired, which took place in Nazi Germany and other occupied territories throughout the Second World War, stands as one of the saddest – and least known – episodes in human history.

Chapter 7

Resisting Evil

By the beginning of 1942 rumours of the atrocities committed by the Nazis had started to spread amongst the civilian population. Some members of the Hitler Youth itself began to question the morality of Hitler's actions and whether he was indeed going to keep his promises of a strong, prosperous state and one pure, strong nation.

Slowly, scepticism wormed its way in. However, challenging Hitler's vision and claiming he was wrong, let alone writing anti-Nazi literature, was considered a crime and required huge courage. If caught, the punishment was death. Very few people were willing to risk their own life, or those of their loved ones in order to try to overturn an established dictatorship.

Unlike countries like Poland, Yugoslavia, France, Italy and Norway, there was no unified resistance movement in Germany during the war. It consisted of mainly small and isolated groups unable to mobilise political opposition. Except for individual attacks on Nazis or acts of sabotage, the only real strategy was to persuade leaders of the *Wehrmacht* to stage a coup against the regime. The 1944 assassination attempt against Hitler was intended to trigger such a coup, but as we shall explore in the next chapter, it never succeeded.

Very often executions, particularly hangings, were carried out publicly and the bodies left to dangle from gallows or trees as a warning to others of what would happen to them if they tried to oppose the regime or desert from the army. Passive resistance, such as refusing to join the Nazi party or to salute, was perhaps the most common example of defiance. German composer and conductor Wilhelm Furtwängler was very critical of Hitler's appointment as chancellor and was convinced he would not stay in power for long. In 1932 he said of Hitler, 'This hissing street pedlar will never get anywhere in Germany.'

Orphelia Maschmann. Courtesy of O.Maschmann.

Above left: Claudette Bauer with one of her goats. Courtesy of C.Bauer.

Above right: Sophie Scholl.

Above left: Claus Philipp Maria Schenk Graf von Stauffenberg.

Above right: Claus von Stauffenberg with his children.

Above: General Ludwig Beck.

Left: Dietrich Bonhoeffer.

Above: The co-conspirators of July 20 1944. (German Resistance Memorial and Museum, Berlin)

Right: Hitler at the Wolf's Lair, 1944.

The launch of the *Wilhelm Gustloff*.

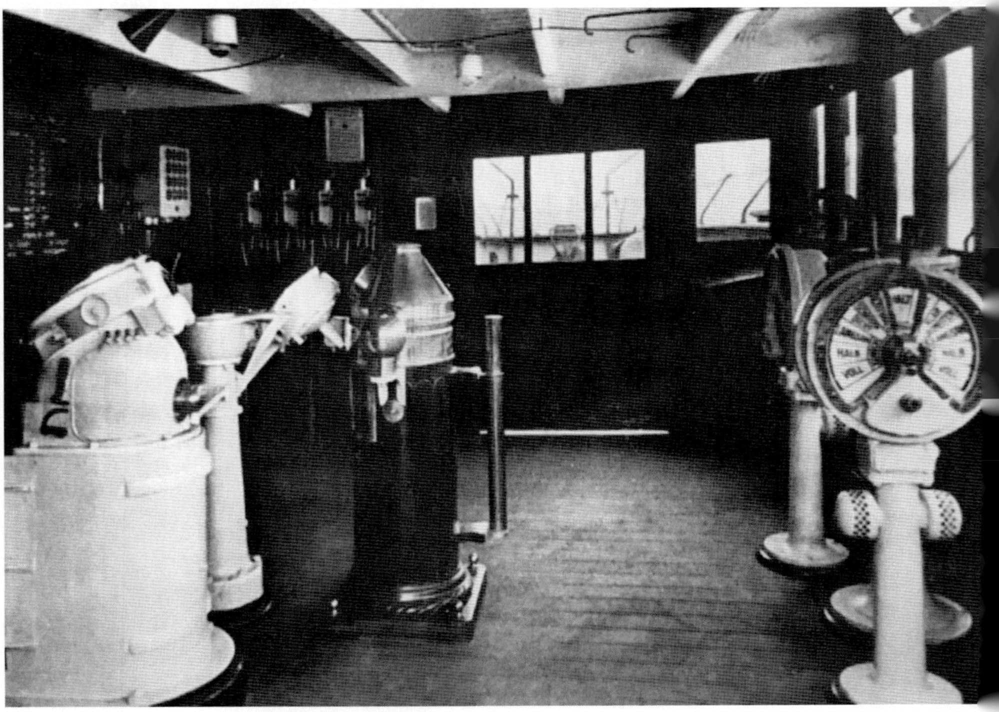

The command deck on the *Wilhelm Gustloff*.

The smoking room aboard the *Wilhelm Gustloff*.

The glass promenade on the *Wilhelm Gustloff*.

The swimming pool on the *Wilhelm Gustloff*.

Above left: Captain Petersen.

Above middle: Captain Zahn.

Above right: Commander of the *S-13* Alexander Marinesko.

Left: Young German soldier Wilhelm "Willi" Hübner is awarded the iron cross in Lauban, Silesia March 1945.

Above: The great flight from East Prussia.

Right: Victims of the Nemmersdorf Massacre.

Below left: Elke Gerns, five years old. Danzig Stolzenberg, December 1944.

Below right: German refugees boarding a train.

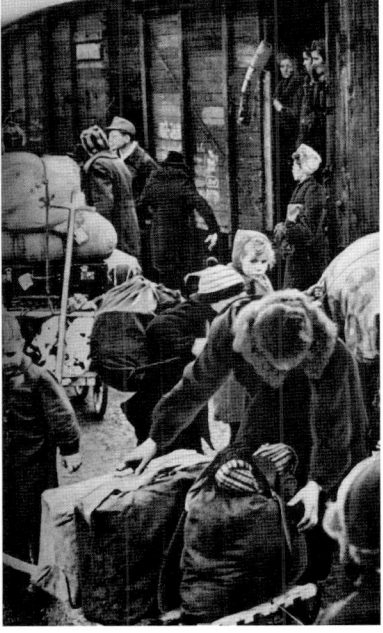

German refugees boarding a ship: scene from *Darkness Fell on Gotenhafen* (1960).

Left: German refugees.

Below: German refugees fleeing Königsberg.

German refugees.

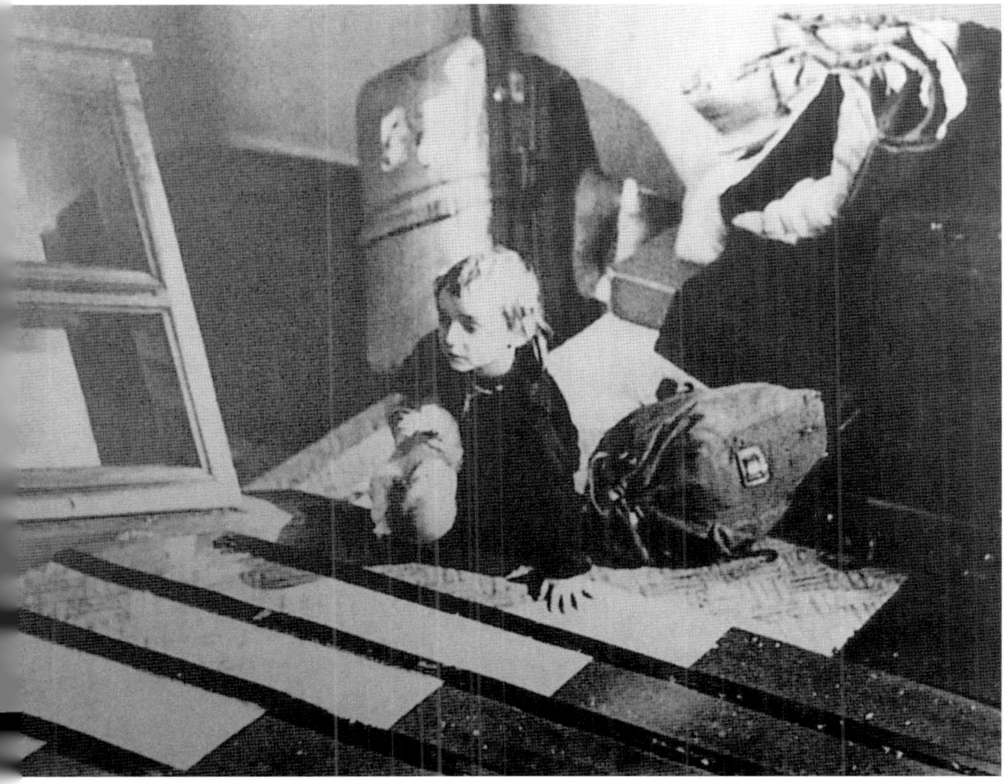

A young German refugee.

Refugees boarding the *Wilhelm Gustloff* at Gotenhafen.

The *Hansa*.

The *Walter Rau*.

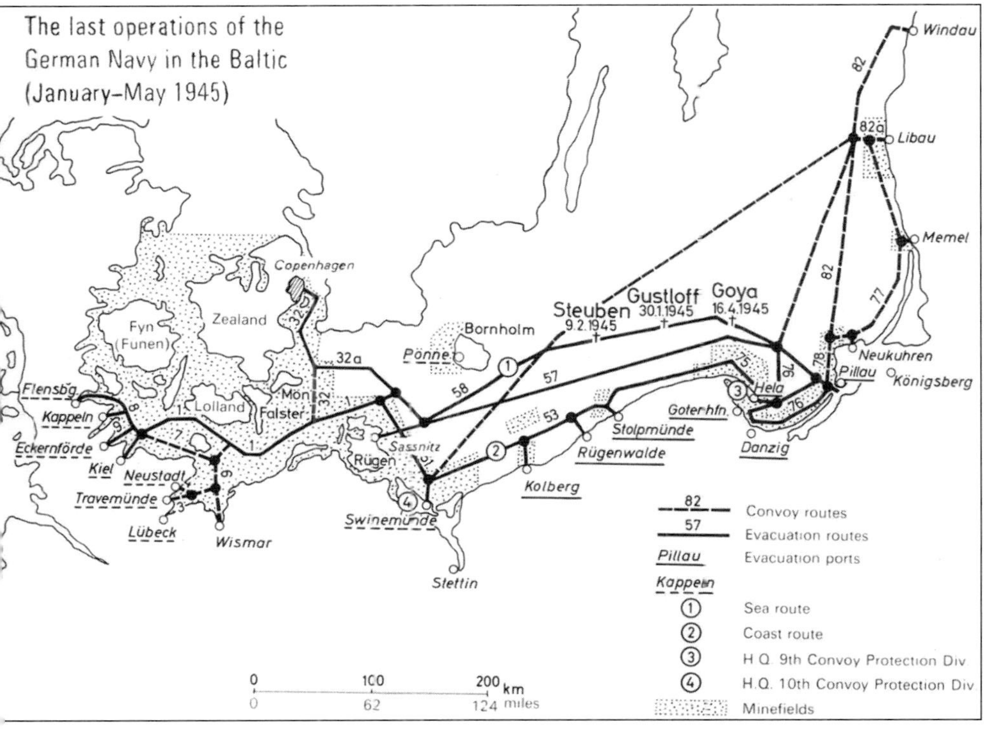

Operation Hannibal.

Above left and middle: Horst Woit and his mother.

Above right: Horst Woit.

Left: Heinz Schön.

Peter Fick with adopted parents.

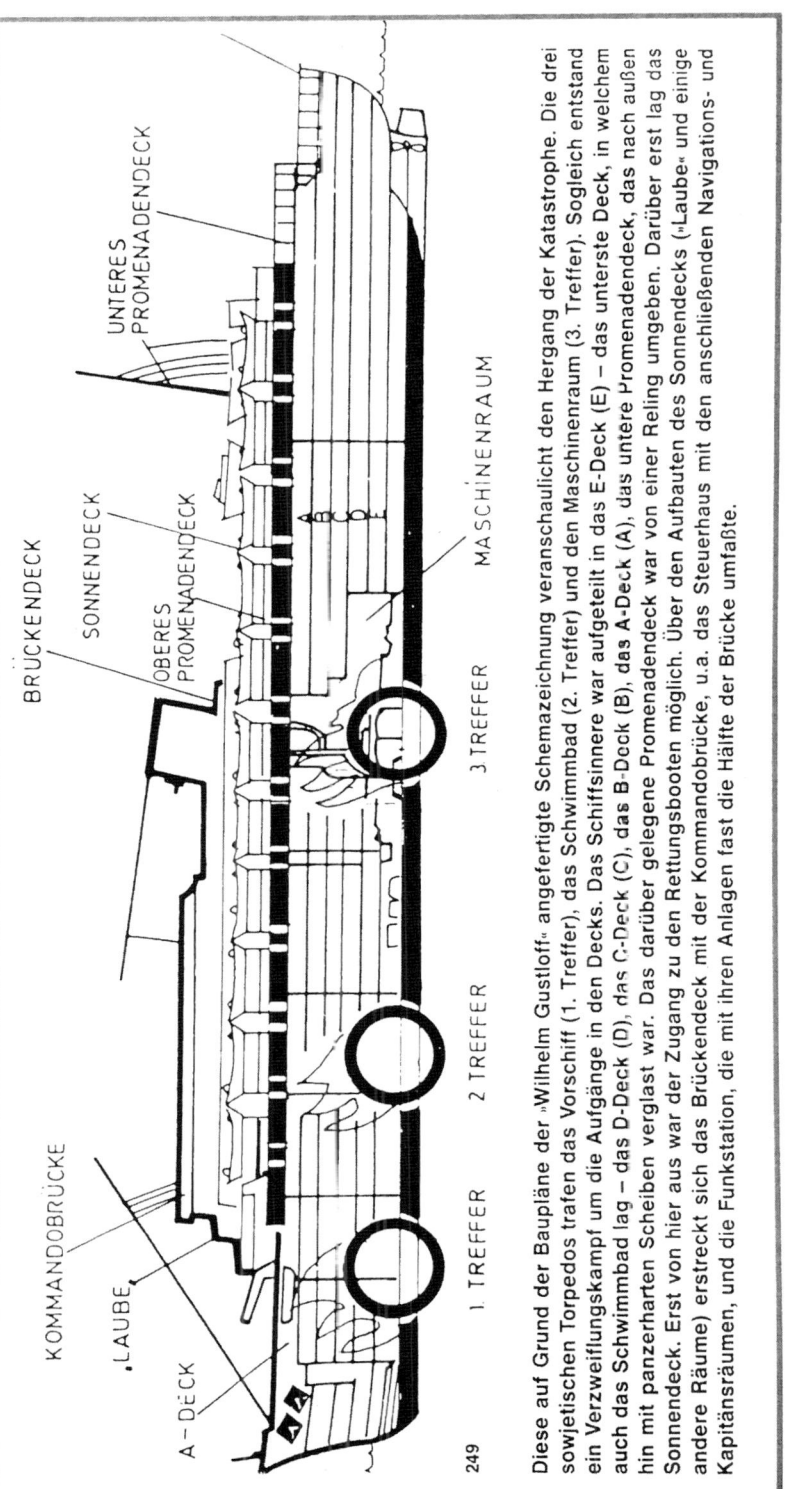

Diese auf Grund der Baupläne der „Wilhelm Gustloff" angefertigte Schemazeichnung veranschaulicht den Hergang der Katastrophe. Die drei sowjetischen Torpedos trafen das Vorschiff (1. Treffer), das Schwimmbad (2. Treffer) und den Maschinenraum (3. Treffer). Sogleich entstand ein Verzweiflungskampf um die Aufgänge in den Decks. Das Schiffsinnere war aufgeteilt in das E-Deck (E) – das unterste Deck, in welchem auch das Schwimmbad lag – das D-Deck (D), das C-Deck (C), das B-Deck (B), das A-Deck (A), das untere Promenadendeck, das nach außen hin mit panzerharten Scheiben verglast war. Das darüber gelegene Promenadendeck war von einer Reling umgeben. Darüber erst lag das Sonnendeck. Erst von hier aus war der Zugang zu den Rettungsbooten möglich. Über den Aufbauten des Sonnendecks („Laube" und einige andere Räume) erstreckt sich das Brückendeck mit der Kommandobrücke, u.a. das Steuerhaus mit den anschließenden Navigations- und Kapitänsräumen, und die Funkstation, die mit ihren Anlagen fast die Hälfte der Brücke umfaßte.

Plan of the *Wilhelm Gustloff*, marked up to indicate the targets of the three torpedoes. (credit Heinz Schoen)

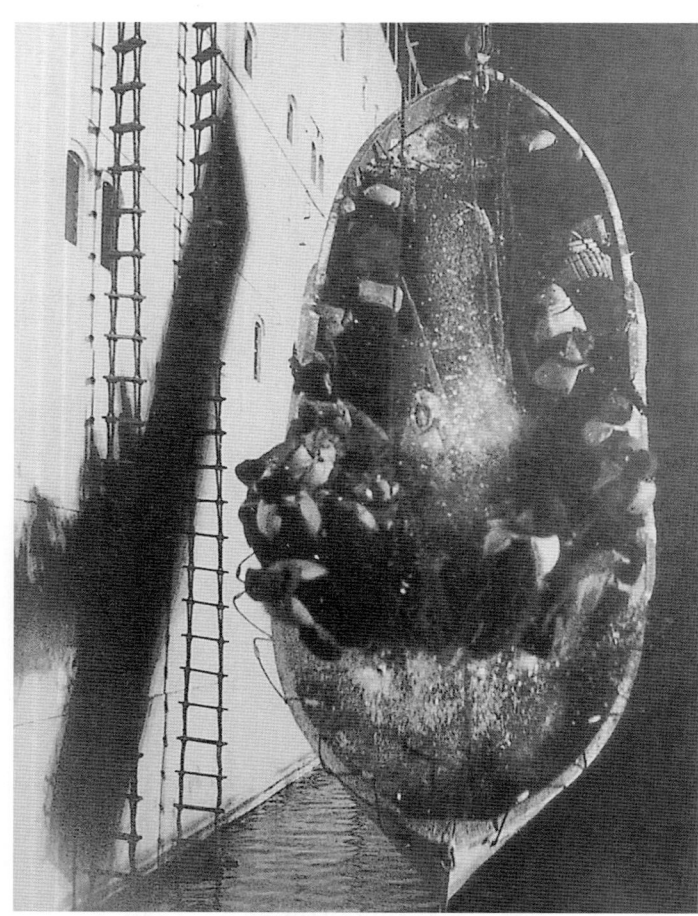

Left: The sinking of the *Wilhelm Gustloff* - scene from *Darkness Fell on Gotenhafen* (1960).

Below: A lifeboat scene from *Darkness Fell on Gotenhafen* (1960).

Above left: Another scene from *Darkness Fell on Gotenhafen* (1960).

Above right: Danzig in 1945.

Above left: Danzig, 1945. The Town Hall.

Above right: Danzig, 1945. The medieval crane.

Above: Danzig, 1945.

Right: Refugees fleeing Danzig.

German PoW's in allied camp.

As antisemitic policies started to take effect in the Third Reich, many Jewish musicians left Germany. Because of his high profile, Furtwängler's public opposition prompted a mixed reaction from the Nazi leadership. Himmler wanted to send Furtwängler to a concentration camp, while Goebbels and Göring wanted to give him the impression that they were listening to his requests to keep Jewish players in the main orchestras. The Gestapo built a case against Furtwängler, noting that he was providing assistance to Jews. Furtwängler never joined the Nazi party, he refused to give the Nazi salute, wouldn't conduct the *Horst-Wessel-Lied* (also known by its opening words '*Die Fahne Hoch*', or 'Raise the Flag', which was used as the anthem of the Nazi Party), and refused to sign his letters with 'Heil Hitler', even those he wrote to Hitler himself. Rather than removing Furtwängler, the Nazis looked for another conductor to counterbalance him and found the young Austrian Herbert von Karajan, who had joined the party earlier and was more willing to take part in propaganda activities.

Many more examples of opposition by Germans to the Nazi regime could be added to the one of Wilhelm Furtwängler. Approximately 77,000 German citizens were killed for one or another form of resistance by special courts, court martial, people's courts and the civil justice system. Among them were the members of the White Rose, notably Sophie Scholl and her brother, Hans, who, due to the strong and committed Christian influence of their parents, became the driving force behind the student anti-Nazi movement at Munich University.

The fourth of five children, Sophie Scholl was born to Robert and Magdalene Scholl on 9 May 1921 in Forchtenberg-am-Kocher, a riverside town east of Heilbronn, where her father was mayor. Known for her bubbly personality, she was a likeable child and made friends very easily. In Sophie's eyes, race and religion were no barrier to friendship. In 1932 the family relocated to Ulm, where Sophie's father had acquired a business and a tax-consulting office. Sophie possessed her mother's quiet sensitivity and her father's strong personality. In 1932, at the age of eleven, she entered secondary school. The following year Adolf Hitler stormed to power with his Nazi party. He immediately began to implement new reforms in the education system, urging both girls and boys to join the Hitler Youth. At the age of twelve, along with her brothers and sisters, classmates and friends, Sophie joined the Hitler Youth for Girls (JM/BDM). Sophie's father was under no illusion of the game Hitler was playing, asking the children, 'Have you considered how he's going to manage all that he has promised? He is expanding the armaments industry and building barracks. Do you know where that's all going to end?'

Sophie was initially enthusiastic about the Hitler Youth movement, but she soon began to question many of the organisation's ethics. She was very concerned by the Nazi attitude towards her Jewish school friends, who were not permitted to join the Hitler Youth. While her brothers and sisters became group leaders in their respective organisations, Sophie became increasingly sceptical. She was aware of the dissenting political views of her father, friends and some of her teachers. Following the Nuremberg party rally of 1935, where he was given the honour of bearer of the flag of Ulm, her brother, Hans, grew extremely despondent at the constant drilling, hate-filled oration, stupid conversations and vulgar jokes. He, like Sophie and their father, understood now more clearly what Nazism really meant. To make matters worse, awful stories were beginning to filter back into Germany of what was happening to Jews in German concentration camps. Sophie found that she could no longer integrate with those who supported the Nazi ideal, instead seeking the company of those who shared her views.

The arrest of her brother and some of his friends in November 1937 for their membership of a youth group (known as the 'dj1.11' after the date of its founding, 1 November 1929) banned by the Nazis left a very strong impression on Sophie. She greatly admired their courage and conviction to stand by their personal beliefs. After their arrest, the Scholl household was searched by the Gestapo. Nothing was found, as Frau Scholl had managed to cleverly dispose of any incriminating material, on the pretext that she had to visit the bakery. She had managed to hide the illicit documents, which the secret state police had been searching for, under a cover in her basket, then left the Gestapo to search the house.

Sophie had a great talent for drawing and painting, enjoying anything to do with art. She was also a compulsive reader, developing a growing interest in philosophy and theology. Aged nineteen in the spring of 1940, and with the Second World War still in its infancy, Sophie graduated from secondary school. She was very fond of children and became a kindergarten teacher at Frobel Institute in Ulm-Solfingen. Sophie had chosen this position as she hoped that the authorities would recognise it as an alternative service to *Reicharbeitsdienst* (National Labour Service), which was compulsory for all females and a prerequisite to any university education. This was a misjudgement and from the spring of 1941 she had to enrol for six months' auxiliary war service as a nursery teacher in Blumberg. The military-like regime of the RADwf (Labour Service) only made her more determined to practise passive resistance and non-conformity. In May 1942, at the age of twenty-one, Sophie eventually enrolled at Munich University to study Biology and Philosophy. Her brother, Hans, was also at the university studying medicine. It was here that he introduced her to his group of friends. The group later became known for their political activities, though they had been drawn together initially by a shared love of art, music, literature, philosophy and theology. It was during her time in Munich that Sophie met artists, writers and philosophers such as German publisher and writer Carl Muth, and writer and critic Theodor Haecker.

The one thing of prime importance to Sophie was the issue of how one should act under the rule of dictatorship. During the early summer of 1942 she had become involved in the production and distribution of a series of political leaflets of 'The White Rose', the name given to their student resistance movement, which was supported by philosophy lecturer Kurt Huber. Huber was already under suspicion and the Nazis had been watching him closely. Though unable to lead them, he gave them much moral and material support, editing the last two of the six leaflets produced by the students.

Sophie and her friends shunned violence as a means of protesting against the government, aiming to change the way that people viewed Nazism and its militaristic ideal through non-violent, passive opposition. The group constantly worked in fear of betrayal or discovery by the Gestapo, but they were driven by their desire to fight National Socialism and the spectre of Adolf Hitler. Sophie also feared greatly for her family's safety, wondering what might happen to them if her activities were discovered.

On 13 January 1943 an interesting incident occurred at the Munich University while it was celebrating its 470th anniversary. The district Nazi *Gauleiter* of the city, Paul Giesler, gave a speech in which he insulted the girl students by telling them 'It's better that they get on with giving the Führer a child than wasting time on books.' He then insulted them further by offering some of his men to oblige in this cause. Several girls immediately left the assembly hall in disgust, but they were arrested at the exit. A disturbance broke out, the first protest against the Nazis to be held by students. Sophie knew time was running out. The next morning Hans and Sophie went to the university to attend a lecture by Huber. Near the entrance someone had inscribed the word 'FREEDOM' in huge lettering on the wall.

Meanwhile, fliers and handbills had been distributed by other members of the White Rose around Cologne, Stuttgart, Berlin and Vienna. The authorities had been alerted and they began to search for the authors of the circulated material. The Gestapo assumed that the authors were from the Munich student set. Thousands of leaflets, which gave details of the Holocaust and supported ideals of democracy, freedom and religious tolerance were printed. The text of the sixth leaflet, written by Kurt Huber, was smuggled out of Germany to Britain. The leaflet encouraged the German people to rise up against the 'enslavement of Europe at the hand of National Socialist terror'. Copies of this particular leaflet were then dropped by RAF Bomber Command aircraft over Germany. Additional excerpts were read out over the BBC Sender Radio.

On 18 February 1943, just before 10am, Sophie and Hans distributed over 1,700 leaflets on their university campus. As they were coming out the main building, they stopped before deciding to run back in to distribute the remaining leaflets. This is when they were seen by the university caretaker, Jackob Schmidt, who caught them on the stairway and shouted 'You are under arrest!' Sophie and Hans were taken first to the bursar and then to the SS Oberführer, Dr Walter Wrist, a lecturer in Aryan language and culture.

The Scholls were taken in handcuffs to the Gestapo headquarters for interrogation. Christoph Probst, another member of the White Rose and father of two young children, was arrested the following day. Sophie and Hans knew that they would now have to pay a very high price for denouncing the National Socialist regime and for their resistance movement's written attacks on Hitler.

The White Rose had caused considerable embarrassment to the Nazi regime. Over a four-day period, Hans, Sophie and Christoph underwent intensive interrogation at Gestapo headquarters at Wittelsbach Palace in Munich. Nothing could be done to secure their release. It was obvious what their fate would be. They had committed treason against the Reich and its Führer. The fact that 'The Hanging Judge', Roland Freisler, was going to conduct their court trial only confirmed the fears of most.

Resisting Evil

Nazi judge Freisler was known to be an intimidating, raging bully who represented the evil of Nazism at its most virulent. There was no way Sophie, Hans and Christoph would receive a fair hearing.

On 22 February 1943 the trial began at 9am and closed at 1pm. Hans and Sophie's parents were not allowed to attend as they had not been issued with passes to enter the courtroom. Freisler, for all his theatrical shouting and abuse, could in no way break Sophie. Her wit and intelligence, together with her challenging composure, unsettled Freisler. For once he was facing someone who was not afraid of him or the consequences of her beliefs. Her last words to Freisler were, 'You know the war is lost. Why don't you face it?'

Judge Freisler sentenced Sophie, Hans and Christoph to death by guillotine before they were taken to Stadelheim Prison. Robert and Magdalene Scholl were able to spend a few final minutes with their children. Robert embraced his son and said to him, 'You will go down in history. There is another justice than this.' Magdalene embraced her daughter saying, 'I will never see you come through the door again.' Sophie replied, 'Oh, Mother, after all, it's only a few years' more life I'll miss.'

Sophie's short life ended at 6pm on 22 February 1943, when she, Hans and Christoph were executed by guillotine, only a few hours after they were sentenced. As she was led away from her cell to the execution chamber, Sophie remained defiant to the end, winning the admiration of the prison officials. Her last words were, 'It's a beautiful sunny day and I have to go'. The guards later recalled how courageous she was and how she showed no fear of dying for her cause. Sophie and Hans were buried in Perlach Forest Cemetery on 24 February 1943.

Sophie Scholl was a remarkable human being, one the Nazis could never defeat. On 12 October 1987 the *Weisse Rose Stiftung*, or White Rose Foundation, was founded in Munich to keep her legacy of the wartime resistance movement alive, while reminding today's youth of the importance of fighting for human rights. A contemporary German theatrical production was also staged to celebrate the short lives of the members of the White Rose. Today's young German girls especially recognise Sophie's selfless bravery and sacrifice.

Other scattered resistance movements and individual attempts to oppose the National Socialist regime developed in Germany in the early 1940s and within the military as early as the mid-1930s. Many of these Germans had served in government, the military or in civil positions, which enabled them to engage in subversion and conspiracy. The Canadian historian Peter Hoffman (*The History of the German Resistance, 1933–1945*) counts 'tens of thousands' in concentration camps who were either suspected of or actually engaged in opposition. Small-scale attempts to overturn the Nazi regime were often swiftly and brutally suppressed by Himmler's secret police, the Gestapo.

Between 1932 and 1944 no fewer than forty-two plots to assassinate Adolf Hitler have been uncovered. The majority involved people serving amongst Hitler's elite, where the Gestapo least expected them. The exact number, however, cannot be accurately determined due to an unknown number of undocumented cases.

Perhaps the most famous attempt on Hitler's life was the 20 July 1944 plot carried out by Claus von Stauffenberg. This was the culmination of efforts by several groups in the German resistance to wrest political and military control from the Nazi Party and to make peace with the Western Allies as soon as possible.

In the summer of 1944 East Prussia was still a beautiful and prosperous land of rich countryside, crystal-clear lakes and dark forests. It was in one of those forests that Hitler had established his Eastern Front Headquarters ahead of Operation Barbarossa in 1941. The population of East Prussia could not possibly imagine that the Führer had his '*Führerhauptquartiere*' in the Masurian Woods, about 8km east of the small town of Rostenburg, now Gierloz, Ketrzyn, Poland. The top secret, high-security site, known as '*Wolfsschanze*', consisted of a central complex where Hitler's bunker was located, surrounded by three security zones guarded by personnel from the SS *Reichssicherheitsdienst* and the *Wehmacht*'s armoured *Führerbegleitbrigade*. It was there, despite the high security, that the famous assassination attempt against Hitler was made on 20 July 1944.

Claus Philipp Maria Schenk Graf von Stauffenberg was a German army officer and a leading member of the failed 20 July plot to assassinate Adolf Hitler. Along with Henning von Tresckow and Hans Oster, he was a central figure in the German resistance movement within the *Wehrmacht*. Born in 1907 to Alfred Klemens Philipp Friedrich Justinian Graf von Stauffenberg and Caroline Schenk Graefin von Stauffenberg (born Graefin von Uxkull-Gyllenband) into one of the oldest and most distinguished aristocratic Catholic families in the eastern part of Swabia, in Bavaria, Claus Philipp Maria Justinian 'Count of Stauffenberg' was one of four brothers, including twins, Berthold and Alexander, and his own twin brother, Konrad Maria, who died one day after birth. Among his maternal Protestant ancestors were several famous Prussians, including Field Marshal August von Gneisenau.

Claus and his brothers were inseparable, physically and intellectually. They grew up in the privileged comfort of the German nobility under Keiser Wilhelm II at the Lautlingen Estate, around fifty miles south of Stuttgart. During the First World War, Caroline regularly took tea to the soldiers passing through the local station. In the summer she urged the boys to help local women – now deprived of their men who were busy fighting on the Western and Eastern fronts – with the harvest. In their spare time the boys played music and read poetry. They were members of the *Neupfadfinder*, a German Scout association which was dissolved in 1933 and its members absorbed into the Hitler youth.

As Stauffenberg's biographer, Peter Hoffamann, notes, 'The Stauffenberg brothers were extraordinarily unlike their contemporaries – in their own families, in the nobility, within the Catholic community, in their school, in their profession. The more closely a witness was acquainted with the Stauffenbergs, the more cautious they were in describing them, in uttering judgments beyond respect and admiration. The Stauffenbergs themselves were aware of being unlike other people, partly because of their strong family and aristocratic traditions.'

In 1926 Claus von Stauffenberg took up a military career and joined the traditional family regiment, the Bamberger Reiter und Kavalerieregiment 17, in Bamberg. Around this time he was introduced to the influential circle of poet and author Stefan George (author of *Das Neue Reich*), from which many notable members of the German resistance later emerged.

Stauffenberg was commissioned as a second lieutenant in 1930. His regiment became part of the German 1st Light Division under General Erich Hoepner, who had taken part in the plans for the 1938 Oster Conspiracy, which has been cut short by Hitler's unexpected diplomatic success in the Munich Agreement. The unit was among the *Wehrmacht* troops that moved into Sudetenland following its annexation to the Reich in accordance with the Munich Agreement.

Although Stauffenberg initially agreed with the Nazi Party's racist and nationalistic aspects, and supported the colonisation of Poland, he never became a member. He remained a practising Catholic and was torn between a personal dislike of Hitler's policies and a respect for his military acumen. Following the Night of the Long Knives and *Kristallnacht*, Stauffenberg became even more disassociated from the party. He realised that Hitler had no intention to pursue justice and his systematic ill-treatment of Jews and religious suppression had outraged him and offended his strong sense of morality. Traditions like family honour, service to the state, and shared responsibility were deeply rooted in Claus. These, together with the ideals of Stefan George's circle, eventually led to a recognition of the criminal nature of Hitler's war.

Following the outbreak of war in 1939, Stauffenberg and his regiment took part in the attack on Poland. At first he supported the occupation of Poland and the use of Poles as slave workers to achieve German prosperity. The belief common in the German aristocracy was that the Eastern territories, which were partly absorbed by Prussia in partitions of Poland but taken from the German Empire after the First World War, should be colonised, as the Teutonic Knights had done in the middle Ages.

Although Stauffnberg's uncle, Nikolaus Graf von Uxkull-Gyllenband, had approached him before to join the resistance movement, it wasn't until after the Polish campaign that he began to consider it. During Operation Barbarossa, the German invasion of the Soviet Union, Stauffenberg did not engage in any coup plotting, although he and his brothers maintained contact with anti-regime figures such as the Kreisau Circle.

After being wounded outside Moscow, Baron Philipp von Boeselager, the second-to-last survivor of the 20 July plot to assassinate Hitler, began to work for Field Marshall von Kluge. He recalls: 'Then arrived a note from the SS saying, "the five gypsies had received special treatment". So von Kluge asked "What does that mean?" "We killed them." "After a Courts Martial?" "No. We shoot all gypsies and Jews." That was the first time I heard about it. From a high-ranking SS officer. I was shocked'. It wasn't until 1941 that the news of the systematic killing of gypsies and Jews by SS officers reached the highest ranks of the *Wehrmacht*.

Stauffenberg openly commented on the ill-treatment of Jews and expressed outrage and shock on this subject to fellow officers in the General Staff Headquarters in Vinnitsa (Ukraine) during the summer of 1942. Stauffenberg's friend, Major Joachim Kuhn, was captured by the Red Army and during interrogation on 2 September 1944 claimed that Stauffenberg had told him in August 1942 that 'they are shooting Jews in masses. These crimes must not be allowed to continue.' After his arrest in July 1944, Stauffenberg's older brother, Berthold, told the Gestapo that he and his brother had basically agreed with the principle of National Socialism but found it to be exaggerated and excessive.

Since 1938 there had been groups plotting an overthrow of some kind within the German army and in the German military intelligence organisation. Early leaders of these plots included Major General Hans Oster, deputy head of the Military Intelligent Office, Colonel General Ludwig Beck, former Chief of Staff of the German Army High Command (OKH), and Field Marshal Erwin von Witzleben, former commander of the German 1st Army and former Commander-in-Chief of the German Army Command in the West. They had established contacts with several prominent civilians, including the former mayor of Leipzig, Carl Goerdeler, and Helmuth James Graf von Moltke, the great-grandnephew of Moltke the Elder, hero of the Franco-Prussian War.

Groups of military plotters exchanged ideas with civilian, political and intellectual resistance groups in the *Kreisauer Kreis* (Kreisau Circle), which met at the von Moltke estate in Kreisau. Plans to stage an overthrow and prevent Hitler from launching a new world war were developed in 1938 and 1939 but never materialised, partly due to the failure of the Western powers to oppose Hitler's aggression until 1939.

Despite his ethical opposition to an aggressive war, General Ludwig Beck understood that it was not his place to come up with spiritual or political arguments, so he approached his superiors and declared that Germany wasn't ready for a world conflict, neither economically nor militarily. When his arguments fell on deaf ears, he tried to convince his fellow *Wehrmacht* officers to threaten the Führer with a collective resignation if he was not willing to give up on his aggressive foreign policy. When all his efforts ended in vain, Ludwig Beck resigned from his post as Chief of Staff in 1938 as a final protest. The seeds for his future role as leader of the military anti-Nazi resistance had been sown.

In 1942 a new conspiratorial group formed, led by Colonel Henning von Tresckow, a member of Field Marshal Fedor von Bock's staff (he commanded Army Group Centre in Operation Barbarossa). Tresckow systematically recruited opponents of the regime to the group's staff, but little could be done against Hitler as he was heavily guarded and none of the plotters could get near enough to him. Nevertheless, Oster and Tresckow succeeded in building a strong resistance network, recruiting General Friedrich Olbricht, head of the General Army Office headquarters at the Bendlerblock in central Berlin, who controlled an independent system of communications to reserve units all over Germany.

By late-1942, the tide of war was turning decisively against Germany. The army plotters and their civilian allies became convinced that Hitler should be assassinated so that a government acceptable to the Western Allies could be formed and a separate peace negotiated in time to prevent a Soviet invasion of Germany. Tresckow had been planning to eliminate Hitler since the early 1930s and had previously attempted to assassinate him on at least two occasions. The first plan was to shoot him during dinner at the army base camp, but this plan was aborted because it was believed that Hitler wore a bullet-proof vest. He also considered poisoning him, but this was not possible because his food was specially prepared and tasted. He concluded that a bomb was the only option.

In March 1943 Tresckow and Olbricht, together with Hans von Dohnanyi, drew up a plan to assassinate Hitler during his visit to the headquarters of Army Group Centre at Smolensk by placing a bomb on his plane (Operation Spark). The bomb failed to detonate, and a second attempt on the Führer's life a week later, at an exhibition of captured Soviet weaponry in Berlin, also failed.

Since 1942 Stauffenberg had come to share two basic convictions with many military officers: that Germany was being led to disaster, and that Hitler's removal from power was necessary. After the battle of Stalingrad in December 1942, and despite his religious beliefs, Stauffenberg concluded that the Führer's assassination was a lesser moral evil than him remaining in power. However, his active involvement in the 10th Panzer division in North Africa prevented him from putting any plans into action.

In November 1942 the Allies landed in French North Africa and the 10th Panzer Division occupied Vichy France before being transferred to fight in the Tunisia Campaign as part of the Afrika Korps. In 1943 Stauffenberg was promoted to Obersleutnant (lieutenant-colonel) and was sent to Africa to join the tank division. On 19 February Rommel launched his counter-offensive against Allied forces in Tunisia. On 7 April Stauffenberg was driving from one unit to another, directing their movement. Near Mezzouna his vehicle was part of a column strafed by

Kittyhawk (P-40) fighter bombers of the Desert Air Force – most likely from N.3 Squadron, Royal Australian Air Force – and he received severe multiple wounds. He spent the following three months recovering in hospital in Munich, having lost his left eye, his right hand and two fingers of his left hand. He jokingly remarked to his friends never to have really known what to do with so many fingers when he still had them all. For his injuries he was awarded the Wound Badge in gold on 14 April and for his courage the German Cross in gold on 8 May. Claus' wife, Nina von Stauffenberg commented: 'It was a turning point for him. When I saw him in the hospital in Munich he said "It's time for me to save the German Reich". That was the moment when he chose to become involved.'

Stauffenberg's convalescence was slow but steady. Around that time, the position of Chief of Staff to General Fromm at the Reserve Army Headquarters on Bendlerstrasse in Berlin became available. General Olbricht, well aware of Stauffenberg's commitment to remove Hitler, quickly arranged for him to be offered the post. Stauffenberg immediately agreed.

In August 1943 Treshkow met Claus von Stauffenberg for the first time. This encounter brought a new tone of decisiveness to the ranks of the resistance movement. When Tresckow was assigned to the Eastern Front Stauffenberg took charge of the planning and execution of the assassination attempt. Meanwhile, Olbricht had put forward a new strategy for staging a coup against Hitler.

The Replacement or Reserve Army (*Ersatzheer*) had an operational plan called Operation Valkyrie, which was to be used in the event of the disruption caused by the Allied bombing of German cities causing a breakdown in law and order, or an uprising by the millions of forced labourers from occupied countries that were being used in German factories and shipyards. Olbricht suggested that this plan could be used to mobilise the Reserve Army for the purpose of the coup, and in August 1943 he drafted a 'revised' Valkyrie plan and new supplementary orders. A secret declaration began with these words: 'The Führer Adolf Hitler is dead! A treacherous group of party leaders has attempted to exploit the situation by attacking our embattled soldiers from the rear in order to seize power for themselves.' Detailed instructions were given for the occupation of government ministries in Berlin, Heinrich Himmler's headquarters in East Prussia, radio stations, telephone offices and other Nazi offices in military districts and concentration camps.

Operation Valkyrie could only be put into effect by General Fredrich Fromm, commander of the Reserve Army, so he needed to be part of the conspiracy or be neutralised. Like many other senior officers, Fromm was generally aware of military conspiracies against Hitler, but neither supported them nor reported them to the Gestapo. As the war situation deteriorated in 1944, Hitler no longer appeared in public and rarely visited Berlin. He spent most of his time at his headquarters at the *Wolfsschanze* (Wolf's Lair), near Rastenburg in East Prussia, with occasional breaks at his Bavarian mountain retreat, *Obersalzberg*, near Berchtesgaden. At both places he was very heavily guarded and rarely met people he did not know or trust. Himmler and the Gestapo had become increasingly suspicious of plots against the Führer and rightly suspected the officers of the general staff, who had been the source of many previous conspiracies. By the summer of 1944 the Gestapo was closing in on the conspirators.

It is possible that Himmler, who by 1943 knew the war was unwinnable, allowed the plot to go ahead in the knowledge that if it succeeded, he would be Hitler's successor. Treschkow and the other plotters, however, had no intention of removing Hitler only to see him replaced by the ruthless SS chief. They had to kill them both if possible. The plan was for Stauffenberg to plant a briefcase with the time bomb in Hitler's conference room, excuse himself from the meeting, wait for the explosion then fly back to Berlin and join the other plotters at the Benderblock. Operation Valkyrie would be mobilised, the Reserve Army would take control of Germany and the other Nazi leaders would be arrested. Beck, who was well respected by officers as well as politicians in opposition circles, would be appointed provisional Head of State, Goerdeler would be chancellor and Witzleben commander-in-chief of the armed forces.

A first attempt was made on 11 July 1944, but was aborted because Himmler was not present. A second attempt followed four days later, but was called off at the eleventh hour. Himmler was present but Hitler was called out of the room at the last moment. Stauffenberg was able to intercept the bomb and prevent its discovery. On 18 July rumours reached Stauffenberg that the Gestapo had knowledge of the conspiracy and that he might be arrested at any time. This was later proved to be untrue, but there was a sense that the net was closing in and that the next opportunity to kill Hitler must be taken.

Resisting Evil

Stauffenberg was instrumental in the organising of Valkyrie and therefore was needed in Berlin, but at the same time he realised that he had to be the assassin as well. So, on 20 July 1944, he carried out the final attempt to assassinate Adolf Hitler. In the early hours, together with his aide, Werner von Haeften, Stauffenberg left the house in which they were staying, at Tristanstrasse in Berlin, and headed back to the *Wolfsschanze* to attend a military conference. He had been summoned to report on the implementation of the Replacement Army on the Eastern Front. In his briefcase Stauffenberg was hiding an English-made plastic explosive provided by plotters in German military counter-intelligence. He was also carrying a pair of tongs (which he would use to break the capsules and release the acid that would eat away wiring and ultimately detonate the explosive), a spare shirt and various papers. He had practised manipulating the bomb for hours with his only three-fingered hand.

The flight, arranged by General Quartermaster Eduard Wagner, lasted just under three hours and they landed at Rastenburg airport shortly after 10am. Stauffenberg told the pilot to be ready for an immediate take-off any time after 12pm. At around 12pm Stauffenberg arrived at the 'Wolf's Lair' and met with field marshal Wilhelm Keitel, who informed him that Hitler had moved the conference from 1pm to 12.30pm because Benito Mussolini was expected in the early afternoon and Hitler needed to be free to receive him. The conference would also no longer take place in the sealed bunker, but would instead be held in the open-windowed barracks. Stauffenberg asked if he could change his shirt and was shown to a separate room. Here he opened the briefcase and quickly broke the capsules, but was interrupted by a knock on the door before he could prepare a second, smaller bomb. He put the briefcase under his arm and rejoined Keitel, who had started to become rather impatient. The bomb would go off in about ten minutes. During General Heusinger's briefing Stauffenberg placed the briefcase under the table, near Hitler, before slipping out to take a phone call. It is believed that Colonel Heinz Brandt, who was standing to the right of Hitler, accidentally kicked the briefcase and decided to move it further right, behind the leg of the conference table.

At 12.42pm the bomb detonated, demolishing the conference room and killing one stenographer and three officers. More than twenty people were injured in the blast. Hitler survived with a perforated eardrum and other minor injuries, as did everyone else who was standing to his left, partly shielded from the explosion by the table leg. In the turmoil that followed the explosion, Stauffenberg saw a body covered by Hitler's trenchcoat being carried out on a stretcher. After passing through the first two security checkpoints, Stauffenberg managed to go through the last checkpoint, by which time the Wolf's Lair was in complete lockdown. At Rastenburg airport his plane was waiting to carry him back to Berlin.

Meanwhile, at the Bendlerblock in Berlin, news had reached them that the plot might have failed. General Olbricht decided to wait until Stauffenberg had reported in before launching Operation Valkyrie. When Stauffenberg arrived at the Benderblock, he was furious that nothing had been done. General Fromm, Commander of the Reserve Army, refused to activate Valkyrie. He had just spoken to Keitel, who informed him that Hitler was alive. Fromm ordered all conspirators arrested but, believing he was one step ahead, Stauffenberg ordered Fromm arrested instead. Together with Olbricht, Stauffenberg decided to activate Valkyrie, ordering each army unit to move to their assigned position. At the same time a communiqué on Radio Berlin stated that there had been an attack on Hitler's life but the Führer was alive and would speak on the radio shortly. Back at the Wolf's Lair, it was at first believed that the assassination attempt had been carried out by workers at the complex, but the sudden disappearance of Stauffenberg made him a suspect. Hitler knew that a number of army officers had been responsible.

Around 9.12pm, on orders from General Paul von Hase, Major-General Remer went to Goebbels' house to arrest him, but to his great surprise, Goebbels informed him that Hitler was alive. To prove this, Goebbels telephoned Hitler at the Wolf's Lair and passed him over to Remer. Hitler ordered Remer to crush the plot in Berlin, but to capture the perpetrators alive. The plotters were then arrested and Fromm released. Valkyrie was lost. Had the meeting been held in the concrete bunker rather than the wooden conference block, everyone in the room would almost certainly have been killed.

Contrary to Hitler's wish, Fromm ordered the conspirators executed so that none of them could implicate him in the investigation that was soon to follow. He also confronted General Beck, placing a gun on the desk in front of him and encouraging him to 'accept the consequences', but Beck's attempted suicide failed. At the same time, Hitler was making his radio address from the Wolf's Lair. Hitler saw his survival as confirmation of the task that providence had given him to continue his life's goal.

An execution squad was formed in the Bendlerblock courtyard, lit by the headlights of SS vehicles. At 1am on 21 July 1944, Olbricht, Stauffenberg, von Quirnheim and von Haeften were escorted down the steps to the courtyard to be shot. When Stauffenberg was standing in front of the firing squad, he shouted 'Long live our holy Germany!'

After the execution Fromm ordered a staff officer to give Beck the *coupe de grâce*. Soldiers then loaded the five bodies onto a lorry and took them to the Matthaikirche cemetery in Schoeneberg, where they were buried with their uniforms and decorations. The next day Himmler had them exhumed, cremated and their ashes scattered on an open field in a location unknown to this day.

On the Eastern front, von Treskov, on hearing that Hitler's assassination attempt had failed, decided to commit suicide by detonating a hand grenade under his chin. His parting words to his aide Schlabrendorff were, 'The whole world will vilify us now, but I am still totally convinced that we did the right thing. Hitler is the arch-enemy not only of Germany but of the world. A man's moral worth is established only at the point where he is ready to give his life in defence of his convictions.' The officers who died in the bomb blast at the Wolf's Lair were hailed as heroes and given a state funeral. Hitler personally went to see the injured officers in hospital.

On the morning of 22 July 1944 Fromm was arrested by Nazi officers and jailed to await trial. It was clear to them that his actions immediately after the coup's collapse may have been an attempt to use his authority to silence those officers directly under his command who might have implicated him in the plot. Fromm was discharged from the German Army on 14 September 1944. As a civilian, he was tried on 7 March 1945, found unworthy for military service, convicted of cowardice before the enemy and sentenced to death. However, because he had executed the conspirators within reach, he was spared torture and execution by thin rope and given a military execution instead.

Other arrests followed, including Claus von Stauffenberg's brother, Barthold, Fritz-Dietlof, Count Schulenburg and Commander Alfred Kranzfelder. On 10 August 1944 they were tried, together with other four conspirators, at the People's Court and sentenced to death by Roland Freisler (the same judge who had ordered the execution of Sophie and Hans Scholl two years earlier). They were hanged with piano wire on the same afternoon and died in the cruellest way after being resuscitated several times. The entire execution was filmed for Hitler to view at his leisure.

The topic of the resistance in Nazi Germany is a very complex one and the subject of much debate. One question naturally comes to mind: where was the church in all this? In the south of Germany, where National Socialism had its origins, the main religion was Catholicism. From the beginning, Catholic political groups resisted Hitler's rise, but by the summer of 1933 their fear of a loss of freedom under a Hitler government brought Catholic leadership to the negotiation table. Nazi leaders met with representatives of the Vatican, including Cardinal Eugenio Pacelli, the future Pope Pius XII. Together they signed a concordat promising the church's autonomy in exchange for its pledge not to organise against the regime. This was possible because the majority of Catholic bishops assumed that Hitler was a Catholic and that he would behave legally and conservatively. But the excesses of the Nazis, their use of force in their pursuit of power and their intrusion in the works of the church, began to disturb even the most loyal Protestant pastors. Over time, 7,000 pastors began to voice their opposition to Hitler's racial policies, though the majority of nearly 20,000 pastors refused to do so. Equally, most officers and civil servants, even those uncomfortable with Hitler's policies, obeyed their oaths, simply stayed in their lanes and did their job. But there were others that, for a number of reasons – noble or pragmatic – decided to break the oath they had sworn to Hitler in 1933.

The question of whether breaking one's oath and killing a dictator in order to save innocent lives can be acceptable or even justified was not taken lightly by any of the conspirators. They would have to violate their military oath, they would have to lie, to be duplicitous, and they would have to plan to murder the head of state. However, they found great moral support and inspiration in the teachings of the German pastor, theologian and anti-Nazi dissident Dietrich Bonhoeffer. Born in Breslau, Silesia, in 1906, Dietrich Bonhoeffer was known for his staunch resistance to Nazi dictatorship and his vocal opposition to Hitler's euthanasia programme and genocidal persecution of the Jews. After obtaining a master's degree in theology from the University of Tübingen, he went on to complete his Doctor of Theology degree from the University of Berlin, graduating in 1927. He was offered a parish in Berlin in 1933, which he refused in protest at the nationalist policy, accepting a two-year appointment as pastor of two German-speaking Protestant churches in London instead: the German Lutheran Church in Dacres Road, Sydenham, and the German Reformed Church of St Paul's in Goulston Street, Whitechapel.

In 1935 he returned to Berlin, running underground seminaries and travelling from one eastern town to another to conduct 'seminaries on the run' for students who were working illegally in small parishes within the old-Prussian ecclesiastical province of Pomerania. In 1938 the Gestapo banned Bonhoeffer from Berlin. He was forbidden to speak in public, or to print or publish material and was required to regularly report his activities to the police.

In 1941 he was invited by his brother-in-law, Hans von Dohnanyi, to join the *Abwehr*, a German military intelligence organisation, thus avoiding conscription into active service. Despite the fact that the Treaty of Versailles prohibited the Germans from establishing an intelligence organisation of their own, they formed an espionage group in 1920 within the Ministry of Defence, calling it *Abwehr*. Its initial purpose was defence against foreign espionage. The *Abwehr* claimed that Bonhoeffer's wide ecumenical contacts would be of use to Germany. Led by Wilhelm Canaris, it quickly became a hub of resistance activity against Hitler. Joining this organisation, however, was a big problem for somebody coming from a very religious background. It was a tremendous conflict to be part of a complot. The main question was the fundamental Christian principle 'Thou shall not kill'. How could it still stand? In answer to this vexed issue, Bonhoeffer wrote:

> Are we still of any use? We have been silent witnesses of evil deeds; we have been drenched by many storms; we have learnt the art of equivocation and pretence; experience has made us suspicious of others and kept us from being truthful and open; intolerable conflicts have worn us down and made us cynical. Are we still of any use?

Bonhoeffer travelled extensively to America, Italy, Switzerland, Scandinavia and England. Together with Von Dohnanyi, he helped save several Jewish people by disguising them as agents of the *Abwehr* on a mission in order to leave Germany only to never return.

Under cover of the *Abwehr*, Bonhoeffer served as a courier for the German resistance movement to reveal its existence and intentions to the Western Allies in hope of gaining their support, and, through his ecumenical contacts abroad – particularly his friendship with George Bell, Bishop of Chichester and British MP – to secure possible peace terms with the Allies for a post-Hitler government. The Allied governments greeted these peace planners with distrust. The military members of the resistance wanted guarantees of German territorial integrity and their own positions as leaders of a post-war Germany. Allied diplomats and leaders found this demand unacceptable and never seriously considered support for a German coup. No promises in advance could be expected from the Allies. In January 1943 Churchill and Roosevelt announced that only the unconditional defeat of Germany would eradicate Nazism. It was perhaps this refusal of the Allies to back the German resistance that reinforced even more in Stauffenberg and the other conspirators a determination to act alone. As Christians, both Bonhoeffer and Stauffenberg believed that they could not remain insensitive to suffering and injustice, and so they were called to compassion and action.

Bonhoeffer's niece, Marianne Liebholz stated: 'I think the most important thing my uncle did was to realise from the start how evil Nazism was. Then I think how brave it was of this small group of people to think that they could fight together with other companions this monstrous machine, and that they were prepared to give their lives to do this.'

Following the failure of the 20 July assassination attempt, it was months before the Nazis realised the extent of Bonhoeffer's involvement in the resistance circles. He was eventually arrested by the Gestapo in October 1944, together with other members of his family who were also actively involved in the resistance. He was then taken to Buchenwald concentration camp before being moved to Flossenburg concentration camp where, on 9 April 1945, at the age of thirty-nine, he was hanged. The SS doctor who witnessed Bonhoeffer's execution later recalled a man 'devout [...] brave and composed. His death ensued after a few seconds [...] I have hardly ever seen a man die so entirely submissive to the will of God.'

Bonhoeffer sent one final message to George Bell in England: 'This is the end, for me the beginning of life.'

The authors would like to conclude this chapter with a quote by General Ludwig Beck, which is displayed on a panel at the German Resistance Memorial Centre (former Bendlerblock) in Berlin. 'It is a lack of character and insight, when a soldier in high command sees his duty and mission only in the context of his military orders without realising that the highest responsibility is to the people of his country.'

Chapter 8

Blood and Fire

'Through blood and fire, we came, with vengeance burning in our hearts.'
Joseph Stalin

Germany's military campaign against Soviet Russia in the East was without doubt Hitler's greatest gamble of the Second World War. Although in the early phases of Operation Barbarossa the Germans rapidly overwhelmed their ill-prepared enemy, many German commanders were certain the glory would not last given the ignominious history of enemy forces invading Mother Russia. Hitler was convinced that the *Blitzkrieg* (Lightning War) principles, which had served him so well throughout the campaigns in the West, were an unstoppable force. He was confident the Germans could defeat the Russians before the onset of the winter of 1941.

The idea of such a rapid victory was as ill-conceived as it was foolhardy, and the terrible winter of 1941 exposed the technical and logistical difficulties that would have to be overcome if victory in the East was to be secured. The fact that the German forces began to falter as the temperatures plummeted proved to the Russians that though they were facing a formidable enemy, it was one that could be beaten when favourable tactical situations presented themselves. The Russians utilised their harsh winters to good effect, and when the German war machine began to grind to a halt, the Russians went on the offensive. Another factor in the Russians' favour was the sheer size of their military forces. It would be overwhelming numbers that would defeat the Germans in the East. By the end of 1943 the writing was almost certainly on the wall for the German forces. Hitler's persistent interference in tactical matters, combined with blunders made by commanders on the ground, saw Germany rapidly lose the initiative. Under the Soviet onslaught the Germans were forced to give up ground to their enemy and steadily retreat. For the German inhabitants of Prussia, the consequences of the country's failing fortunes could not have been more frightening.

One and a half years before the end of the Second World War, following the Anglo-Soviet invasion of Iran, the US president, Franklin D. Roosevelt, Britain's prime minister, Winston Churchill, and the Soviet dictator, General Josef Stalin, met at the Tehran Conference to discuss, among other things, the conditions under which the Western Allies would open a new front in northern France (as Stalin had pressed them to do since 1941) and the launch of a massive Soviet offensive on Germany's Eastern Front to divert German forces from northern France. In the course of the conference of the 'Big Three', which took place from 28 November to 1 December 1943, Stalin set the course for the violent occupation of Eastern Germany by Poland and the Soviet Union, attaching particular importance to East Prussia. Churchill wanted to dismantle the German Reich and reduce its territory significantly and suggested moving Poland's western border further to the west. The USSR was to receive North-East Prussia with Königsberg. Stalin's argument, that in order to prevent 'minority-building' in this area the Germans residents 'had to be resettled', found the approval of both the United States and Great Britain. A few months later, on 27 July 1944, the Soviet Union concluded a secret agreement with the Communist Polish Committee of National Liberation, which would decide the future western border of Poland and the division of East Prussia.

Two other important conferences followed. At Yalta on 4–11 February 1945, during the discussion of Germany and Europe's post-war reorganisation, Stalin justified the Soviet claims on East Prussia not only as a 'necessity' for the USSR to occupy the ice-free port of Pillau but also by saying that the Soviets had suffered so much at the hand of the Nazis that they were anxious to retain a portion of German terriroty. Unlike Poland, which before the war had justified its expansionist intentions on East Prussia on 'historical grounds', the Soviet Union was openly demonstrating the power of its massive military force. Among other important issues discussed at Yalta were the division of defeated Germany into zones of occupation and the shifting of the 'western border of Poland' to the Oder-Neisse Line. The third and final conference of the Allies took place after the end of the war in Potsdam, near Berlin. In addition to issues relating the treatment and trial of the defeated German military, the dismantling of Germany's industrial war potential and war reparations, the Potsdam Agreement established the transfer of North-East Prussia to the USSR, the placement of other areas of Eastern Germany under Polish administration, and the orderly and humane expulsion of the German population. Following these decisions by the victorious powers, the Soviet Union and Poland, therefore, had permission to expel the Germans residents from East Prussia.

War in Russia had effectively started on 22 June 1941, when German soldiers crossed the Soviet western border. This marked the beginning of the pre-emptive strike against the Soviet Union, which was in the final preparatory phase of its attack on the German Reich and Europe. At first, the German advance was quick. Resistance could be overcome, losses were limited and land could be conquered village by village, city by city. The *Wehrmacht* was often welcomed by the population as a liberator from the yoke of Bolshevik rule. Adolf Hitler and his general staff hoped for a quick victory, but then came the Russian winter, which turned out to be even more severe than usual, and the advance faltered as the cold and icy storms claimed their victims. In the spring of 1942 it was hoped that the victories of the summer and autumn of 1941 could be continued by an offensive towards the Caucasus and the Volga, but things went slower than in the previous year. The resistance of the Soviet defenders had become stronger and more determined, and Hitler's dreams of finally defeating the Red Army remained unfulfilled.

The capture of Leningrad, which had been under siege since September 1941, failed due to the spirited defence of the city and the fact that Hitler didn't want to deploy larger German units for this strategically unimportant goal. In August 1942 German troops advanced on Stalingrad. The city was the key to the Volga and one of the main supply lines of the Soviet war economy. Much of the city was captured, but it could not be fully occupied, and in November 1942 the Soviet counter-offensive began. The German troops were encircled and forced to surrender in February 1943. The *Wehrmacht* suffered its heaviest defeat of the war: 150,000 soldiers died in the battle, and more than 90,000 were captured by the Soviets. Only 6,000 of those prisoners saw their homeland years later. The German defeat at Stalingrad represented a turning point in the war on Germany's Eastern Front, initiating the slow retreat of her troops, which was constantly interrupted by counter-offensives. Despite the many partial successes of the German military, its triumphant march through Russia had come to an end.

On 22 June 1944, three years after the beginning of the Eastern campaign, the Soviets' biggest counter-offensive began, involving 126 infantry divisions, forty tank brigades, sixteen motorised brigades and six cavalry divisions, supported by three air units with 6,000 aircraft. A total of 2.5 million Soviet soldiers attacked the German side, which consisted of the 2nd Army under Colonel-General Walter Weiss, the 9th Army under General Hans Jordan, the 4th Army under General Kurt von Kirch, and the 3rd Panzer Army under the command of Colonel-General Georg-Hans Reinhardt: a total of forty divisions with about 500,000 men. In this imbalance of powers, the defeat of the German defenders was inevitable, especially due to their insufficient and inadequate armaments. After the collapse of twenty-five of the German divisions and the loss of 298,000 German soldiers who either fell or were taken prisoner, the Soviet units moved like a 350-km-wide tidal wave to the West, approaching the Reich borders and soon to arrive in East Prussia.

Adolf Hitler, who was in his *Wolfschanze* HQ near Rastenburg, was forced to order the 'temporary evacuation of the non-combatable population' of the Memel region and some 50,000 East Prussians were brought by ship from Memel across the Baltic Sea to Pillau, Danzig and Gotenhafen. Erich Koch, *Gauleiter* and Reich Defense Commissioner, was well aware of the danger posed by the Soviets. For months he had been supervising the building of a 1,000km-long 'Eastern Wall'. Not a wall in the true sense of the word, but a series of anti-tank ditches built in strategic locations along the Reich's south-eastern border. Consisting of a 6m-wide and 6m-deep ditch, it was intended to be used to stop the Soviet tanks advance. Tens of thousands of workers were deployed to build the 'wall'.

On August 24 Erich Koch reported to Adolf Hitler at his headquarters: 'My Führer, the East wall has been completed in the basic form. The homeland now joins the front on a fanatical will to win, not a metre of German soil will be given to the Bolshevik hordes. East Prussia is German and will always remain German. If necessary, men, women and children will defend their homeland with their fists. I have no plans to evacuate East Prussia. Our task is to defend it until the last breath.' On his way back to Königsberg, Koch was informed that his representative at the office had started to draw up an 'East Prussia Evacuation Plan' during his absence. Koch immediately stopped the plan from being forwarded to any of the district offices. Koch is today cited as a prime example of a typically deluded National Socialist.

During the night of 26–27 August 1944 the inhabitants of Königsberg were taken by surprise and confronted with the terror of the air war. The air raid sirens howled. The night sky over the East Prussian capital was suddenly as bright as daylight. Several hundred magnesium lights, dropped by British bombers, hung from small parachutes and floated slowly to the ground, allowing the bomber pilots to better recognise the target area. To avoid the expected flak fire, the British aircraft were flown in via Denmark and neutral Sweden. The pilots of the 167 Lancaster bombers, who had 460 tons of bombs on board, were given clear orders: not to bomb military targets, industrial plants or the port area, but exclusively residential areas and the city centre.

For the first time since the war started, British bombers were using new blasting bombs, which had devastating effects. The bombs first hit Maraunenhof, between Cranzer Allee, Herzog-Albrecht-Allee and the Wallring. In just a few minutes the attack turned Königsberg into a sea of flame. Entire rows of houses and irreplaceable cultural and historical buildings collapsed. Despite the firefighters' attempts to contain the fires, they spread rapidly through the city. One house after another went up in flames. Several thousand civilians were left homeless that night; many killed by the flames, many others buried under the rubble. The number of wounded and those with severe burns was also alarmingly high. All hospitals in the city were overcrowded. The next day efforts were made to rescue those who had been buried by the collapsing buildings and to shelter the displaced in emergency quarters.

While many thousands of people in Königsberg mourned their relatives and tended to the seriously injured on the morning of August 28 1944, the *Manchester Guardian* published the 'successful story' of 'The Lancaster Bombers' 1,000-mile flight to Königsberg with new incendiary bombs'. Commander-in-chief, Arthur 'Bomber' Harris reported: 'Royal Air Force Lancaster bombers made a 2,000-mile flight on Saturday night to launch their first attack on the capital of East Prussia and currently the main supply port to the Germans fighting 100 miles east against the Red Army. The bombers were in the air for ten hours.

They carried a large number of flaming firebombs. The attack was limited to nine and a half minutes. After that time the bombers left behind what one of the pilots described as the biggest fire he has ever seen. Flames were visible from 250 miles.'

The shock and horror of this first night of bombing was still vivid in the minds of the people of Königsberg. The smouldering fires had not yet died out in many houses, the last victims had not yet been recovered, and the walls of damaged houses were still collapsing when the sirens howled again on the night of 29 August as 189 British bombers flew in over Sweden, in violation of the neutrality laws, and attacked Königsberg again, dropping 492 tons of bombs on the historically important buildings in the city centre. In the following hours huge fires raged through the streets, engulfing fleeing women, children and elderly who could not run fast enough to reach the shelters in time. Firefighters, doctors and nurses who rushed to help the injured were also killed or injured in the attack. The blazing fires unleashed an inferno that left firefighters almost powerless. The castle, cathedral and twelve churches, the old and the new universities, museums, the stock exchange, the opera house and the city library went up in flames. The three medieval districts of the old town – Löbenicht, Kneiphof and the picturesque Speicherviertel on the Pregel – were also ablaze. The industrial quarter, the port and the main rail station remained undamaged. More than 5,000 people lost their lives in this second British attack, twice as many were injured, and around 150,000 residents were left homeless. Nearly half of all the buildings in the city were completely destroyed or severely damaged. The old Königsberg no longer existed; British air mines, explosive bombs and phosphorus bombs had wiped it out. The city's famous Knights' Castle, the pride of the East Prussian capital, had been virtually destroyed.

The *Oberbaurat* (Chief Surveyor) of Königsberg, Hans Gerlach, who carried out an inspection of what remained of the castle, reported to the Lord Mayor, Hellmuth Will: 'The air attacks, especially those on the night of 29 August 1944, resulted in an almost total destruction of the castle. As a result of the large number of phosphorus firebombs, all roof trusses immediately caught fire. The fire has then eaten inexorably through the floors of all wings down to the basement. All floors in the four wings of the castle and in the tower were destroyed, the vaults of the castle church and part of the remaining ceilings have collapsed.

Only the basement in the eastern part of the south wing, in which the boxes with the dismantled amber room are located, is undamaged.'

The two devastating air strikes triggered unrest in the Königsberg population. Not only were further bombardments expected, but an advance by Soviet troops into the border area of East Prussia was also feared. Trust in *Gauleiter* Koch's statement that no Russian would ever enter East Prussian was lost. Rumours started to spread that Soviet troops were assembling beyond the border. In September 1944 anxiety over the uncertain future prompted many mothers who had lost their homes in the night of the bombing to leave Königsberg with their children to stay with relatives 'in the Reich'. Despite buying a return ticket – so that their journey was not considered an 'escape' – they had no plans to return before the end of the war.

Several thousand children were sent back to the Reich from East Prussia in September and October 1944. A previous agreement of 1942–43 between Erich Koch and the Berlin *Gauleiter*, Dr Joseph Goebbels, had made it possible for children from Berlin, which was endangered by air raids, to be transferred to the safer East Prussia and to Königsberg in particular, where they were taken in by local families. This child repatriation programme at the end of September 1944 proved to be a somewhat far-sighted move, as the chances that East Prussia would become a theatre of war were increasing by the day.

In the light of a possible Soviet-East Prussian clash, *Gauleiter* Koch was pushing for the completion of the 'Eastern Wall'. There were signs that the Soviets could begin an autumn offensive in October. East Prussia was not ready to defend itself as most of its soldiers were still fighting on other fronts. Hitler therefore signed a decree on September 25 1944, calling all local men between the ages of sixteen and sixty, who had previously been exempt from military service for health, old-age or occupational reasons, to take up arms: 'The enemy believes they can strike the final blow but we are determined not to allow this to happen. Building on our strength alone, our *Volkssturm*, we must not only break the enemy's will to defeat us but throw it back and keep it out of the Reich until victory for Germany and therefore peace throughout Europe can be secured.'

On October 17 1944 Erich Koch reported to Adolf Hitler at his *Wolfschanze* HQ, 'The first Volkssturm battalion is up!' Koch's 'Goldaper Battalion' consisted of 499 men divided into four companies,

Hitler's Lost State

with twenty-five trucks driven mainly by Polish drivers. The *Volkssturm* men were equipped with guns, bazookas and light machine guns; uniforms were not issued, only *Volkssturm* armbands, and no dog tags. Several departments of the party were responsible for the establishment, arming and supply of the *Volkssturm* units while *Gauleiter* Koch appointed himself the 'leader of the East Prussian *Volkssturm*'.

The military situation in East Prussia was more serious than Koch wanted to admit. Only a month before the British air raids on Königsberg, Tilsit had also been attacked, this time by Soviet aircraft. There were dead and injured among the population, and 154 buildings were destroyed. On 29 and 30 July 1944 the important rail hub of Insterburg experienced a massive Soviet air strike with devastating consequences. Then, on 7 October, the Memel region was completely cleared at the hand of the Soviets.

On 16 October the Soviets began the autumn offensive expected by the German defenders. Soviet troops managed to enter East Prussian soil, pushing back the 4th Army led by General Friedrich Hoßbach. The 3rd Belorussian Front, under the command of General Ivan Danilovich Chernyakhovsky, invaded the area south of Ebenrode and north of the Romain Heide (Romincka Forest). The East Prussian border lands became a battleground. On 20 October the Soviets deployed new armoured units of the 11th Guards Army, overrunning the weak German defence front. A few tanks passed through the Rominter Heide at Großwaltersdorf, crossing the Angerapp stream the next day before pushing their way through the district of Gumbinnen and occupying Nemmersdorf, a village that few people today will have heard of.

Nemmersdorf lies in present-day Mayakovskoye, in Kalinigrad Oblast, and was one of the first pre-war ethnic German villages to fall into the hands of the advancing Russian Red Army in the Second World War. The horror and violence visited upon the inhabitants of Nemmersdorf on 21 October 1944 makes particularly disturbing reading. When soldiers of the Russian 25 Guards Tank Brigade belonging to the 2nd Guards Tank Corps of the 11th Guards Army crossed the Angerapp bridge, they established a bridgehead on the western bank of the river. The German forces defending the bridge attempted to retake it, but several attacks were repelled by the Russian tanks and their supporting infantry. During an air attack, a number of Russian soldiers took shelter in an improvised bunker already occupied by fourteen local men and women.

According to a testimony given by Gerda Meczulat, who had been badly wounded, a Russian officer ordered everybody out of the bunker. The Russians then shot and killed the German civilians. During that night, the Russian 25th Tank Brigade was ordered to retreat across the river and take up defensive positions along the Rominte river.

When the *Wehrmacht* regained control of Nemmersdorf they were shocked at what they discovered. It became evident that the Russian forces had immediately embarked on a rampage of rape and murder, the savagery of which shocked even hardened combat veterans. Many German soldiers broke down at some of the sights that confronted them in the village. A total of 122 civilians had been massacred; seventy-two were German girls and women aged from eight to eighty-four years. It was stated in the report that every dead female at Nemmersdorf had been raped before being killed, including the children. Fifty French and Belgian prisoners of war who had been in the village at the time had also been murdered.

German authorities quickly organised an international commission to investigate the incident, headed by Estonian Hjalmar Mae, plus other representatives of neutral countries, such as Francoist Spain, Sweden and Switzerland. The commission heard from the medical authorities at Nemmersdorf, who confirmed that all of the dead females in the village had been raped. The fifty French and Belgian non-combatant prisoners of war had been present in the village to take care of some thoroughbred horses. When the bodies of these POWs were examined, it was ascertained that their deaths were caused by blows from entrenching shovels or rifle butts.

The former chief of staff of the German 4th Army, Major-General Erich Dethleffsen, testified on 5 July 1946 before an American tribunal in Neu-Ulm. He recalled:

'When in October of 1944, Russian units temporarily entered Nemmersdorf, they tortured the civilians. They nailed them to barn doors and then shot them. A large number of women were raped and then shot. During this massacre the Russian soldiers also shot some fifty French prisoners of war. Within forty-eight hours the German forces re-occupied the area.'

Karl Potrek, a resident of Königsberg and leader of a *Volkssturm* (people's militia) company present when the German army retook the village, testified in a report in 1953: 'In a farmyard stood a cart, to which more naked women were nailed through their hands in cruciform position. Near a large inn called the 'Roter Krug' stood a barn and to each of its two doors a naked woman was nailed through the hands, also in a crucified posture. In the dwellings we found a total of seventy-two women, including children, and one old man, all dead, some babies had their heads smashed in. Another family had been shot and their remains dumped in a pig sty, and the pigs were feeding off their rotting bodies.'

The massacre at Nemmersdorf was, as one might expect, hijacked by the Nazi propaganda ministry in an effort to further mobilise the German people. Marion Grafin Donhoff, the post-war co-publisher of the weekly *Die Zeit*, recalls at the time of the reports of the Nemmersdorf massacre that she was living in the village of Quittainen (Kwitany) in Western East Prussia. She wrote: 'In those years one had become so accustomed to everything that was official being lies that at first I took the pictures from Nemmersdorf to be falsified. Later, however, it turned out that it was no falsity at all, that it was all true.'

To many Germans, the massacre of Nemmersdorf became a symbol of the Russian terror and an example of the Red Army's worst excesses in Eastern Germany at the time. As many more German civilians volunteered for the *Volkssturm*, panic set in with East Prussian women. News about the atrocities committed by the Russians led to a massive evacuation attempt by civilians in the months to come.

At the beginning of November 1944, the Soviets occupied an area on the East Prussian border some 40km deep and 150km long and the German defenders had failed to push the Soviets back. Some villages and towns had been lost, including Eydtkau (formerly Eydtkuhnen), which was almost completely destroyed. By the end of November eleven German infantry divisions, two armoured divisions and two cavalry divisions were lost, and five armies with forty rifle divisions and strong armoured formations were confronted by the Soviet divisions. During the night of 19–20 October 1944, the bridge to Tilsit, which juts out into the Memel region, was being used to evacuate German troops. After the last of the soldiers had been withdrawn both the Luisen Bridge and nearby railway bridge were blown up by the Germans.

Hitler was troubled. Memel had been lost and only the fortress remained; he knew it was just a matter of time before this, too, must be given up. The next Soviet offensive could be expected in the coming weeks and months. Looking at the map, Hitler realised that the Soviet autumn offensive had also brought his headquarters at Rastenburg in East Prussia dangerously close to the war zone. On 6 November 1944 German units succeeded in recapturing the city of Goldap, which had already been occupied by the Soviets, but the map clearly showed that the *Wolfschanze* HQ was only 70km away. The question about how to best protect the Führer's headquarter as the war progressed was, however, a redundant one as Hitler wanted to move it to the Western Front in order to lead the Ardennes offensive against the Western Allies. Success in the West would also have lessened the danger for East Prussia, because troops from the West could then have been relocated to the Eastern Front. So, on 20 November the *Wolfschanze* was evacuated. As commander-in-chief of the *Wehrmacht*, Hitler had led the Eastern campaign from there. Only four months earlier, he had survived an assassination attempt, though his health had been seriously compromised. When leaving the *Wolfschanze* Hitler moved his Führer Grenadier Brigade, which had been stationed at the former headquarters, to the Eastern front.

After a short stay in Berlin, on December 10 Hitler moved into 'Adlerhorst', his new headquarters in Ziegenberg near Bad Nauheim. The bunkers of the *Wolfschanze* were taken over by General Friedrich Hoßbach and the staff of the 4th Army, but as the Soviets continued to advance into East Prussia at the beginning of 1945 Hitler ordered its demotition. The abandoned remains were captured by the Red Army on January 27 1945 without a shot being fired. That same day, Auschwitz was liberated farther south. It would take until 1955 to clear the over 54,000 land mines that surrounded the complex.

By the winter of 1944 it had become clear that the war was lost. Hitler had previously forbidden civilians from fleeing, as this would have been seen as a sign of defeat for the Reich. As the Red Army pushed forward into East Prussia, rumours about the atrocities they committed were spreading fast.

Most East Prussians wanted to leave the country during the fierce fighting. In December 1944, with the snow and icy winds of winter fast approaching, the military commanders once again asked the *Gauleiter* to lift the flight ban and instead authorise the activation of the evacuation plans, which many district leaders and mayors had already finalised. Koch again refused, declaring, 'East Prussia will not be evacuated. East Prussia will be defended to the very end,' adding that the soldiers' sole task was the military defence of East Prussia. The commanders insisted that a successful defence would only be possible if women, children, the sick and elderly in the endangered areas left their homes and the streets were free of vehicles. Koch, on the other hand, argued: 'If I agree to evacuate the civilian population and allow for East Prussia to be evacuated, our soldiers' and *Volkssturm*'s determination to fight will decrease as they would not want to risk their lives to defend an empty, uninhabited land.'

Meanwhile, at the beginning of November, Stalin, who was disappointed by the Soviet's autumn offensive in East Prussia, met with Marshal Alexander Vasilevsky to plan the next large-scale offensive. On November 12 1944 he appointed Marshal Georgy Konstantinovich Zhukov as commander-in-chief of the 1st Belorussian division, Marshal Konstantin Rokossovsky as commander-in-chief of the 2nd division and Marshal Ivan Chernachovsky as commander-in-chief of the 3rd Belorussian division. Although they were all highly experienced, Stalin reserved the right to lead Operation East Prussia himself. He planned to gain control of East Prussia within a few weeks and to destroy it in a swift military campaign. Eighteen days after the attack began, his Red Army soldiers stormed Königsberg. Some 1.6 million soldiers, 25,400 guns and grenade launchers, 3,800 tanks and artillery on self-propelled guns, 3,000 aircraft, 13.5 million grenades, 620 million cartridges and 2.2 million projectiles for rocket launchers were supplied for the battle in East Prussia. The largest assault army deployed thus far during the Second World War was soon to fulfil Stalin's intention of destroying the towns and villages of East Prussia and extinguishing all life. In Stalin's own words: 'We shall turn East Prussia into a desert!'

The Chief of the German General Staff of the Army, Colonel-General Heinz Guderian, knew about the Soviet preparations for the winter offensive and their superiority of men and resources. He considered it his duty to inform Hitler. This took place on 26 December 1944 at Hitler's new headquarters, from where he was directing the current offensive on the Bulge. During his speech, Guderian pointed out the strength of the Soviet force, which was preparing for an imminent attack in the East Prussian border region. Once again, Guderian asked for the speedy reinforcements of troops in Eastern Prussia to replace those that had been relocated to other fronts. Guderian went into great detail, outlining the supremacy of the Soviets: eleven-to-one in infantry, sevene-to-one in tanks, and twenty-to-one in aircraft.

Although Hitler was aware of the dangerous situation, he could not draw troops back from the Ardennes offensive, because it was there – and not in East Prussia – that the outcome of the war would be decided. In addition to East Prussia, there was a lack of troops on all fronts, but the Führer had set all his hopes on the success of the Ardennes offensive. By the end of 1944 Stalin's troops reached the East Prussian border. However, before launching their offensive they had to wait for the winter, which, with its constant temperatures of minus 20–25°C, would consolidate the roads, make fields and meadows passable for tanks, and cover lakes, rivers, ponds and streams with ice. On 31 December the temperatures in East Prussia dropped further. What would happen in East Prussia to the soldiers, the *Volkssturm* men, and civilian women and girls in thirteen days' time still remains an episode of unprecedented cruelty in the history of the Second World War.

The East Prussian offensive, though often overshadowed by the Vistula-Oder operation and the later battle for Berlin, was in fact one of the largest and costliest operations fought by the Red Army. It lasted from 13 January to 25 April 1945 (although some German units did not surrender until 9 May) and cost the Red Army 584,788 casualties, and 3,525 tanks and assault guns. The Soviets had two main objectives. One was to move as rapidly as possible to the west and meet the Allies as far west as possible in order to maximise the post-war Soviet sphere of influence. The main objective, though, was to capture Berlin. The two were complementary because possession of Russian-controlled territory could not be won quickly unless Berlin was taken. Another consideration was that Berlin itself held strategic assets, including Adolf Hitler and part of the German atomic bomb programme, which German physicists had been working on since the late 1930s.

In the first days of January 1945 the military commanders in East Prussia once again tried to persuade Koch to relax the flight ban or lift it altogether. They pointed out that rail transport to the Reich was still working and that it would be possible to carry mothers, children and the sick to safety from the endangered East Prussia. It was also still possible for the military to organise the population living near the frontline into trekking to the west. But these arguments did not convince Koch. He firmly believed that East Prussia could still be successfully defended and was not prepared to give up the province. As Reich Defence Commissar of East Prussia, he was forced to invite the commanders of his staff and various other units to his headquarters to once again argue for the active defence of East Prussia. His passionate appeal ended with the words, 'Königsberg remains German! East Prussia will not be evacuated! Our duty is to fight back to the last man!'

In spite of this appeal, evacuation plans were already being drafted by some mayors and district councillors, who, having had an in-depth look at the situation on the ground, bravely decided to override party orders. Individual attempts to evacuate civilians, especially women and children, from East Prussia across the Danzig Bay to the West had already been made throughout 1944.

Dirk Kersthold owns a hotel-restaurant in Puck, the capital of Puck County, part of Kashubia, north-west of Gdańsk. He recalls:

> One day a man and his son came in and explained that he wanted to show his son where his mother was born and told me this incredible event. At the end of 1944 he was stationed on Hela as an artillery officer, and his wife worked there in a refugee camp looking after the children. The time was pretty panicky already, and people were hanged left, right and centre when expressing the wish to flee. At that time there were six new U-boats in the harbour, destined for an attack on America. The order came to equip the U-boats and make them ready to ship out. The officers of the U-boats held a secret get-together to devise a plan and agreed not to follow orders, but to rescue the refugees. In the dark of the night they smuggled women and children past the noses of the alert SS and on board the U-boats. After a dangerous underwater flight, where they had to dodge the mines, Russian U-boats and their own military, they arrived safely in Kiel, Germany, and released their precious cargo.

In January 1945 millions of civilians, mainly women, children and the elderly, fled through ice and snow, an exodus of such proportion the world had never seen before. On foot over the frozen gulf of East Prussia, aboard ships heading west through the icy waters of the Baltic sea, along the roads of Silesia and Pomerania, or moving south towards

Bavaria, in temperatures of minus 20°C, they set off on a journey of hope and despair, cold, hungry, tired and scared. The lucky ones who had a horse-drawn cart would take bedding and blankets, but also household goods, pots, dishes and, above all, laundry, clothing and shoes. Children and the elderly would travel in the back of the cart, covering their heads and hands to protect them from frostbite. In the next few weeks more than twelve million Germans would lose their homeland; two million of them also their lives. Those who survived would never forget their ordeal.

Helga Schneider was one of the evacuees: 'It was horrendous. I have never seen anything like that again in my life, miles and miles of caravans, the women and the children and horses and everything […] frozen bodies on the side of the road, everywhere […] no human being can possibly imagine what it was like.'

Hunger, thirst and cold soon started to strike children, the elderly, the sick, the frail, pregnant women and those who had recently given birth. Inevitably, many were left behind. But no Soviet planes were yet in sight to fire at people or drop bombs on them. There was still no danger of being run over by tanks. The streets were still reasonably free from military vehicles. There was still hope that the refugees could reach the West unharmed by Red Army soldiers. It was this hope that helped many refugees face the hardships and made them easier to bear. Those who managed to flee East Prussia in the first twelve days of January 1945 had the best chance of survival, but all this was soon to change for the worst.

On January 12 1945 Stalin launched the Soviet winter offensive against Germany with 6.2 million Soviet soldiers, the largest offensive ever carried out in a war. The primary objective of the operation was to occupy East Prussia and destroy the 'fascists'. To do so, he planned to storm the Königsberg fortress and reach the Baltic coast. The last months of 1944 and the first ten days of 1945 were used by the Red Army leaders to systematically brutalise the soldiers and convince them to commit atrocities against all Germans. This was done through lectures and films showing the atrocities committed by German fascists in the Soviet Union and the siege of Leningrad. The aim of this 'theoretical preparation for attack' was to incite hatred against the Germans.

Marshal Ivan Tschernjachowskij, commander-in-chief of the 3rd Belarussian Front, said goodbye to his soldiers in East Prussia with the following order: 'We marched two thousand kilometers and saw the destruction of all that we have built in twenty years. Now we are standing in front of the cave of the fascist aggressors. We shall have no mercy as they had no mercy for us. They blaze with hate and rage. The land of the fascists must be destroyed like they have ravaged our land. The fascists must die just as our soldiers have died.' Iwan Alymow recalls: 'We had only one thing in mind, doing to the Germans what they had done to us. Now they had to experience that too.'

The Jewish writer, Ilja Ehrenburg, had also called on Soviet soldiers to use violence, and to kill and rape women and girls. Hundreds of thousands of Red Army soldiers were carrying the following appeal in their breast pocket: 'Kill! There is nothing innocent about the Germans, not the living and the unborn. Follow the instructions of Comrade Stalin and crush the Fascist animal in their cave! Break the racial pride of Germanic women! Take them as legitimate prey!' The Soviet Minister of Defence issued the 'order to plunder' as early as 26 December 1944. According to this, solders who 'behaved well' were allowed to take home extra packages of plundered goods once a month via the field post office. Infantrymen and NCOs were entitled to up to 5kg, officers 10kg and generals 15kg. From the middle of January 1945 to May 8 1945 East Prussia became the main battleground on German soil.

On January 12 1945, at 1.30am, the 1st Ukrainian Front, under the command of Soviet Marshal Ivan Konjew, with sixty infantry divisions and eight tank corps, began to storm the weakly occupied German positions. The Soviets showered them with a hail of steel and fire and rolled like an avalanche through the defence lines of the 4th German Panzer Army, under the command of General Fritz-Hubert Grasses. The Soviet soldiers, tanks and guns, supported by hundreds of fighter planes, succeeded in ripping up the 150km-long German front in a few hours. Thousands of German soldiers perished in that first attack. Only one day later, on 13 January, in the early morning hours, the 3rd Belarussian Front began its advance in the Gumbinnen area towards Königsberg. Some 350 Soviet batteries stormed the German defences and delivered a two-hour assault, after which the fourteen rifle divisions and two tank brigades were unstoppable. On the same day, the 2nd Belorussian Front, under Marshal Roskossovski, stormed into East Prussia. Six Armies, two tank corps, a pioneer corps and the 3rd Guards Cavalry Corps crushed the positions of the German 2nd Army. Rokossowski's goal was the occupation of the city of Elbing on the Frisches Haff. Should he succeed, the Germans would be cut off from the west and East Prussia would be turned into a cauldron. On 14 January 14 1945, Marshal Zhukov attacked the 9th German Army with his 1st Belorussian Front, consisting of five fully replenished armies, including the 1st Polish Army. The big Soviet winter offensive with its three fronts was in full swing. The objective was to cut off East Prussia from all land connections, encircle and annihilate the German troops, reach the Baltic Sea coast within two weeks, and conquer the Königsberg fortress.

The first three days of the Red Army's campaign in East Prussia saw the Soviets' offensive being directed not only against German soldiers, but also against the civilian population. Women, girls and babies were raped on a massive scale, many of them killed afterwards. One hundred thousand women were killed within a few days. It was an orgy of violence not seen since Nemmersdorf. They looted and burned down entire villages leaving many dead on the roadside. One Russian soldier, Sergej Schwyzkij, reported: 'We mowed down carts, we didn't care if they were civilians. We had to go forth and forth and forth.'

On 16 January 1945, the 43rd Army of the 1st Baltic Front, from the Tilsit area, launched its attack on East Prussia. On the same day, Schlossberg (formerly Pillkallen) was occupied. On 18 January a Soviet tank formation managed to break through 18km north of Insterburg and quickly move towards Königsberg. On 19 January the Red Army occupied Ragnit, then Gumbinnen on 20 January, and Insterburg on 21 January. On 22 January the Red Army reached Wehlau, Anappap (former name Darkehmen) and Goldap, only 40km from Königsberg. On 31 January 1945, only eighteen days after the attack had started, the assault of Königsberg began. It would last until 9 April.

Chapter 9

Harbour of Hope

By mid-January 1945 rumours about the atrocities committed by the Soviets in East Prussia began to spread further west. Telephones at the House of Government in Königsberg were ringing incessantly. Party officials, local mayors and district administrators were bombarded with questions, but had no answers. Koch, who had been against the evacuation of civilians from the start of the Soviet offensive, finally agreed to lift the ban.

The 3rd Belorussian Front had surrounded Königsberg on the landward side, cutting off the road down the Samland peninsula to the port of Pillau, and trapping the 3rd Panzer Army and approximately 200,000 civilians in the city. Basic provisions were so meagre that civilians were faced with three bleak alternatives: to remain in the city and starve (rations were cut during the siege to 180g of bread a day); to cross the front lines and leave themselves at the mercy of the Soviets; or to cross the ice of the Frisches Haff to Pillau in hope of finding a place on an evacuation ship.

On 21 January, in a cordoned-off section of the port of Pillau, the steamer *Pretoria*, bearing the markings of a hospital ship, was still empty. Koch's party employees would be the first passengers, followed by the severely wounded and, the following day, several hundred refugees. In another harbour in Pillau lay the former flagship of the KdF fleet, the *Robert Ley*. On 25 January the *Pretoria*, *Robert Ley*, *Ubena* and *Duala* left Pillau with more than 20,000 passengers on board, heading west. Many ships would follow in what became known as 'Operation Hannibal', the evacuation of civilians and injured soldiers from East Prussia and the Polish Corridor to the West, from mid-January to May 1945. Over a period of fifteen weeks between 500 and 1000 merchant vessels of all types, including fishing boats, and Germany's largest remaining naval units, carried between 800,000 and

900,000 civilians and 350,000 soldiers across the Baltic Sea to Germany and German-occupied Denmark. This was more than three times the number of people evacuated in the nine-day operation at Dunkirk.

Evacuation by train was no longer possible. On 22 January the last scheduled D-train of the *Deutsche Reichsbahn* had left Königsberg central station in the direction of Berlin. On 23 January, ten days after the start of the Soviet offensive, Russian armies reached the town of Elbing on the western border of East Prussia. Roads into Elbing, as well as rail lines, were blocked off by the Red Army so that it would not be possible to escape to the West either by road or by train.

All trains traveling to Elbing had to be stopped in Braunsberg, Heiligenbeil and Ludwigsort and sent back to Königsberg. On the evening of 23 January, Briesen, the railroad junction at Goßlershausen, Bischofswerder, Freystadt, Rosenberg, Prussian Holland and Mühlhausen were lost and occupied by the Soviets. The following morning Allenburg, Labiau, Tapiau, Gutenberg, Arnau, Riesenburg, Christburg and Liebstadt were also lost to the Soviets. The city of Königsberg had become a fortress. Hitler appointed the Iron Cross-bearer General of the Infantry, Otto Lasch, as fortress commander and ordered Lieutenant-General Hans Schittnig and his staff of the 1st East Prussian Infantry Division to defend the city to the last man and the last bullet cartridge, completely excluding a surrender of the fortress.

On 24 January Soviet troops invaded Samland and occupied Löwenhagen. The same day, the provisions that had been stored there over a period of three months for the supply of 36,000 soldiers become the loot of the Soviet invaders. On 26 January Red Army units south of Tolkemet arrived at Steinbeck and up to Frisches Haff, occupying Waldau, Gamsau, Mölsehnen and Liska-Schaaken. The Red Army had succeeded in enclosing East Prussia and separating it from the West. Soldiers unable to escape would face death or imprisonment. Those refugees who were spared death would be threatened with deportation to forced labour camps behind the Urals in Siberia. The last few possible escape routes left were to the north, over the frozen bay of Frisches Haff (Vistula lagoon) to Frisch Nehrung (the Vistula Spit) and from there to the West, or to find a boat sailing west from Pillau. Another way west was to reach the two larger ports of Danzig-Nuefahrwasser and Gotenhafen in the Danzig Bay, where several ships were waiting to take in refugees and bring them to safety across the Baltic Sea to the port of Kiel.

On 27 January, as the Soviet artillery began the bombardment of Königsberg, the 65th and 69th infantry divisions arrived to reinforce the fortress defence. By then, more than 150,000 civilians had left their hometown, but there were still some 11,000 seriously injured soldiers in the local hospitals, waiting in the hope of getting on a ship across the Baltic Sea and being transferred to a homeland army hospital in the West. They had been waiting for weeks, in vain. As Koch prepared to leave his office in Pillau-Neutief at 1.30am, a terrible noise rang out. Fort Steele, situated on a small hill by the port of Pillau, was blown up with all the ammunition stored in it. Was it sabotage? In the warehouses immediately adjacent to the fort more than 300 refugees waiting for the ships that would carry them to safety were killed, and more than 600 injured. Most of those would not survive. The same night, Rastenburg was occupied by the Soviets, the fortress of Memel fell, and with the town of Sensburg also taken by the Russians, the last city of Masuria was lost.

The artillery fire had already started early in the morning, followed by air strikes later in the day, and commander General Lasch asked Koch to clear the fortress of civilians and ensure their removal to Pillau. The general explained the gravity of the situation to Koch, adding, 'I expect the Russians to storm the fortress in the next few days.' In a speech on Königsberg radio station, Koch urged the civilian population to leave the fortress town immediately in the direction of Pillau, as an attack on the fortress was to be expected at any time.

The closing down of the city's Albertus University on 28 January came as no surprise: its relocation to Greifswald had been planned for some time. The University Women's and Children's Hospital was also included in the move. For the evacuation of the clinic, with its patients, doctors and nursing staff, two large ships were used, which, up till that point, had served the *Kriegsmarine* as *Wohnshiffe* (residential ships). These were the former KdF ship *Der Deutsche* and the steamer *General San Martin*. In addition, both ships took a few hundred refugees, and arrived at the port of Stettin (Szczecin) a few days later.

On 28 and 29 January the containment ring around Königsberg would be narrowed further. Around noon on the twenty-eighth the motorway bridge north of Gollau was blown up, and Ludwigswalde, Neuhausen and Tannenwalde were lost, though the 5th German Panzer Division succeeded in shielding the south of the city. On the night of 29 January Sohna and the Altenburg substation were also lost.

Harbour of Hope

Despite fierce resistance, especially from the *Volkssturm*, Bischofsburg and Rößel fell into Soviet hands. Fierce fighting took also place around the railway junction at Korschen. On 29 January the Red Army advanced from Brandenburg and Haffstrom to the Frisches Haff (Vistula lagoon), occupying Godrienen Trankwitz and Wargen, thus enabling the attackers to take Samland and Königsberg from the 4th German Army. Without any resistance, the Soviets seized Seerappen (Ljublino) the following night. Crossing the railway line to Pillau, they invaded the Königsberg suburb of Metgethen (present-day Imeni Alexandra Kosmodemyanskogo in Russia's Kalinigrad Oblast), surprising the inhabitants in their sleep. Nobody could have woken or warned them. A nocturnal massacre took place.

If Nemmersdorf had set the template for terror in the East, then Metgethen would certainly surpass it in its brutality. German forces would recapture the suburb on 19 February in a successful attempt to reopen the vital road and railway line that ran between Königsberg and the Baltic port of Pillau. According to official reports, they discovered the mutilated corpses of civilians.

There are several contemporary reports by German military personnel stating that, among other things, women had been brutally raped and mutilated by having their genitals or breasts cut or shot, and that thirty-two civilians had been rounded up on the local tennis court and killed by an explosion, probably from a grenade or grenades being thrown at them. In one eyewitness report, Captain Hermann Sommer, former staff officer of the fortress commander of Königsberg, Otto Lasch, stated:

> I made my own observations on 27 February 1945 when I came to Metgethen on official business. When I drove my motorcycle just before the railway crossing into a gravel pit, in order to inspect the building for its usability, I found behind it the corpses of twelve women and six children. All were completely undressed and huddled up in a pile. Most of the children had their skulls broken with a blunt object or their bodies perforated with innumerable bayonet stabs. The women, mostly older ones between forty and sixty years, had also been killed with knives or bayonets. On all of them black-and-blue marks of beating were clearly visible.

It is believed a total of 3,000 German civilians were murdered at Metgethen. Other incidents that can best be construed as Russian vengeance upon the German population followed, including one that took place at Treuenbrietzen, in the Brandenburg area of Germany.

The town was first occupied by the Russian 5th Guards Mechanised Corps on 21 April 1945, until being beaten back for a short period by *Wehrmacht* and Waffen-SS troops. When the German units were finally forced to retreat for good, Russian soldiers entered the town and murdered an estimated 1,000 civilian inhabitants during the last days of April and early days of May. Again, many women and young girls were subjected to brutal rape ordeals. The rape of very young girls and very old women was widespread through the territories recaptured by the Russians in the closing stages of the Second World War. It was something that, together with looting, the burning of houses and killing of civilians, would continue all the way to Berlin.

Many of the Germans civilians who had moved into Prussia in the wake of Operation Barbarossa were mainly families of Nazi administration staff, Gestapo agents and high-ranking officers. Despite Koch's ban on evacuating civilians from East Prussian territories, several officials had the foresight to at least try to evacuate their families before the Russians came. For many ordinary ethnic Germans in Prussia, their only means of escape was on foot, a nightmare journey through fields, swamps and forests, with the Red Army in close pursuit. During this period there were undoubtedly other incidents where German civilians were caught and executed.

Wehrmacht soldier, *Gefreiter* Peter Baumanis, who lived in Evesham in Worcestershire after the war, recalled:

> The Russians would take a village or town off us and after a few days of fighting we would get it back only to lose it again. Every time we retook a place, we would find more graves that were not there before. We would find bodies in ditches or buried in shallow graves in fields. When unearthed, we discovered these were not the graves of soldiers, theirs or ours, but civilians; our civilians. These graves had not been there previously, so these people had to have been killed by the Russians. That is what it was like, a game of cat and mouse. Only they became stronger

in numbers than us; they were the cat while we were the mouse. The most frustrating part of all was that we could not defend our people. We would shout at them "Go now, get out of here". Some would go, others refused. When we left, we left them behind and I remember thinking, those people, the old man, the old woman and the four or five children, they are all going to be killed. I saw some terrible things, what they used to do to people, it was horrible. But then they used to say, "Well, look what you have done to our people, how many thousands upon thousands have you Germans murdered?" The point is, they were right. There is no denying that fact. A soldier seeking vengeance cannot be judged by any civilian. Only a soldier understands how his emotions become muddied by what he sees in his own personal war. The Russian soldiers would have been just the same in their thinking. This is what happens in wars where ideology and race become defining factors in a soldier's behaviour. There is often no mercy, no remorse and no compassion.

Not all civilians, however, were subjected to the vengeful violence of the Russian army.

Siegfried Quandt remembers: 'We were about 30 hiding from the Russian tanks. We were petrified, dead still. Then comes a Russian, "Uri! Uri!" He wanted watches. In a fraction of a second everybody took their watch off or looked for whatever they had to give. He took the lot, thanked us and left. We were all bewildered, we thought he was going to shoot us or do something to us. Nothing.'

With the occupation of Metgethen an important link between Königsberg and Pillau was lost and the escape route was no longer an option. Over half of East Prussia was in enemy's hands.

Thousands of people were still marching over the ice or snow-covered land hoping to reach the port of Gotenhafen, near Danzig, and board one of the ships that would take them to safety. Temperatures were as low as minus 20°C. Cold, tired and hungry, these refugees had nothing left to lose apart from their lives. Children developed fever, old people who could no longer continue the journey dropped to the ground and let themselves freeze to death. Mothers didn't want to let go of their dead children or had to bury them by the edge of the road. Those trying to cross the frozen bay of Frisches Haff were constantly faced with the danger of air strikes. Russian planes were firing at the ice, creating big craters in which horses, carts and people were falling in. One survivor, Gerd Scheffler, recalls, 'I was fleeing with my mother and brother. My brother was shot by a plane. "I can't move my legs," he said. Moments later he was still.'

Many thousands of civilian, as well as hundreds of wounded soldiers, were hoping to leave Gotenhafen on board a ship. On 21 January Admiral Karl Dönitz had ordered all available ships to the bay of Danzig: 2.5 million people would be evacuated in the following months. One ship stood out among the others: the MV *Wilhelm Gustloff*, the dream ship of the 1930s. As we saw in Chapter 5, the *Wilhelm Gustloff* had a capacity of around 1,500. By 30 January 1945 over 10,000 people had boarded the ship, over six and half times her capacity (three times the full capacity of the *Titanic* and six times the number of passengers actually on board the *Titanic* when she sank on April 15, 1912).

During the first few days the people with passes were getting along nicely, but in the following days more and more refugees arrived at Gotenhafen. They were assigned to the music hall and the glass promenade, people were quickly filling corridors and cabins were overcrowded. A few female naval auxiliaries like Waltraud Grüter were lucky enough to be assigned a cabin, while most were assembled in the empty swimming pool. She recalled: 'Everyone wanted to go on the *Wilhelm Gustloff*. Everyone thought that if they went on the *Gustloff* nothing bad would happen. There were young mothers who had their dead children in their arms and didn't want to part with them. People had to be pushed back, everybody wanted a little place on the *Gustloff*, everybody wanted to leave Gotenhafen.'

Wilhelm Gustloff survivor Ursula Schulze recalled: 'There were old people, mothers, children. The cabins were full. They came and cleared the large halls, there was no furniture left. Everyone got a mattress and they were lying next to each other like sardines. For me and my sister the ship was a safe haven. We thought, now we are off, we are going to be ok.'

The crew included sixty-seven-year-old merchant navy captain Friedrich Petersen, thirty-four-year-old lieutenant commander, and captain of the U-Boot (submarine) complement housed on the Wessel,

Wilhelm Zahn, senior merchant navy officers Captain Kohler and Captain Weller, first officer Louis Reese, purser Gerhardt Luth, and chief engineer Franz Löbel. In addition, there were 173 naval armed forces auxiliaries, 918 officers and men of the 2 *Unterseeboot-Lehrdivision* (Submarine training division), 373 female naval auxiliaries, 162 wounded soldiers and 8,956 civilians, of which an estimated 5,000 were children: a total of 10,582 passengers and crew. Just under 1,000 would survive.

We owe most of what we know about the sinking of the *Wilhelm Gustloff* not only to the accounts given by the survivors and the people involved in their rescue but especially to one survivor, twenty-year-old purser assistant, Heinz Schön, who dedicated all his life to the researching and archiving of the events, contacting survivors, compiling lists of passengers and raising awareness about the biggest maritime disaster in naval history.

On 21 January, according to Schön, Captain Zahn summoned the leading officers to a conference in the wardroom to inform them, 'Gentlemen, I have brought you here to deliver an order which affects both the Training Division and the *Wilhelm Gustloff*. He explained the Dönitz order to evacuate civilians from East and West Prussia at some length and stressed the importance of speed in preparing for sea. The ship was to be ready to sail in forty-eight hours. Many of the naval personnel on board were to go ashore to help defend the port until the evacuation was complete.

The first task would be to embark seriously wounded soldiers who had arrived in Gotenhafen aboard a hospital train from the East. Then the refugees were to be taken on board. 'This will be no Strength through Joy cruise,' warned Zahn, 'All of us, both Navy and Merchant Navy officers, have a difficult task and bear heavy responsibility. It is our duty to do everything possible to make things easier for the refugees.'

The build-up to the 'German Dunkirk' had been rapid and efficient. Dönitz himself had taken over control of all the merchant ships that could be gathered together for the evacuation. Ships of all shapes and sizes were assembled in Pillau and Gotenhafen, among them the big ships that had once been the pride of the KdF: the *Hansa*, the *Hamburg*, the *Deutschland*, the *Cap Arcona*, and, of course, the *Wilhelm Gustloff*. Another eight liners and twenty-five cargo ships were ordered to join in the evacuation. The *Hansa* (former *Albert Ballin*) was to carry the equipment of the training divisions, the officers and 3,000 refugees.

The *Wilhelm Gustloff* was to embark the 2nd Training Division, a contingent of women auxiliaries and a number of badly injured soldiers. The remainder of the naval personnel were to go aboard the *Hamburg* and *Deutschland*. Then civilian refugees would follow.

Gauleiter Koch regularly made his men comb the shipyards for deserters disguised as refugees, and other able-bodied workers to serve in the army, often boys as young as thirteen.

By the evening of 22 January the crews of the *Gustloff* and *Hansa* were hard at work preparing the ships to receive thousands of passengers, many of them wounded, all of them cold and exhausted. Some of the refugees coming from as far as Masuria and Silesia had been walking for days in freezing temperatures. On the way to Gotenhafen, some had lost parents, grandparents or children. Arriving at Gotenhafen, they thought the worst was over.

Horst Woit was ten years old when he left Elbing with his mother and her friend. On the morning of 23 January 1945 he watched from his window as Soviet tanks entered Elbing city centre. His mother, worried that they themselves would become victims of rape and murder, packed a few belongings in preparation for an escape to the West. Horst remembers: 'What my mum did, she ran across the corner to her friend's house and they decided that we were going to flee. While I was alone, and knowing we were going to go soon, I went into the trunk of my uncle and there was a jack-knife. I stole it and stuck it into my ski pants. But I didn't tell my mum. Later on, it became a life-saving story.' After collecting Horst, his mum and her friend walked to the Elbing river. Facing extreme weather conditions and the hardships of war, they reached Danzig on a small cutter and managed to obtain passes for the *Wilhelm Gustloff*.

In the chaos that prevailed at the time, the authorities had been unable to come up with a decision regarding the status of the famous ship. Was she to be considered a troopship? A refugee liner? A hospital ship? She was probably a bit of each. She was indeed a hospital ship, but there is some controversy as to whether she was marked with the red crosses that identify a hospital ship. If she had been, this would have been a breach of the Geneva Convention, as she was a ship of the German navy and equipped with anti-aircraft guns.

The evacuation operations took far more than the forty-eight hours Zahn had planned. On 27 January thousands more refugees had reached the port of Gotenhafen, hoping to find a place on one of the ships and preparing to sail away from the Fatherland and their childhood memories. Many of them had lost family members, their homes and all their possessions. Some of them had locked the door and were still carrying the key, hoping that one day, after the war ended, they would return to their homes.

On board the *Gustloff* there were already 4,000 refugees, with 2,500 on the *Hansa*. Grey naval trucks were busy delivering provisions to the ships. Each refugee was to receive one hot meal a day. Though this doesn't seem much of a luxury, for most of the refugees it was more than they had enjoyed in weeks.

In the winter of 1945 the German navy had two convoy protection units in the area: the 9th Escort Division in Gotenhafen, led by Commander Adalbert von Blanc, and the 10th Escort Division based in Swinemünde, commanded by Commander Hugo Heydel. Both units consisted mainly of three flotillas of minesweepers. From time-to-time escort destroyers and torpedo boats were used for other purposes, including the evacuation of troops and civilians.

At this point the main obstacle to the evacuation operations was the Royal Air Force.

In January 1945 the RAF had dropped 668 mines, sinking eighteen ships. It had also laid 1,345 mines, mostly concentrated in the area around Swinemünde, the headquarters of the 10th Escort Division, but also as far as the coast of Pomerania, causing long delays to the convoys while the mines were swept.

By 28 January the Gustloff still had no escort ships and only twelve lifeboats. The authorities managed to gather together another eighteen small boats, most of them cutters, and a number of naval rafts were stuck up on the upper decks next to piles of mattresses for the refugees. People were pouring into the harbour of Gotenhafen. Marine auxiliary Eva Dorn was twenty years old at the time. She was stationed near Gotenhafen: 'We were asked do you want to stay and fight for the Fatherland or do you want to leave? I am no hero so I said I wanted to leave. I arrived at Gotenhafen; people, people, people, abandoned sledges, dead horses, sick children, pregnant women. It was chaos.'

Around 250,000 refugees had arrived in Gotenhafen that week. One of them was Irmgard Harnecker: 'We packed a few belongings in the pram, then we pushed it through the snow to the ships. My sister came with us too.' Irmgard's daughter, eleven-month-old Ingrid, was with them. 'Ingrid, yes, well, she was like a doll. Sweetest baby. Was just starting to walk.'

In the early morning of 29 January most ships of the 9th and 10th Escort Division were still at sea and unavailable to escort the *Wilhelm Gustloff* and the *Hansa* to the west. However, the continuous presence of fully occupied ships at Gotenhafen was posing an increased threat of enemy air strikes.

Later that morning, an order arrived from U-boat commander, Captain Schutze: the *Wilhelm Gustloff* and the *Hansa* were to be ready to sail together '*in geleit*' the following day. The order brought some relief to the bridge, for the officers were well aware of the frustration of their crew, the growing tension of the passengers packed below decks and the resentment and desperation of those refugees who had not yet managed to acquire an identity pass for the *Wilhelm Gustloff*.

A larger transport with wounded soldiers arrived at Gotenhafen, together with medical vehicles. The ladies' salon on the *Gustloff* was cleared of refugees in order to set up an emergency hospital. The Lord Mayor of Gotenhafen Schlichting, who had occupied the 'Führer's Cabin' with his family, disembarked the ship to assist in the operations of embarkation of the wounded. At 11am a number of drills were carried out, including emergency drills for closing the water-tight bulkheads. Similar preparations were taking place a few hundred metres away on the *Hansa* led by forty-four-year-old U-Boat commander, Captain Karl Neitzel, and his crew.

Pregnant women and mothers of children under the age of three who had boarded the *Hansa* were asked to move to the *Wilhelm Gustloff*. With a maternity ward, a creche and a large supply of infant milk, The *Wilhelm Gustloff* was better equipped to provide for infants and young children. Families were often split, mothers and young children on the *Gustloff*, older children and grandparents on the *Hansa*.

More refugees arrived at Gotenhafen later in the day and were pushing to board the *Gustloff*, the *Hansa* or the whaling factory ship *Walter Rau*. Piles of abandoned prams could be seen by the harbour. Women were trying to smuggle their husbands and sons on the ships, disguising them as women or hiding them in trunks while the SS squads patrolled the crowds in search of men suitable for war service.

Marine auxiliary Eva Dorn recalled: 'I was working at the reception until the morning of 30 January. Until midnight 29 January, all refugees arriving on board were registered and their names entered in notebooks. We worked in groups of three or four marine helpers. We then ran out of paper, we had to stop at around 6,300 refugees. The refugees that came on board on 30 January were not registered by us. They were registered by the soldiers, a list of around 2,000 mainly refugees but also helpers and wounded soldiers. It was complete chaos.'

Gisela Teschke was one of those trying to board:

> There was a big commotion on the wharf. I had never seen so many people. My mother and her friend went to find out which ship we would be assigned to. They came back very upset. We had to go onto the whaling ship *Walter Rau* together with about 5,500 other people. My mother was angry, "Our men have to fight on the Russian front and all those women whose husbands have soft jobs can get onto the luxury liner," she said. Once on board the ship we ended up where the big kettles were, deep inside the ship's belly. They had been used in the production of whale oil. The smell was nauseating. There were no beds. We had to lie down on the bare, icy floor, where we spread some of our clothes and tried to at least get some rest. It took a long time for the ship's departure and even then we had to stop and wait for the icebreakers to arrive. With all those 5,500 people on board, the toilets were soon blocked. We were locked in and not allowed to go on deck.

Chapter 10

The Cruellest Night

On the night of Tuesday, January 30 1945 a couple of small boats had arrived in Gotenhafen to escort the *Gustloff*, *Hansa* and *Walter Rau*. They were supposed to rendezvous with an evacuation convoy that had left Pillau the previous day and included the heavy cruiser *Admiral Hipper* and her escort ship, T-36.

While the *Wilhelm Gustloff* had finished embarking refugees and was carrying six times her capacity, the *Hansa* was still taking people on board. Mothers were desperately trying to board the ship with their infants, deserters disguised as women were taking young children who had been separated from their mothers, or snatching infants and passing them off as their own to try and board the liner.

At 1200hrs the sea dutymen closed up and secured the hatches. The *Gustloff* still only had twelve lifeboats instead of the required peacetime complement of twenty-two. At 12.15pm, together with the *Hansa*, the *Walter Rau* and two torpedo boats, she was ready to leave Gotenhafen bound for Kiel.

Four tugs began pulling her bow away from the pier. A number of small boats drew alongside, each one filled with refugees, mainly women and children, imploring, 'Take us with you! Save the children!' It was their last hope. The liner stopped while crew put out gangways as desperate refugees frantically struggled to get on board. The ships were overcrowded and, because of very high temperatures and humidity inside, many passengers defied orders not to remove their life jackets.

Marine auxiliary Waltraud Grüter remembers: 'It was my twenty-first birthday and the cook heard that, and said to me "It's your birthday? Then I'll bake you a cake for tonight. You must celebrate your twenty-first." So I was really looking forward to the evening.' Marine Auxiliary Eva Dorn: 'It felt safe in the big ship, you know, because it was a tremendous big ship for those times. Everybody felt nothing could ever happen to it. But me ... I was always afraid.'

As the *Wilhelm Gustloff* and her convoy started their journey towards Flensburg, north-west of Kiel, just beyond the bay of Danzig, east of Kolberg, was a desperate Soviet submarine captain, Alexander Marinesko, and the crew of the S-13, hunting in the open sea.

Captain Marinesko was a complex individual. He was a hurt man, victimised and somewhat bitter. He was much loved by the Russian people, though, who identified with him. Although widely regarded as a brilliant commander, Marinesko was facing a court martial due to, among other issues, his problems with alcohol. One month before the *Gustloff* set off on her final journey, the crew of the S-13 were celebrating New Year's Eve near their base in south-west Finland. The crew, who were in trouble with the Red Army authorities and only hours away from their forthcoming mission, were left without their commander. He had spent the night in a local brothel and was nowhere to be found. In wartime, the Soviet naval command would have considered this an act of treason, but after careful review by naval authorities, Marinesko's post as captain of the S-13 was restored. However, his court martial was not cancelled.

Leaving on this mission at the end of January 1945, Marinesko knew that he must restore his own integrity and the reputation of his crew, who would also be punished severely. He knew that if he failed, he would have to leave the fleet for good. With his career at stake, Marinesko was ordered to patrol the Baltic off the coast of Lithuania, but after days of fruitless hunting, he ordered the S-13 to the gulf of Danzig where the evacuation of German refugees had begun. By the time the *Gustloff* had left Gotenhafen, on the afternoon of the thirtieth, the S-13 was approaching the Hela peninsula.

Just off the Hela-Reede peninsula, the refugee ships stopped and the T-boats that had accompanied them from Gotenhafen returned to port. Panic started to break out. An announcement was made through the loudspeakers, 'We are waiting for the escort ships. No need to worry.' For the trip across the Baltic Sea, *Gustloff* and *Hansa* needed security boats fitted with submarine locating devices. Three security vessels had been requested to the Hela-Reede peninsula to escort the convoy. Meanwhile, bad news came from the *Hansa*: 'Hansa has machine damage. Departure is delayed.' Lieutenant commander Zahn could not resist commenting on this message with 'Damned crap!' The damage was soon fixed and the anchor lifted, but another problem with the steering gear awaited. Strong winds were driving the *Hansa* onto the wreckage of the battleship *Schleswig-Holstein*. There was a risk of collision. The *Hansa* managed to narrowly avoid collision and pass by the wreck. Moments later, however, another message from the Hansa reached the *Gustloff* command deck, 'Hansa not ready to leave. Repair time indefinitely. Continue on your own. Have a good trip.' On the command bridge of the *Gustloff*, Captain Zahn and Captain Petersen were discussing whether they should continue unaided or wait for the damage on the *Hansa* to be repaired. That would have likely meant waiting another night. Before a decision could be reached, the escort ships arrived, though only two vessels instead of three turned up, the destroyer *Löwe* and torpedo recovery boat (*Torpedofangboote*) TF-1. Upon arrival, TF-1 immediately reported a water leak due to a tear in the welding and requested dismissal to Gotenhafen. TF1 was dismissed and it was decided that the *Gustloff* should continue alone with only the destroyer for protection.

The two captains on the *Gustloff* were arguing about which course the ship should take. Petersen pointed out that shallow waters along the coast were infested with mines, but Zahn stressed the fact that deep waters carried a high risk of a submarine attack. As the ship sailed round the Hela peninsula, Captain Zahn decided that the Gustloff should proceeded to deeper waters.

In the late evening the S-13 surfaced. The signaller, standing in the conning tower, saw two large ships travelling out of the bay. One of them stopped while the other continued her journey out of the bay. This was the ship that Marinesko started to follow. Fiodor Danilov, one of the S-13 crew, recalled: 'Our task was the same one as always. We needed to look for transport ships and sink them. We didn't know if they were transport ships or military ships.' Ivan Schnabzew was also on board the S-13: 'It sounded like a passenger ship. A military ship would have sounded very different.'

When they received news of an oncoming German minesweeping convoy, commanders on the *Wilhelm Gustloff* decided, for safety reasons, to turn the position lights on around 6pm, making the giant vessel visible to any nearby submarines. In the following hours the weather deteriorated, and at 8pm a communication from a nearby headquarters warning of a potential submarine attack was never received.

As soon as Marinesko spotted the ship, he ordered the submarine to keep an almost parallel course with the target. To catch up with the liner, the S-13 had to achieve maximum speed. Fiodor Danilov noted: 'The ship was very fast for us, 15 knots or so.'

Eventually, about 30km (19 miles) offshore, between Grossendorf and Leba, the S-13 caught up with the *Gustloff*. Marinesko ordered his crew to turn the submarine almost perpendicular to the ship's course and to fire torpedoes at her port side. At 2100hrs Horst Woit and the other children on board the *Gustloff* were settling to sleep. The crew was celebrating the safe departure with a round of cognac on the bridge. Over the ship's loudspeakers, Hitler's final radio broadcast about a delusional 'victory' marking the twelfth anniversary of his rise to power was coming to an end.

Surgeon Ralph Wendt was the doctor on board the ship, and he had delivered five babies that day already: 'I was lucky that I had a colleague to help me. I mean, I was a soldiers' doctor not a ladies' doctor.' Some of the female auxiliaries were helping the nurses in the hospital, too. Eva Dorn was one of them: 'I was in the hospital. It was a large room and we had a birth next door. And he [Ralph Wendt] came into the room and said, "Dornchen, you don't have to worry anymore. We are out of danger now, out of reach of the Russians". Then the one door opened, and the nurse came in and said, "Doctor, you must come in, the head is showing". And then the torpedoes came.'

The S-13 launched four torpedoes, each of them painted with a different dedication: 'For the Motherland', 'For Leningrad', 'For the Soviet People', and 'For Stalin'. Three torpedoes came out their tubes and sped towards the *Gustloff*. The fourth torpedo, 'For Stalin', failed to launch. What happened next is very rare in naval warfare: all three torpedoes hit their target.

The first torpedo struck *Wilhelm Gustloff*'s bow, causing the watertight doors to seal off the area that contained quarters where off-duty crew members were sleeping. The second torpedo hit the accommodation for the women's naval auxiliary in the ship's drained swimming pool, dislodging the pool tiles at high velocity and causing heavy casualties; only three of the 373 auxiliaries survived. The third torpedo was a direct hit on the engine room located amidships, disabling all power and communications.

The radio operator was forced to use an emergency transmitter to dispatch an SOS. The less powerful radio had a range of only 2,000m. Crewmen began shooting red flares into the night sky and, though some distance away, Lieutenant commander Paul Prüfe, on board the *Löwe*, hurried to reach the area. Horst Woit recalled: 'My mother shook me awake after the first crash, which I did not hear. But I did hear the second crash and the third crash. Now, being ten, I didn't know what that could be. Panic broke out. We tried to get out the cabin as fast as we could.'

Thousands of people rushed to the stairways at that same moment. As a result, some people were trampled to death as others ran over them to get to the top. As Eva Dorn told us, 'Each cabin was for four people and had eight people in it and they all came out, dressed or in their nightgown, with or without shoes, the children in their arms and so on. They all tried to get into this small corridor, and they stepped on each other.'

Horst Woit added: 'The detonation of the torpedoes caused the fire extinguishers to break loose and the stairs we were trying to get up to go to the outside were all covered in foam. I made it to the top of the stairs, but my mum fell down all the way to the bottom. I was standing on the top screaming "Mum! Mum!" Then she was able to get hold of the railing and pull herself up and eventually she made it to the top of the stairs, and we were outside looking down onto the lifeboats.' There were children who lost their mothers in the chaos, crying out for them, and mothers crying out the names of their children.

About twenty minutes after the torpedoes struck, the ship started to list. Hundreds of people poured onto the glass promenade deck, hoping to reach the outside. It was a fatal mistake. The windowpanes were made of safety glass and could not be broken. There was no way out. Ursula Schulze recalls: 'I took my shoe off and I hit it against the window several times. I wanted to break that glass. But I couldn't. My sister said to me, "Ulla, we are now going to die". But I said, "No, I don't want to die. I want to live."'

Soldiers were firing at the glass panes to try to break them, but with no success. Nobody could help. A few people managed to go back and reach the upper decks, but for the majority the glass promenade deck had become a deadly glass cage. On the upper decks people were pushing to secure a place in one of the lifeboats. Only thirty minutes after the

Gustloff was hit, the lower decks were already submerged. Eva Dorn recounted: 'I went to the boats and I helped put women and children in and lower the boats. Then I saw that on one of the boats one of the davits was loosening up and the other davit was frozen. And all the people from that boat fell into the water, just one over the other.'

Reportedly, only nine lifeboats were able to be lowered; the rest had frozen in their davits and had to be broken free. Horst Woit again: 'The problem my mum and I had, and the other seventy people in that lifeboat, was that the ropes of the lifeboat were frozen to the boat. All of a sudden they started to scream, "Who's got a knife? We are frozen, we can't get away!" I remembered the knife I stole from my uncle and had in my ski pants – my mum didn't know I had it – and I gave it to the marines, and they managed to cut the ropes. And that's why I am alive today.'

Eva Dorn: 'I helped women and children into the boats, then one of the soldiers said "Now it's your turn, you are going in now." So I went into the boat and we were lowered safely onto the water. You could hear the screams of people jumping from the top and landing near our boat.'

As the *Wilhelm Gustloff* continued to list on her port side, women, children and the elderly were holding onto each other, waiting for the ship to sink further in order to jump into the water or being swept away by the waves. Irmgard Harnecker was on board: 'The waves came nearer and nearer and I had my child in my arms, my sister was holding on to me and she said, "Irmgard we are going down."' As Heinz Schön recalled:

> The ship was listing badly and as she was listing the engines were cutting out. The ship moved forward with a lurch. I had to try to hold on to something and I managed to hang onto the superstructures of the sundeck. Next to me was a man in party uniform. He was hanging from the same structure. Next to him hung his two children and his wife. The woman shouted at him, "Put an end to it!" Holding on to the railing with one hand, he pulled his gun out with the other and shot the two children first, then his wife. Then he put the pistol next to his own temple, pulled the trigger, but nothing happened. There were no bullets left. He then shouted at me, "Give me your pistol!" and I replied, "I don't have one." He then let go and slid over the deck, following his dead children and wife into the water".

The water temperature in the Baltic Sea at that time of year is usually around 4°C (39°F); however, this was a particularly cold night, with an air temperature of minus 18°C (0°F) and ice floes covering the surface. Many deaths were caused either directly by the torpedoes or by drowning in the onrushing water. Others were crushed in the initial stampede caused by panicking passengers on the stairs and decks. Many others jumped into the icy sea, and the majority of those who perished succumbed to exposure in the freezing water. Horst Woit remembers, 'We started to pull away from the ship. We were about 80 to 100 metres away, the Gustloff was two-thirds sunk when suddenly all of the lights came on and within minutes the lights went lower and lower and lower. And then it was dark.'

As the *Gustloff* sank, Waltraud Grüter was able to climb into a small lifeboat with thirty-five children and women and get away from the sinking ship. 'The last few minutes, I remember, she laid on her side, the lights were flickering and the sirens came on … and then she was gone.' Eva Dorn added: 'I heard it, too. It was a somber scream, a death scream. The scream of all those people who were still trapped there and knew that it was the end. I can still hear that scream today.' Less than an hour after being struck, the *Wilhelm Gustloff* sank bow-first in 44m (144ft) of water.

The ship went down in just under an hour. People who had survived the fall into the water were frantically trying to get onto one of the few lifeboats that had been lowered into the sea, but the boats were already overloaded. Those who could not be pulled into the boats had to be pushed back or hit on their fingers to stop them from tipping the lifeboats over. Irmgard Harnecker recounted: 'The waves came, people in our boat were falling on top of each other. I still had the baby and my sister then. But the next moment a big wave came and they were gone. If only I could have held on tighter to them … but the waves were just so strong.'

Nobody could survive for longer than a few minutes in the icy water. Ursula Schulze tragically recalled: 'The worst thing was the children. I could never sing "*Alle Meine Entchen*" ['All my Ducklings', a traditional nursery rhyme] to my children. They had their life vests on, but their heads were heavier than their bodies. Their heads were under the water and their little feet up in the air.'

Around half an hour after the *Gustloff* sank, Horst Woit was picked up by the *Löwe*. He was one of the first children to be rescued.

They took me to the engine room and gave me a hot drink to warm up. When they eventually pulled Mum up, she was asking the marines, "Have you seen my son?" and they asked, "How old is he?" She said, "He's ten years old." They said, "There are some children in the backboard, let's go and take a look." So they walked to the backboard and lifted up the tarp and those children were dead. Of course, my mum started to get a little panicky, but she searched the ship and eventually she found me.

The heavy cruiser, *Admiral Hipper*, and her escort T-36 had left Pillau the night before and were approaching the spot where the *Gustloff* had sunk. The commander of the T-36 was twenty-seven-year-old Captain Robert Hering: 'There were boats with people screaming, waving their arms, desperate to be rescued. Boats with dead people. Empty rafts. Boats that had capsized. It was a terrible situation because if we stopped for too long what happened to the *Gustloff* could, of course, happen to us. But I said to myself "The rescue continues, you must risk it."'

The crew of the T-36 spent around forty-five minutes pulling people onto the boat. It wasn't an easy task. The sea was still rough, and it was cold and dark. Most people were wearing heavy, soaked coats. Some were injured. Captain Robert Hering again: 'And then, to my great surprise, among the people we pulled up was the captain of the *Gustloff*. That was quite something. Dry! Then the commander of the submariner division. Dry!' Captain Petersen had been amongst the first to abandon the ship, together with is colleague, Lieutenant commander Zahn. Hans Joachim Elbreicht, a soldier on board the *Gustloff* was not impressed, 'When we heard the news [of Petersen and Zahn's rescue] we were outraged. Because for an officer, a captain, to put himself first like that was just disgraceful.'

The men on the T-36 rescued over 500 people that night. Amongst them was Doctor Ralph Wendt: 'When I was picked up, I informed them I was a doctor. They said, "That's good, we have a woman in labour, please follow us." I followed them to one of the cabins and the woman there was so happy to see me. "Oh, doctor," she said, "now that you are here everything will be fine." I smiled and thought to myself, "You think so? I am not an obstetrician, I am a surgeon". A few minutes later I delivered a healthy baby boy. That's life. That's nature. Even in the most tragic circumstances, it doesn't stop, it goes on.'

Captain Hering's concerns about a possible submarine attack were not unfounded. After celebrating the successful sinking of the *Wilhelm Gustloff*, the crew of the S-13 were back on the hunt for more ships to target. They tried to fire at the T-36 but the torpedoes were successfully intercepted. With a heavy heart, Captain Hering had to abandon the rescue mission and continue the journey to Sassnitz, where 564 refugees were finally brought to safety.

Naval auxiliary Waltraud Grüter recalled, 'Then I realised that the people in our boat were no longer screaming. They had all died from the cold and the shock. When we were saved, there were five of us left alive. Three officers, a Berliner, and myself.' The rescue vessel that picked up Waltraud was the small freighter *Göttingen*, commanded by Captain Freidrich Segelken, along with his second lieutenant, Heinz Schulz. They dropped the twenty-eight survivors they picked up that night in Swinemünde (Swinoujscie) on 2 February. Ursula Schulze again recalled:

> 'We saw a small light in the distance. It was very small but then it became bigger and bigger. It was coming closer to us and we started to shout like crazy. And then we were pulled up, we were rescued. I noticed that one of the officers on the ship was staring at me and then asked me "Do you have a sister? There's a young woman on board who's been looking for her sister and she looks very much like you." Then he disappeared and came back with this young woman. I jumped up. I didn't even realise that my clothes were torn, and the cover they had put over me had slipped off. I didn't care. We jumped into each other's arms and laughed and cried. We were both alive.'

Seven ships worked throughout the night to rescue survivors from the icy waters of the Baltic Sea. German forces were able to pick up 996 survivors from the attack: the torpedo boat T36 rescued 564 people; the torpedo boat Löwe 472; the minesweeper M387 rescued 98; the minesweeper M375 rescued 43; the minesweeper M341 rescued 37; the steamer Göttingen 28; the torpedo recovery boat TF19, rescued 7;

the freighter Gotenland two; and the patrol boat VP-1703 rescued one baby. At 5.30am on 31 January the VP-1703 came upon a dark shape bobbing in the waves. All on board the lifeboat appeared frozen dead, but when Petty Officer Werner Fick jumped into the boat to make an inspection, he was astonished to find an infant wrapped in a warm blanket snug alive between the frozen corpses. The child Fick rescued that morning was the last official survivor of the *Wilhelm Gustloff*. Some time later the officer and his wife adopted the baby and called him Peter.

Why was the *Wilhelm Gustloff* attacked? As one survivor, Irmgard Harnecker, put it: 'I wanted my child back. At least if I had known that she was dead ... but she was recorded as a missing person and she is still missing. Why? Why did they do that? There were many women, children, pregnant women, wounded ... there was nothing else on the ship. The ship was not posing a threat to anybody.'

The first Western scholar to research the Red Army's activities and the mass flight of Germans from the East was an American lawyer, historian and former secretary of the United Nations Human Rights Committee, Doctor Alfred de Zayas:

> 'As a lawyer, I was interested in the question "Was this a war crime?" Obviously, this ship was a big target for a submarine. The Baltic was littered with ships evacuating refugees. Everybody knew these were refugee ships. These were civilians; human beings fleeing ethnic cleansing. There again, you could say they assumed the risk, they knew that they could have been sunk. Obviously, there was a fear that they could be sunk. On the other hand [...] there is a very important reason for these people to be on the ship and the cause of that is the Soviet Union'.

Alexander Astachov, one of the crew of the S-13, stated: 'We didn't know it was a passenger ship. We only knew it was a large ship. We first found out it was a passenger ship from the Swedish and Finnish newspapers.'

All four captains on the *Wilhelm Gustloff* survived her sinking, but an official naval inquiry was only started against Wilhelm Zahn. His degree of culpability was never established, however, because of Nazi Germany's collapse in 1945.

During the testimony, Zahn blamed the Croatian members of the crew's lack of understanding of orders given in German for the high number of casualties during the sinking. Zahn also mentioned that he had not received any orders regarding the performance or avoidance of zig-zag manoeuvres, saying that he just got three phone calls and told to leave. He also said that he had concluded that there were no submarines in the area after discussions with fellow officers. This conclusion, he said, was further reinforced by his belief that if the presence of submarines had been detected in the area the naval command would have informed him. Zahn testified that immediately after impact the ship started listing about 5° at the port side. For about twenty minutes the angle of list remained small, but then started increasing, causing panic. Zahn testified that he told the refugees that the ship had run aground so as to minimise panic. When the ship kept turning more and the tilt angle increased to 25–30°, Zahn abandoned any further attempts at coordinating the evacuation efforts and went to the stern to board a lifeboat and leave the ship.

Zahn also testified that ice had accumulated in the lifeboat launchers and made the lowering of the boats difficult. In addition, he blamed the Croatian crew for leaving, saying: 'The davits were iced and the Croats were absent.' He further testified that, 'only four to six lifeboats were lowered with the help of soldiers under difficult circumstances.' Zahn told the inquiry that at first he and the other officers had gathered on the bridge and then instructed the refugees to go to the upper deck and not to panic. But as the stern began tilting upwards and the bow started penetrating the surface of the water, Zahn realised the ship was not going to remain afloat for much longer and left from the bridge. The inquiry was never completed before the German surrender.

To this date, many people still consider the sinking of the *Wilhelm Gustloff* a war crime as thousands of civilians died as a result of the Russian submarine attack. Counterarguments were made, however, stating that the ship made no attempt to show that she was carrying civilians, also that she was carrying around 1,000 active military personnel. Alfred de Zayas stated: 'I am afraid that in this particular field of history, it is all politicised. Historians deliberately ignore whole aspects. They give you maybe twenty per cent of the truth and the rest is basically politics.'

Did Alexander Marinesko commit a war crime? According to the commander of the T-36, Robert Hering: 'He did his job. At that time the

Gustloff was not a hospital ship. She was carrying a U-boat division. That's soldiers. That's war.' Marinesko and the S-13 crew stayed in the deep waters off the Pomeranian coast for several days. The *Walter Rau* and the *Steuben* were now its next targets. In her book, *Of Prussian Heritage*, Gisela Teschke wrote:

> Suddenly machine-gun fire sounded from above. I held on tightly to my little brother. There seemed a war of survival going on outside the ship in the darkness of the night. Then came the sickening thud as the torpedo hit our ship, the Walter Rau, cutting off the lights and engines instantly. People started to scream in terror. Some shouted: "For heaven's sake be quiet!" We sat frozen in fear, waiting for the inevitable explosion to follow, holding our breath.
> Flickering lights, hissing sounds. Horst and I went to investigate. A heavy iron door was half open and we peeped through. The room was half-filled with water. A bilge pump was operating out of view. A man in a black diving suit was using what looked like an oxy cutter, cutting a circle around a large, cone-shaped object that stuck in the wall and looked like a torpedo head. Horst and I went back in the darkness to our sleeping place as the lights had not come back on. In the morning the hatches were opened and hundreds and hundreds of people used the opportunity to stream outside, get some fresh air and exercise and walk on the deck. Then we heard what happened the night before. The Wilhelm Gustloff had been hit by three torpedos from a Russian U-Boat and had sunk.

Those on the *Walter Rau* eventually made it to Eckernförde. Gisela and her family reached Heide in Schleswig-Holstein before emigrating to Australia. On 9 February 1945 the passenger liner *General von Steuben* sailed from Pillau for Swinemünde with 2,900 wounded soldiers, 800 civilians, 100 returning soldiers, 270 navy medical personnel, 64 crew for the ship's anti-aircraft guns, 61 naval personnel, radio operators, signal men, machine operators and administrators, plus 160 merchant navy crewmen. Because of the rapid evacuation ahead of the Red Army's advance, many German and East Prussian refugees boarded the *Steuben* without being recorded, putting the total number of those on board at around 5,200.

Just before midnight on 9 February Alexander Marinesko ordered the crew of the S-13 to fire two torpedoes with a fourteen-second interval: both hit the *Steuben* in the starboard bow, just below the bridge where many crewmen were sleeping, killing most of them on impact. She sank within twenty minutes, bow first. An estimated 4,500 people died. Thanks to the torpedo boat T-196, which hastily pulled up beside *Steuben* as she sank, about 300 survivors were pulled straight from the ships's listing decks and brought to Kolberg, Pomerania. Another 650 people were rescued.

Heinz Schön commented: 'People today, even in Russia, have a different awareness of the injustice of war than they did in 1945. The Russians have their heroes and Marinesko is for them the submarine hero of the Second World War. Although, if you count the total number of dead on the Steuben and the Gustloff, he killed 14–15,000 people. But German submariners did that, too. So you have to keep things in perspective and you cannot blame one or the other. In my opinion, the war is guilty for everything that happened between 1939 and 1945 throughout the world.'

The evacuation of military and fleeing civilians continued during the following months right up to the end of the war. Many other passenger liners were deployed during Operation Hannibal, including *Robert Ley*, *Deutschland*, *Monte Rosa*, *Potsdam*, *Oceana*, *Antonio Delfino*, *Iberia*, *Emden*, *Meteor*, *Nautik*, *Memeland* many more smaller ships. Each one had a different fate: the lucky ones arrived at Western ports and refugee centres, having lost their homes, belongings, family members, sometimes even an arm or a leg, to enemy fire or to the frost; the not-so-lucky were claimed by the freezing waters of the Baltic Sea.

Some people narrowly escaped death. On 31 January, the SS *Berlin* left Pillau with a convoy heading west. She struck a mine off Swinemünde and was put in tow for Kiel. She then hit another mine and was beached in shallow waters. There was one fatality. All usable equipment was salvaged by 5 February and the ship was abandoned before the Soviets refloated her in 1949 and renamed her *Admiral Nakhimov*, after the nineteenth-century Russian naval commander who played a prominent role in the Crimean War.

The Cruellest Night

When it comes to loss of life in maritime disasters, the *Goya* certainly deserves a mention. MV *Goya* was a Norwegian motor freighter built in 1940. Following the invasion of Norway in April 1940, she was seized by Germany and passed into service of the *Kriegsmarine* as a troop transport ship. MV *Goya* took part in Operation Hannibal loaded with thousands of refugees and *Wehrmacht* soldiers. On 16 April 1945 she was torpedoed and sunk by the Soviet submarine L-3. It was one of the largest single losses of life during the Second World War and one of the largest maritime losses of life in history: only 183 people survived out of around 6,700 passengers and crew.

Although the position of the wreck had been known to Polish fishermen for over fifty years and simply referred to as 'obstacle 88', it was not formally identified until 16 April 2003 when an international expedition, under the direction of Ulrich Restemeyer, located the shipwreck with the help of 3D-Sonar scanning. Soon after her discovery, she was officially declared a war grave by the Polish Maritime Office in Gdynia and it is therefore illegal to dive within 500m of the wreck. MV *Goya* lies in upright position at a depth of 76m (49ft) below the surface of the Baltic Sea and is in remarkably good condition.

Noted as 'obstacle 73' by Polish navigation charts and classified as a war grave, the wreck of the *Wilhelm Gustloff* rests at about 35km (22 miles) offshore, east of Leba and west of Wladyslawowo. It is one of the largest shipwrecks on the Baltic Sea floor and has attracted much interest from treasure hunters searching for precious panels of the Amber Room, which rumours say were taken from Königsberg, and loaded onto the ship at Gotenhafen. Following the end of the war, Soviet authorities had forbidden anyone to dive near the wreck.

It wasn't until the 1990s that official international diving expeditions were carried out and the findings were shocking. Unlike the *Goya*, the *Wilhelm Gustloff* appeared completely stripped of everything from portholes to washbasins. No signs of humans or belongings were found, no bones, nothing. Following her recognition as a war grave, diving around the *Gustloff* wreck is now illegal, except for bona fide scientific or historic expeditions. Polish maritime authorities say, however, that their lack of resources makes them powerless to keep divers off the wreck.

In the Northern Polish sea sort of Leba, 22 miles from the wreck, several diving clubs openly advertise day trips to the *Gustloff*, the *Goya* and the *Steuben*. One diver who knows the wreck better than most is Jerzy Janczukowicz. Every room of his house in Gdańsk is cluttered with dusty artefacts from Second World War wrecks that he has salvaged over the years. But the items the sixty-six-year-old is most proud of are from the *Gustloff*. These include the blackened shell of a chandelier from the ship's ballroom, which he has turned into a coffee table, part of the ship's compass and, propped up outside his house, an algae- and mollusc-covered rusty stair rail. 'I don't consider what I do to be illegal, or disrespectful to the dead,' he said, 'It's about preserving the past, stopping people from destroying evidence of it; just like the British Museum thinks it is important to preserve sarcophagi.'

Soon after the sinking of the *Gustloff*, Heinz Schön was ordered back to Gotenhafen to assist with the German evacuations before relocating in northern Germany. He passed away in 2013 and his dying wish was to be buried at the *Wilhelm Gustloff* shipwreck where so many of his friends, and thousands of people, had tragically perished. A team of scuba divers, including Dimitris 'Dima' Stavrakakis and Tomasz 'Tomek' Stachura from Poland, managed to fulfill Heinz Schön's wish. They put a commemorative plaque as well as an urn containing Schön's ashes at the wreck of the *Wilhelm Gustloff*. Stavrakakis said: 'Our dive at the Gustloff had a special significance for all of us: German diver Matthias Schneider overcame all bureaucratic obstacles in order to dive at the protected site of the wreck and three divers from Poland were part of the team.'

The *Gustloff* was not only the biggest loss of life in maritime history, but the story of Heinz Schön, who dedicated his whole life to making the story known to people, both inside outside Germany. For decades people didn't talk about it. Eva Dorn said: 'For forty years I didn't talk about it. Then I started to talk about it and only because I met people who had the same experience [...] My husband was Jewish and, you know, and they all had family that got killed [...] So, I thought, I'd better shut up. But later, after fifty years I started to talk about it.'

After being rescued, Eva Dorn returned to Hamburg for a while before emigrating to the United States. Horst Woit, his mother and her friend were unloaded in Kolberg (now Kolobrzeg) before settling in the north-eastern German city of Schwerin. The city was first captured and controlled by US forces, but was transferred to Soviet control in the summer of 1945. During that time, ten-year-old Horst had to witness rape, as Soviet soldiers entered his home, pulled their guns out, and raped his mother's friend, forcing Horst and his mother to watch. The family then moved further west and, in the early 1950s, after completing his apprenticeship, Horst decided to emigrate to Canada, where he finally settled and started a family.

Sadly, during the writing of this chapter, the authors were informed by Horst's wife, Grace, that after a short illness, he passed away on December 21 2018, and it is to his memory that this chapter is dedicated.

Chapter 11

A Tale of Two Lost Cities

The defeat of the German garrison at Königsberg proved to be the burial shroud not only for East Prussia but the whole German state of Prussia itself. The Battle of Königsberg, or Königsberg Offensive as some historians refer to it, was one of the final military operations of the East Prussian Offensive of the Second World War. Although the siege started in mid-January, when the Soviets surrounded the city, the final battle itself would last no more than fifty-six hours. Yet those fifty-six hours saw some of the most savage urban fighting of the entire war.

Soviet forces had continued to advance and by March 1945 Königsberg was hundreds of miles behind the main front line. The German forces in the city numbered some 60,000 to 130,000 troops, 4,000 artillery guns and mortars, 108 tanks and assault guns plus 170 aircraft. The Russians had 137,000 troops, of which 24,500 were to participate in the actual fighting (with the remainder held in support), 5,200 artillery pieces and mortars, 528 tanks and self-propelled guns, plus 2,174 aircraft. These figures confirm just how hopelessly outnumbered the German defenders of Königsberg were.

The final assault on the city began on 6 April 1945 at sunrise with a three-hour artillery barrage, before the first wave of Russian troops began their advance. The Russian infantry divisions tore through the first German defensive line with little difficulty as most of the Germans had been eliminated by the artillery bombardment. Those who were wounded or survived unharmed had been so demoralised that they offered no resistance. By noon that first day Russian troops reached the second German defensive line. It was here that the Russian forces met more stubborn resistance. forcing Russian commanders to bring in their reserve forces. Three more hours of brutal fighting, often at close quarters, ensued before this second defensive line was overrun in several places.

Some of the worst fighting took place in the vicinity of Fort Eight, a structure that had been built at the end of the nineteenth century frequently modernised since. The fort had very thick walls which could resist most calibres of Russian heavy artillery and was heavily defended with considerable firepower. The fort also had the advantage of a medieval deepwater moat surrounding it, making any frontal assault on the structure well-nigh impossible. The German forces in the fort held off repeated Russian attempts at approaching the walls. Only when dusk had fallen were Russian forces able to reach the moat and start using explosives in an attempt to breach the walls.

The main Russian attack was in the north. By noon the first defensive line had fallen and the second was badly shaken and broken in several places. In the afternoon, however, the progress of the Russian forces slowed considerably, especially on their right flank, where the Germans stationed in the western suburbs of the city (the so-called Samland Group) attempted several flanking attacks.

Fort Five, which was considered the best fortification of the whole Königsberg position, formed a strong resistance point. Here, the Russian commanders decided to surround the objective and then push on, leaving rearguard forces to prepare a fresh assault.

By dusk the battle had stalled, allowing both sides to consolidate their lines, reorganise their forces and bring in reserves to the front line. That first day of the battle had been one of mixed fortunes for both sides. The Russian forces had not performed entirely to their own expectations and were disappointed at their lack of progress. Furthermore, the Russian use of aircraft for the purpose of precision bombing had not been a great success, mainly due to the poor weather conditions.

On the German side, morale had been severely affected by the day's fighting and some troops, including officers, began to surrender to the Russian attackers. But many fought on and throughout the following night, 7 April, German troops carried out a number of counterattacks, most notably the Samland group in the west of the city. Despite their determination, however, and heavy losses on both sides, the German counterattacks were repelled. An improvement in the weather allowed the Russian army to make good use of its daylight precision bombing. Several hundred bombers of the 1st, 3rd and 15th Air Armies, supported by Baltic Fleet aviation, bombarded the bridgeheads of the downtown and Samland groups.

Meanwhile, Fort Eight, blocked by Russian troops, was still proving a stubborn pocket of resistance. After the failure of several Russian attacks, a more radical plan for attacking the structure was devised. Using smokescreens to conceal their approach and flamethrowers to weaken the defensive positions, several hundred troops managed to cross the deepwater moat and enter the fortress. Heavy fighting ensued as both Russian and German troops engaged one another at bayonet point. The German troops inside the fortress used anything at their disposal. One young German soldier recalled how he had used a piece of metal bar to kill one Russian combatant by striking him about the head repeatedly. In the confined inner areas of the fort German soldiers found their entrenching shovels an ideal weapon for hand-to-hand fighting; a hard blow from one of those could almost decapitate a man. As the outer defences of the fort weakened a massive frontal assault began and after more savage fighting this finally forced the remainder of the German garrison of the fort to surrender.

During the day, the Russian 11th Guards Army attempted to reach the Pregel river, eliminating all resistance on the southern side. However, the Russian advance was slowed in the central area of the city, where every building had to be literally taken apart along with the German defenders inside. At the main railway station a particularly fierce fight broke out. The Germans had placed riflemen underneath, inside and on top of railway carriages, with other troops situated around the platforms and buildings. Subsequently, the attacking Russian forces suffered high casualties and were forced to use their armour and artillery support in order to continue their advance. As darkness began to fall the railway station and immediate area around it was finally cleared of German forces. The Russians were then able to press forward and approach the third defence perimeter, one that was protecting the entrance to the city centre itself.

In the north, Fort Five proved yet another stronghold for resistance, until Russian sappers were able to detonate explosive charges at the base of the walls, allowing them to be breached. The direct assault on the position led to more hand-to-hand fighting, which went on throughout the night and only ceased in the morning when the last German troops surrendered.

German general, Otto Lasch, who was the commander of the defensive forces in Königsberg, understood that the game was over and that offering further resistance would only needlessly sacrifice more lives. Lasch radioed Hitler's headquarters to ask for permission to surrender. As expected, he was told that he had to 'fight to the last soldier'. Lasch defied Hitler's order to fight on and surrendered to the Russian Red Army on 9 April.

On 8 April the 11th Guards Army crossed the Pregel under heavy German fire. By dawn the Russians had established a full bridgehead on the opposite bank of the river. Pushing on northwards, they linked up with the northern troops, completing the encirclement and cutting off the Samland group from the city. In the afternoon, the Russian commander, Marshal Aleksandr Vasilevsky, again offered the Germans terms for surrender, but these were declined. The Germans instead attempted to break out of the Russian encirclement, attacking from both the city centre and the Samland bridgehead. The latter force was able to advance several kilometres before it was stopped. Although another attack was prepared, the German lack of air cover allowed Russian Ilyushin IL-2 ground attack aircraft to destroy large numbers of German troops and armaments. During this phase of the campaign, Russian air power was to prove highly effective. The IL-2, known as the Shturmovik, was primarily a two-seat tank-busting aircraft, heavily armoured to protect it from ground fire and able to carry a huge weight of ordnance. The Shturmovik proved a formidable ground attack aircraft able to drop bombs, fire rockets and relentlessly strafe German ground forces with 23-mm cannon fire.

The *Luftwaffe* had never been short of combat aircraft throughout the war, and new fighter aircraft were being delivered to the frontline fighter squadrons right up until the war's end. The Achilles heel of the German air force in the latter stages of the war was the severe shortage of experienced pilots and fuel. There were small bands of *Luftwaffe* pilots who were able to group together to make token appearances over the battlefront, but these brave pilots found themselves hugely outnumbered and their missions verged on suicidal. One German fighter pilot named Otto Funck recalled:

> You would take whatever aircraft was serviceable and armed and take off. The biggest problem was adequate fuel. This had all but run out. The few remaining crews would often take fuel from wrecked aircraft and transfer it to new ones.

We had hundreds of Focke-Wulf fighter aircraft but no fuel for them. Most of our best pilots were either killed, missing or wounded and no longer able to fly. They would go to the flying schools and order the instructors to fly fighter operations. Many of the instructors were by now old men and incapable of dealing with the physical and mental stress of flying combat operations.

The odds we faced in the East were much the same as in the West. You would take off and within minutes there would be hundreds of enemy aircraft in the sky. You would be looking around for an aircraft with black crosses on its wings and there would not be one. It is impossible to fight against odds of ten to one, no matter how good a pilot you are. You might shoot down one or two enemy aircraft only to find four or five of them on your tail.

Over the East Prussian battlefront the Shturmovik was the biggest menace to our ground forces. It was slow and cumbersome but heavily armoured; they called it the 'flying tank' for good reason. From the air I watched helplessly as the Red Air Force strafed columns of German refugees fleeing from the East. They didn't care that there were women and children; they machine-gunned them all. I attacked one of them from astern and below to avoid the rear gunner being able to shoot at me. All the time I had to look over my shoulder to ensure no enemy was coming up on my tail. I fired a good burst into him with the 30-mm cannon and watched the enemy break up before my eyes. I saw the two crewmen fall to the ground as their aircraft disintegrated. Soon more and more aircraft with the red star on their wings arrived. I climbed hard and turned for home.

When I landed, I was told all the fuel had gone. It was madness. We had lines of brand-new aircraft standing idle with no fuel to fly them. There were groups of boys fresh out of the Hitler Youth all eager to take off and fight. I told them to go home, go back to their families; I was finished. Some of them sat down and wept. The propaganda had convinced them that we could never lose the war. We abandoned the airfield to the Red Army who arrived days later.

A Tale of Two Lost Cities

The Shturmovik reigned supreme over the battlefront of Königsberg. A German infantry officer named Heinrich Busse recalled: 'The Shturmoviks circled overhead like vultures above a carcass. They would break off one-by-one, performing a shallow dive and coming down very low where their heavy 23-mm guns were most deadly and would inflict terrible carnage. The armour-piercing shells would tear through even the thickest walls of a building, and the high-explosive shells were like grenades, exploding and spraying an area with lethal steel splinters. The Shturmoviks were an ever-present threat. They were always there and there were no *Luftwaffe* fighters to stop them.'

By the close of the day it was clear that any attempt by the Samland group to break out of the Russian encirclement would be pointless. It was clear to the Germans that they would soon be overwhelmed and that further resistance was a futile gesture. Furthermore, the coordination between the German forces had rapidly began to fall apart in what was a comprehensive defeat.

The German commander, Otto Lasch, was to act on his own initiative. Refusing Hitler's order to stand firm and fight to the last man, Lasch dispatched emissaries to negotiate a surrender with the Russians. It was an honourable move by Lasch to prevent further heavy losses of the soldiers under his command and the few remaining civilians in the city. At 1800hrs the emissaries arrived at the Russian lines and a delegation was sent to Lasch's bunker. Shortly before midnight of 9 April 1945 the German surrender of Königsberg was acknowledged.

In the aftermath of the battle some eighty per cent of the city had been reduced to rubble. Britain's RAF had bombed Königsberg in August 1944, and Russian artillery had completed the destruction in April 1945. Almost all of the remaining German residents of the city, an estimated 200,000 people (out of a pre-war population of 316,000), were expelled from the city by the Russian authorities. In Moscow the capture of the city of Königsberg was celebrated with 324 Russian guns firing twenty-four shells each. A medal was established for the capture of the city and ninety-eight Russian military units were named in honour of the Königsberg victory.

The city of Danzig (Gdańsk) faced a similar fate. On 30 March 1945 the Soviet Red Army occupied a largely destroyed city. The exact circumstances of the occupation remain a matter of dispute.

While the traditional Polish history stressed the role of the German defence, reports after 1990 of deliberate destruction and arson by the Soviets were published. However, as Soviet sources about events are inaccessible, the topic has not been conclusively clarified.

According to Polish accounts, in the first days of March, the Soviet and Polish armies reached the Baltic coast near Koszalin and Kołobrzeg, cutting in two the German army 'Vistula' division. From that moment the troops of the Second Byelorussian Front directed their assault towards the east in order to 'liberate' Danzig and Gotenhafen (Gdynia). Two defensive belts ran around Danzig, a few kilometres away from the city, and the *Wehrmacht* also adapted old fortifications from the end of the nineteenth century and the First World War in the city of Danzig itself. In the Bay of Danzig, the heavy cruiser *Prinz Eugen*, the battleship Lützow, the light cruiser *Leipzig* and a squadron of destroyers and torpedo boats were supporting the German land troops. About a hundred German planes from the nearby airfields also supported the ground operations. However, the Soviet air force quickly destroyed the majority of Nazi planes and put the rest out of action.

In the fortified area of Danzig and Gotenhafen fifteen divisions of infantry, three armoured divisions, three fighting groups and other smaller units held out, hoping to be evacuated by sea. Hundreds of thousands of refugees, fleeing the Red Army in Eastern Prussia and Pomerania, had gone to Danzig and Gotenhafen looking for a way of escaping to the West. But escape by sea was not always successful, as we saw in the case of the *Wilhelm Gustloff*. Further German forces were cut off by the attack launched on Zoppot (Sopot), which was captured by Soviet troops on 28 March; Soviet troops and the First Armoured Brigade of the Heroes of Westerplatte also occupied Gotenhafen.

At the same time a battle was raging in Danzig, where the majority of troops of the Second German Army were holding out. In the city there were also large numbers of civilians, both inhabitants of the city and refugees. Despite the hopeless military situation, and the certainty that fighting would entail considerable losses among the civilian population, the command of the Second German Army, in accordance with Hitler's personal orders, rejected the call to surrender. On 28 March Polish soldiers ran up the Polish flag at the Artus Court in the city centre. The following day Soviet and Polish troops crushed the German resistance, and on 30 March forced a division of the

German army on Westerplatte to surrender. More than 10,000 soldiers were taken prisoner and large quantities of arms and military equipment were captured. Danzig was liberated, although military operations continued in the surrounding areas. On the Hela (Hel) Peninsula and at the mouth of the Vistula the remnants of the German army continued to hold out, before surrendering on 9 May.

German accounts of what happened differ somewhat. Towards the end of the war, Russian artillery bombardments and concentrated allied bombs were raining down on the city, especially during the whole of the Easter period from the end of March. While causing a great loss of life among the civilian population and the many refugees who had fled the Soviets, such bombardments did not cause serious enough damage to the city's ancient buildings. The wilful destruction of the city started soon after the German soldiers had left at the end of March.

Women and girls of all ages were mercilessly hunted down and raped by Soviets and Poles alike. 'Frau, komm; Frau, komm', was their cry, or 'Uri, Uri, Uri.' (They were always after wristwatches.) There was little, if anything, to distinguish Russians from Poles by their uniforms, except perhaps their caps. They went on a wild looting spree, engaged in wholesale robbing, plundering and stealing of everything and anything of worth that was not nailed down. It was only after the bloody orgies of rape and plunder had died down that the old city was set ablaze as part of a plan to root out and exterminate the German population and all traces of German culture. Many of the buildings in the 700-year-old city, like the Krantor (Crane-gate), were made from ancient timber and were lost. In the inferno that followed, the heat of the fire was so fierce that the bells of St Catherine, St Johan, St Brigitte, Peter and Paul, Trinity, and Corpus Christy churches melted in the belfries. The 72m-high tower of St Mary's church, the tallest brick church tower in Europe, burned from the inside. The fire spread rapidly, helped by tightly-packed buildings in the narrow *gassen* (alleyways). No attempt was made by the Polish authorities to extinguish the flames. They just looked on in glee, and let the city burn for nearly four weeks, until the fire consumed itself and a pall of dark smoke hung over the devastated remains.

Both accounts, however, agree that war damage inflicted to the city and port of Danzig was a tragic sight. The city had been razed. The stumps of burnt-out houses stood out against the sky, piles of rubble covered the streets, and hundreds of human corpses and the decomposing remains of dead animals poisoned the air. Piles of destroyed military and civilian equipment completed the scene of devastation. The oldest districts of the city lay in ruins: the former main town, the Old Town, and the medieval district of Przedmies´cie. The suburbs of Danzig, particularly Langfuhr (Wrzeszcz), did not escape the destruction. The list of valuable historical monuments lost to the war was long, and included the town hall, Artus Court, the Green Gate, the Great Crane, the Great Mill, the Church of the Virgin, St Catherine's Church, the Holy Trinity Church, and many other Gothic churches, city gates, old granaries on Spichlerze island, and hundreds of former burgher houses.

In June 1945, 124,000 Germans and 8,000 Poles lived in the city: from 1945 to 1950 most of those Germans were expelled. Before the end of the war the 'Big Three' leaders at the Yalta Conference had agreed to place the city, under its Polish name Gdańsk, under the *de facto* administration of Poland, and this was confirmed at the Potsdam Conference. A Polish administration was set up in what was left of Danzig on 30 March 1945. New Polish residents were settled: 3,200 in April and more than 4,000 in May and June. By 1948 more than two-thirds of the 150,000 inhabitants came from central Poland, about fifteen to eighteen per cent from Polish-speaking areas east of the Curzon Line who had been annexed by the Soviet Union after the war. Many local Kashubians also moved into the city.

The deportation of the German populace started in July 1945, and so the pre-war population soon became a small minority in post-war Gdańsk. The members of the pre-war Polish minority organised associations dedicated to upholding their past traditions and history. Every last trace of German culture, heritage and other documentation that existed in Gdańsk was destroyed in an attempt to make it appear that the city was, since feudal times, Polish. Poland removed every inscription in the German language from every public building, school and institution, and also adopted Danzig's coat of arms to make it their own. The city's old motto 'Nec temere, Nec timide', dating back to the time when it was part of the Hanseatic League, was also taken.

Poland wantonly vandalised and destroyed all evidence of Danzig's history, even the gravestones in the cemeteries that bore a German name. The former inhabitants of the city were stripped of their dignity and robbed, not only of their personal possessions, but also of their identities, their properties, titles and patrimony. Everything was confiscated, and made the property of the Polish state. Furthermore, every church that was previously Lutheran, whether or not it had been destroyed, was turned into a 'Holy Catholic Church' by the Polish Catholic Church.

Rebuilding started slowly in the burnt-out remains of Danzig, unlike the reconstruction of the ruined German cities, which were rebuilt and totally modernised in less than seven years after the end of the war. In Danzig reconstruction started from about 1960 onwards, and that was only possible, ironically, with the help of German, and other foreign funds. To many surviving Germans who once had inhabited the Free City of Danzig, the new city, with its new name of Gdańsk, was, at best, a poor imitation of the former one. It had no character, no soul. It was gone forever.

Perhaps one of the saddest chapters in the fall of Prussia is that of the German *Wolfskinder* who found themselves left behind in the wake of the fighting. The *Wolfskinder* or 'Wolf Children', of East Prussia have, over the decades since the end of the Second World War, largely been forgotten by history, but these children were as much victims of the war as the soldiers lying dead on the battlefields of the East. Many were left behind in the wake of the German evacuation of East Prussia, or orphaned during the savage fighting which soon followed.

The situation had been made worse by the German *Gauleiter* of East Prussia Erich Koch. Even as the Red Army's invasion of East Prussia was imminent, Koch gave orders that fleeing was illegal. The penalty for defying Koch's order was death by firing squad. Many of East Prussia's German population had begun to prepare for some form of an evacuation well in advance of the Red Army's approach. Due to Koch's 'no flight' order, when the evacuation did begin it was a picture of confusion, fear, disorder and disorganisation.

There were already a huge number of German children who had been orphaned by the fighting and many had few options other than to flee into the forests of East Prussia. Forced to fend for themselves, they often lived together in groups, with older siblings trying to keep younger brothers and sisters together. The dangers they faced were numerous: as well as wild animals such as wolves, bears and wild boar, there was the threat posed by marauding Soviet troops. Any *Wolfskind* unfortunate enough to be taken by Soviet troops could be subjected to all manner of abuses, including beatings and rape.

The rape of young women and very young girls was commonplace; not even the *Wolfskinder* would be spared. It is no wonder so many of these children living wild in the forests of East Prussia made such a determined effort to remain hidden. They would spend the daylight hours hiding deep in the undergrowth, sometimes in holes, then, during the hours of darkness, they would come out on foraging trips to nearby houses or villages. Local farms situated near the edges of the forest provided the easiest pickings. The children could steal eggs, vegetables and even the odd chicken and were able to quickly vanish into the cover of the forest. This was an extremely dangerous undertaking as many of the farms had been abandoned by their original German owners and were now occupied by Russian soldiers who would often shoot at anything that disturbed them during the hours of darkness. Without doubt many a *Wolfskinder* lost his or her life in this way.

The greatest tragedy of the *Wolfskinder*, though, was that hardly anybody cared about them. There were no statistics to measure the death toll, no appeals for help and no plans to even address the problem. It was largely down to the kindness of the Lithuanian population that the desperate situation was alleviated.

Many of the German children who found themselves abandoned in the wake of the evacuation of East Prussia began to cross into neighbouring Lithuania in search of food. Many in the farming communities took pity on the plight of these children and subsequently many were adopted by Lithuanian families. And so the German *Wolfskinder* became known as *Vokietuka*, or 'Little Germans'. The Lithuanian farmers gave the children food and shelter for free. Some of the children who had mothers or other siblings with them often travelled back and forth from the farms to get food to their sick relatives. The children often walked along the railroad tracks to reach the farms, sometimes catching a ride on railroad cars as they ambled slowly through the countryside. They would jump off before reaching the Soviet control stations, continuing the remainder of their journeys on foot.

In the long term the German children proved very useful to the Lithuanian farmers who sold their produce in the townships of East Prussia in 1946. The farmers looked after the children and offered them work on the farms in return for food, shelter and steady employment for the future. Some of the children became so close to their Lithuanian employers that they were later adopted and stayed in Lithuania on a permanent basis. According to the rough statistics, some 45,000 German children and young people stayed in Lithuania in 1948, though that figure could be much higher. Helping these German children could have its drawbacks and Lithuanian farming families who took them into their care risked severe punishment from the Soviet authorities if caught.

There was also a programme of Soviet rehoming of German children. Many found themselves placed in orphanages run by Soviet military officers but staffed mainly by some of the remaining Germans. In late 1947, 4,700 German orphans were officially registered in Kaliningrad. Some of the orphaned children were adopted by Russian families, but the exact figures on the Russian adoption of German children remain unknown as documents are not available to the public.

In 1946, the Soviets began emptying Samland (or Sambia Peninsula) of Germans. In October 1947 the Soviet authorities decided to resettle 30,000 German nationals from Kaliningrad Oblast by trains to the Soviet Occupation Zone of Germany. In 1947 the Soviets sent trainloads of German orphans to the occupation zone; these train journeys took up to a week to reach their destination. Often there was no food or toilet facilities on these trains and some of the children did not survive the journey back to Germany. On 15 February 1948 the Ministerial Council of the USSR decided to resettle all Germans living in the former East Prussia, declaring them illegal residents in their own homeland. If Soviet sources can be trusted, a total of 102,125 German nationals were sent to be resettled in 1947 and 1948, though only 99,481 arrived. Sources in the German Democratic Republic (East Germany) attributed this to 'perhaps a Soviet calculation error'.

In May 1951 another 3,000 East Prussian Germans arrived in East Germany. Some of the orphans were able to escape East Germany and make their way to the Western Allied Occupation Zone hoping for a better life. Some of the German orphans had no idea of their true identities or where they came from and searching for information proved hopeless. It was yet another sad chapter in the history of the war.

The plight of the *Wolfskinder* children was never reported in the press and the outside world remained ignorant of their suffering for a great many years. People living in German towns and cities in the immediate post-war years, however, were painfully aware of their presence. Tia Schuster recalled the *Wolfskinder* of Berlin:

> These children were not invisible. They often lived in small groups and sheltered in the many ruined buildings in the city. People would often try and give them help in the form of food, but they would run away in fright. Others would leave food near to the places where they sheltered. When it was all clear the children would come and collect the food. The thing was these children in many cases had lost everything. Nobody cared about them, whether they lived or died. Me and my friend, Lisa Kraus, often gave them food. After a long time of building trust with them they would be like birds that came and sat in your hand to eat breadcrumbs. They would come and take food from us rather than run away. We were only young girls ourselves at the time and I think they trusted us far more than any adult. Over time we noticed that they slowly disappeared from the broken buildings they called home. I think many were tracked down by relatives or taken in by local German families. Both Lisa and I felt disgusted by the fact that the world chose to forget these children. They were human beings, far too young to have had to shoulder the blame for the Second World War. The journalists never covered it in the national newspapers; not once did a story about them appear in print. It beggars belief that the *Wolfskinder* were only really revealed to the world in the 1990s.

Tia Schuster's friend, Lisa Kraus, agrees with her friend:

> It didn't matter where they came from, they were German nationals. They were children who were left abandoned because of the war and left wide open to abuse and sexual exploitation. I know for a fact that some of those who went into the care of religious orders were sexually exploited. The world didn't give a damn about them; the world ignored them. In Berlin they fared a little better as sympathetic

families would take them in, or relatives came and found them over the months after 1945. For those trapped in the East I feel great sorrow for them, having to live under Socialism with the stigma of being born German. I can't imagine how difficult that must have been.

Hiller Boiten, who was extensively interviewed for the book *Knickers to Stalin*, also recalled the *Wolfskinder* children:

> There were many children who arrived from the east who had been expelled by the Soviet authorities after the war in 1945. Many came from East Prussia and had no one to look after or feed them. In Berlin we used to see small groups of them and we gave them what food we could spare, but few people had food to spare back then. In Berlin I know Soviet soldiers did take pity on these children and did give them food from their rations. Not all of the Russians were bad, some were very kind. The *Wolfskinder* children became almost feral. Their hair looked messy, their faces dirty, and what clothes they had on soon became rags. The problem was at first no one wanted to take responsibility for these children or allocate food and clothing for them. They relied upon the kindness of individuals, the ordinary German people.

Christa Hubst, also interviewed for the *Knickers to Stalin*, book recalled:

> I once watched one Allied soldier trying to coax one child with a bar of chocolate. He was calling to her as if she was an animal, a cat or dog or something, making silly squeaking noises and holding out the chocolate bar in his hand. I watched as the girl snatched the chocolate from his hand and then ran off, disappearing into some ruined buildings. A few seconds later the girl came running out with five or six other kids chasing after her as they wanted the chocolate bar from her. It was only after I followed them and intervened that the girl was able to eat the chocolate in peace. The other kids weren't *Wolfskinder*, just local buggers

who enjoyed tormenting these orphan children. I pondered what to do, and I knew my parents wouldn't be happy, but I took the girl back to my house with me. She remained with us up until when I began working at a hotel in Berlin. I had my own apartment in the city, and she moved in with me. She was like a younger sister and I was always very protective of her.

Those German *Wolfskinder* children who remained in Hitler's lost state had no option but to change their German birth names to Lithuanian ones in order to avoid the scrutiny of the Soviet authorities. It was only after the collapse of the Soviet Union decades later, in 1990, that these young Germans could finally reveal their true identities.

Chapter 12

Nemesis at Potsdam

After Germany's defeat in the Second World War, Europe lay in tatters. Millions of refugees were dispersed across the continent. Food and fuel were scarce. Britain was bankrupt, while Germany had been reduced to rubble. In July 1945 Harry Truman, Winston Churchill and Joseph Stalin gathered in a quiet suburb of Berlin to negotiate a lasting peace: a peace that would finally put an end to the conflagration that had started in 1914, and under which Europe could be rebuilt. The goals of the meeting also included the establishment of post-war order and countering the effects of the war.

The Potsdam Conference was held at Cecilienhof, the home of Crown Prince Wilhelm in Potsdam, in occupied Germany, from 17 July to 2 August 1945. (In some older documents, it is also referred to as the Berlin Conference of the Three Heads of Government of the USSR, USA, and UK.)

A number of changes had taken place in the five months since the Yalta Conference which greatly affected the relationships among the leaders. Firstly, the Soviet Union was occupying Central and Eastern Europe: the Red Army effectively controlled the Baltic states, Poland, Czechoslovakia, Hungary, Bulgaria and Romania, and refugees were fleeing from these countries. Stalin had set up a mock Communist government in Poland, and he insisted that his control of Eastern Europe was a defensive measure against possible future attacks.

Secondly, Britain had a new prime minister. Winston Churchill's Soviet policy since the early 1940s had differed considerably from President Roosevelt's. Churchill believed Stalin to be a 'devil'-like tyrant leading a vile system. A general election had been held in the UK on 5 July and the results were delayed to allow the votes of armed forces personnel to be counted in their home constituencies. The outcome became known during the conference and Labour leader Clement Attlee became the new prime minister.

Thirdly, President Roosevelt had died on 12 April 1945, and Vice President Harry Truman assumed the presidency. His succession saw VE Day (Victory in Europe) within a month and VJ Day (Victory in Japan) on the horizon. During the war, and in the name of Allied unity, Roosevelt had brushed aside warnings of the potential domination by Stalin in part of Europe. He explained, 'I just have a hunch that Stalin is not that kind of a man […] I think that if I give him everything I possibly can and ask for nothing from him in return, 'noblesse oblige', he won't try to annex anything and will work with me for a world of democracy and peace.' An Allied Control Council made up of representatives of the four Allies was to deal with matters affecting Germany and Austria as a whole. Its policies were dictated by the 'five Ds' decided on at Yalta: demilitarisation, denazification, democratisation, decentralisation and deindustrialisation. At Potsdam the Allies took revenge on the Germans, forcing upon them significant territorial losses in Eastern Europe and the transfer of some fifteen million Germans from their homelands in East Prussia, Pomerania, Silesia, East Brandenburg, Czechoslovakia, Hungary, and Yugoslavia.

The closing phase of the war saw millions of refugees and displaced persons wandering across Eastern Europe in one of the most brutal and chaotic migrations in world history. The genocidal barbarism of the Nazi forces has been well documented. What has hitherto been less well researched is the fate of the fifteen million German civilians who found themselves at the mercy of the Soviet armies and on the wrong side of the new post-war borders.

Settled by the Germans in the Middle Ages, the territories of East Prussia, Silesia, the Sudetenland, much of Pomerania, and Brandenburg were emptied, and the historic ethnic communities in Hungary, Romania and Yugoslavia either expelled or killed. Over two million Germans did not survive their forced displacement. Many had supported Hitler, and for Czechs, Poles, Ukranians and the surviving Jews, their fate must have seemed just. However, most of the East Prussian farmers, Silesian industrial workers, their wives and their children were innocent victims of Hitler's dictatorship and their fate, to be accused purely by race, remains a terrible legacy of the period.

Alfred de Zayas was the first to extensively research the fate of the many German communities expelled from the Baltic to the Danube, which marked the terrible end to Nazi fantasies of *Lebensraum*. He explained that, following the Potsdam Conference, it was officially demanded that millions of peaceful inhabitants of the Sudetenland, Prussia, Czechoslovakia and the Ruhr, Germany's most industrialised area, be robbed of their homes and their businesses and then made to travel to Western Germany. The expulsion happened very quickly. The Germans were unable to take most of their possessions, and were generally robbed and abused and/or raped during their journey.

Conditions in Germany were not great either. The land taken by Poland was the rich farmland that could have been used to feed the hungry masses. The American, British and French governments struggled to feed and house the new immigrants, while Poland and Czechoslovakia continued to send more and more Germans despite protests. Hundreds of thousands of Germans didn't survive the expulsion or the imprisonment in camps. They either starved and froze to death or died from diseases and injuries. Many families were brutally slain by Russian soldiers.

Anne O'Hare McCormick, writing for the *New York Times*: 'The scale of this resettlement and the conditions in which it takes place are without precedents in history. No one seeing its horrors first hand can doubt that it is a crime against humanity.'

Bertrand Russell wrote in *The Times*: 'An apparently deliberate attempt is being made to exterminate many millions of Germans by depriving them of their homes and of food, leaving them to die by slow agonising starvation. This is not done as an act of war, but as part of a deliberate policy of "peace".'

The shocking details and photographic evidence that emerged in the 1950s and 1960s was also well documented in James Bacque's *Other Losses*. The pathological hatred of Germany and the German people led to a systematic starvation, abuse and neglect, not only of POWs but also of innocent civilians by the Allies. The death count was shockingly high. The callous disregard for the suffering inflicted seemed to be motivated by a particularly cruel from of spiteful retribution.

One of the worst examples was meted out to the Sudeten Germans by their Czech compatriots. Over a quarter of a million Sudeten Germans were slaughtered by the Czechs. Those who escaped this act of genocide and ethnic cleansing fled for their lives yet were relentlessly pursued by gangs of killers until driven across the border. The majority of these unfortunate souls would never see their homes again.

Scenes such as these were taking place all across Poland, Silesia and East Prussia. Here, the bodies of young women, children and the elderly lay across the countryside in testimony to the steadily unfolding slaughter. The Western Allied powers appeared reluctant to intervene in what was clearly a genocidal process taking place. A measure of the contempt that some of the Western Allied powers possessed even for the innocent was reflected by the United States' treasury secretary, Henry Morgenthau. Morgenthau favoured a proposal whereby Germany could be turned into one huge farming community. There were other, more sinister, proposals also being considered, some of which included the deliberate starvation, sterilisation and mass deportations of those remaining in the ruined cities. It is difficult to imagine that such ideas could have been considered by a liberating power.

Another overlooked area of post-war research is the fate of German prisoners of war and civilians who were corralled into the still-functioning death camps. Dachau, Buchenwald, Sachsenhausen and Auschwitz were emptied of their former inmates, only to be used to accommodate Germans at the end of the war. These camps were permeated by filth and disease and many more lives were claimed in these terrible conditions. Many in the Western Allied hierarchy at that time, however, felt this was fitting retribution for the Germans.

It was only with the revelation of Soviet intent in Europe that the West was forced to change its agenda towards the Germans. The very thought of Communism spreading throughout Europe instilled a greater fear of yet another brutal totalitarian power emerging from the ashes of the Second World War. The Western Allied forces had witnessed for themselves Russian brutality towards perceived enemies within the Western zones of Berlin and Vienna. The Soviets kidnapped and murdered hundreds inside these supposedly safe areas. British Army chaplain Keith Wellings (who was interviewed during the writing of *Hitler's Germany: The Birth of Extremism*) remarked on this situation:

> These fellows [Russian soldiers] operated as a law unto themselves. They showed no regard for age or whether those they attacked were male or female. They frequently took women off the streets, carting them off to their fate. They favoured young German girls in particular. Their mothers

would attempt to hide their daughters only to have them snatched and dragged away from them, screaming. It is obvious that these young girls were being taken away to be violated in a most horrible manner. They saw rape as being the ultimate way that they could vent their anger or revenge. To impregnate German women with Soviet blood was seen as the greatest humiliation for their defeated foe.

Of course, airing one's concerns back then often fell on deaf ears. People didn't want to know about German suffering. The death camps were still fresh in Allied minds and thinking. Yet, as this behaviour continued, the penny, as they say, must have dropped somewhere. I can only imagine at the time that many witnesses to these things began to think what might emerge if the Soviets gained too much influence in the region, and in Europe as a whole. I think it frightened them that someday it could be them suffering a similar fate to the Germans. All I recall is that there was this sudden shift in political allegiances.

As a whole British and US servicemen behaved well. Many felt great empathy, particularly towards the ragged, pathetic hordes expelled from the East who began to arrive in the Western zones. Many felt compelled to help these wretched people who clearly had suffered enough. There were hundreds if not thousands of Germans coming in from the Eastern territories, particularly Prussia. They were mainly women with young children or babies. When asked the whereabouts of their husbands many replied 'dead'. When I had the opportunity to speak with some of these women, they revealed that a systematic process of separating the men from their women was under way. The men were taken away and assessed for their usability in Russian labour camps. The wounded were shot without hesitation in much the same manner that the Nazis shot those of little use to them. The women and girls were subjected to repeated rapes and other sexual abuses before being forced on their way. They received no food or water, and many did not make it back out of the former Eastern territories that were once under German occupation.

These things flew in the face of what I believed were acceptable human principles, yet they occurred on a far greater scale than many people realise today [...] many of those subjected to these abuses had been innocent of any wrongdoing other than being Germans. There were always those who argued that the Germans deserved this. I don't agree, and never have agreed with vengeance in this manner. Put yourself inside the mind of the ten-year-old girl who had been ripped from her mother's arms and then forced to watch as soldiers raped her mother. Then the girl herself was violated while her mother was forced to watch. I know for a fact that, despite General Patton's loathing of what the Nazis did, he soon became outspoken in his admiration for the Germans. That was quite an unexpected turnaround, his thinking fuelled by these exact things. The powers-that-be soon understood what a Russian-dominated Europe could be like and they didn't want that to happen. It frightened them. All of this would lead to the tense division of East from West, and, of course, the onset of the Cold War.

It is also worth examining here the fate of those German soldiers captured by the Allied forces. At the time of the German surrender on 8 May 1945, around twenty allied nations held German prisoners of war. The United States, Great Britain, France and the Soviet Union held the majority of the eleven million members of the German armed forces who surrendered. The ages of the German prisoners ranged from as young as sixteen to elderly men who had fought with the *Volkssturm* or people's militia. Around five million of these prisoners of war were released almost immediately while most of those remaining were transported to Soviet labour camps in the East.

The last German prisoners of war to return from their captivity in Russia was in 1956, some eleven years after the end of the Second World War. The treatment experienced by German soldiers in the Soviet prisoner of war camps or gulags varied. Some German prisoners were treated well, receiving pay for the work they did, while others were literally worked to death in appalling conditions. The majority of deaths in the Soviet prisoner-of-war camps were due to dystrophy, a disease caused by undernourishment. The poor post-war harvests only served to exacerbate the problem, as the Soviets, of course, fed their own people first as a national priority.

According to Soviet sources, some 350,000 to 400,000 German POWs died in Soviet internment. Many historians do not agree that these figures are correct and argue the actual death figures to be around 1.1 million. Poor record keeping on the part of the Soviets makes it very difficult to determine when these deaths actually occurred. An estimated 40,000 Germans died in American captivity due to neglect and hunger between May and July 1945. Many wounded Germans did not receive adequate medical attention for their wounds, and many died unnecessarily as a result. Another 20,000 died while working to rebuild war-ravaged France. The French were particularly callous towards their German captives, often giving them the most dangerous jobs. One example of this treatment was how many were set to work clearing minefields of dangerously unstable explosives.

The ill-treatment of German POWs was clearly a breach of the Third Geneva Convention, which established the provisions relative to the treatment of Prisoners of War. One of the four treaties of the Geneva Conventions, it was first adopted in 1929, but significantly revised at the 1949 conference. It defines humanitarian protections for prisoners of war. Among its rules are the following:

- Article 10 required that POWs should be lodged in adequately heated and lighted buildings where conditions were the same as for German troops.
- Articles 27–32 detailed the conditions of labour. Enlisted ranks were required to perform whatever labour they were asked and able to do, so long as it was not dangerous and did not support the German war effort. Senior NCOs (sergeants and above) were required to work only in a supervisory role. Commissioned officers were not required to work, although they could volunteer. The work performed was largely agricultural or industrial, ranging from coal or potash mining to stone quarrying, or work in sawmills, breweries, factories, railroad yards and forests. POWs hired out to military and civilian contractors were supposed to receive pay. The workers were also supposed to get at least one day a week of rest.
- Article 76 ensured that POWs who died in captivity were honourably buried in marked graves.

There were a fortunate few German POWs who found themselves being transported to Britain. Many of those who were sent to these shores fared far better than those sent elsewhere. Britain's treatment of German POWs was largely humane and as a result many remained here, settling down and marrying British women. Between 1939 and 1945, Britain was home to more than 400,000 prisoners of war from Italy, the Ukraine and Germany. They were housed in hundreds of camps around the country, with five sites in Northern Ireland. Prisoners wore old uniforms with black patches sewn on the legs and backs (allegedly to be used as targets should a prisoner try to flee).

For the most part, the prisoners were content with their version of British life, turning their camps into temporary homes, and sometimes building chapels and other memorials to life in their homelands. A very well-preserved example of an altar built by German Lutheran POWs still exists at the Bonhoeffer Centre in Forest Hill, London.

In order to discourage potential escapees, POWs were paid not in British currency but with 'camp money', paper and plastic facsimiles which they earned for undertaking camp labour. However, somewhat inevitably, a thriving underground industry sprang up. Willi Bungart, a German POW who was captured aged seventeen, and who spent four years in a number of British POW camps, recalls making toys one Christmas to sell to British families, whom he met while at work. Churches, which the POWs were allowed to attend alongside the British congregations, were particularly lucrative for such swaps. POWs who were considered to be 'benign' were given the opportunity to earn 'proper' money by working outside the camps. They were paid a fair wage for this work and many took the opportunity to save for a future outside the camps.

Many German POWs in Britain were set to work on farms or employed as labourers on building projects. Heinz Boetz, who was captured shortly after the June 1944 Normandy landings, found himself on a boat to 'Blighty'. He recalls:

> I was only young, a nineteen-year-old, when I was captured by the British. I was treated more like a naughty schoolboy than a soldier of the German *Wehrmacht*. I was clipped around the ear a few times but other than that I was looked after pretty well. When I arrived in England I was sent to work on a farm in the Kent countryside. I couldn't believe

how beautiful it all was. At first, I was given all of the dirty jobs, so it was, 'Heinz, clean out the horses,' or, 'Heinz, go and see to the pig pens.' As time passed by, they gave me better jobs and treated me with less suspicion. They would ask me about where I lived in Germany, how I got involved in it all and things like that. Of course, I wanted to see my mother and father again, but did not know when I would be returned to Germany. It was the spring of 1946 when I was told I would be released and repatriated back to Germany. One part of me was sad to leave, the other happy that I was going home. Before I left England, the family I had helped on the farm gave me a silver pocket watch to remember them by. They were a lovely couple, their surname was Marsh. I will never forget them.

However romantic the above testimony may appear to the reader, the atrocities that were committed by the Allies against helpless German civilians and disarmed POWs remain a stain upon our history and should never be forgotten. Furthermore, they should be included in modern textbooks, lest we be doomed to repeat those mistakes.

Afterword

I am very grateful to my co-author, Tim, and the staff at Pen and Sword for giving me the opportunity to embark on this new venture. It has been a fascinating and emotional journey of discovery, one which I grew passionate about.

While researching the often tragic facts behind Hitler's rise to power, the German Resistance attempts to overturn it and the evacuation of civilians from the East Prussian territories at the end of the war, I came into contact with the most incredible people and organisations: members of the Stauffenberg family; volunteers at the Dietrich Bonhoeffer Centre; survivors of the *Gustloff* sinking; world-leading historians, authors and journalists; as well as residents of those areas that are now Poland and Lithuania, all of whom had a story to tell and genuinely wanted to help with this project. I was fortunate to visit Danzig (Gdańsk), the city where my mother and grandmother were born, and the port of Gotenhafen (Gdynia) from which they left, never to return. Sadly, as they have now both passed away, they will never know this. I have made several friends in Gdańsk, a city that I grew to love and now consider a second home. In an age where we see more and more countries willing to build barriers instead of bridges, it is essential that we stop and reflect upon the warped ideology that led to the events that unfolded during the Second World War. We must ensure that such events are never repeated nor ever forgotten, in respect and memory of all the victims of war, whatever their nationality, gender or creed.

Michela Luise Cocolin, September 2019.

To say I, too, have learned much from the evolution of this project with my friend, Michela, would be an understatement. This volume represents Michela's first foray into the world of historical literature. She was responsible for conducting the lion's share of the research for

Afterword

this project, research that required both patience and determination. I have immense admiration and respect for the meticulous work she has carried out during the formulation of this volume, one that has endeavoured to bring many different facets into a single work.

On reflection, it is difficult to understand how such a militarily strong nation as Prussia could have shared the same fate that befell the once mighty Roman Empire, enjoying a relatively brief existence in comparison to other European nations that remain intact. Prussia today is all but a whisper in the dark corridors of history. When the end came it was as undignified as it was calamitous. There could be no greater example of the cruelty and horror of war than the fate that befell the *Wilhelm Gustloff* ship during the ill-fated 'Operation Hannibal', the evacuation of German East Prussia. It is even more difficult when I look at the photograph of a smiling little girl taken at Christmas time, just five weeks before the tragedy would unfold. The little girl is much like any other one might see in a collection of old family photographs, only this little girl was Michela's mother. Thankfully, though somewhat traumatised, she survived the horror of the evacuations, but her photo reminds us all that many like her did not. When I reflect upon the last minutes of that doomed ship before it slipped beneath the dark, freezing waters of the Baltic Sea, I think of all those innocent children who perished, trapped within the bowels of the ship, unable to get out. If this book can form even the tiniest of tributes to those souls lost in the greatest tragedy in maritime history, then we can both be happy in the knowledge we have done a fine job.

Tim Heath, September 2019.

Acknowledgements

The authors would like to wholeheartedly thank the following individuals and organisations:

Melanie Frey at The Foundation 20 July 1944 (Striftung 20 Juli 1944); the Imperial War Museum, London; Dirk vom Lehn and Svea Polster at the Dietrich Bonhoeffer Centre, London; Volksbund Deutsche Kriegsgräberfürsorge; Peter and Maria Stahr; the Wilhelm Gustloff Museum; Roger Moorehouse; Ruta Sepetys; Cathryn J. Prince; Realworld Pictures; National Maritime Museum, Gdańsk; the Museum of Second World War, Gdańsk; Emigration Museum; Gdynia; Frank Anton; Edith Wagner; Bundesarchiv; Beate Kreinenborg; Jens Dirks; Niedersächsisches Landesarchiv; Deutsches Schifffahrtsmuseum, Bremerhaven; Ulf-Normann Neitzel; Angelika Nawroth; Zentrum für Militärgeschichte und Sozialwissenschaften der Bw Ansprechstelle für militärhistorischen Rat, Potsdam; Simon Kursawe; Deutsches Schiffhartsmuseum Leibniz Institut für Maritime Geschichte; Dr Jann M. Will; Deutscher Marinebund e.V., Rysiek Klos; Janusz Lenz; Magda Mucha-von Platen; Manuel Fix; Landesarchiv Berlin; Stadtarchiv, Wilhelmshaven; Heinz Schön; Horst and Grace Woit; Eva Dorn Rothchild; Irmgard Harnecker; Waltraud Grüter; Fiodor Danilov; Ivan Schnabzew; Ralph Wendt; Ursula Schulze; Robert Hering; Alexander Astachov; Gisela Teschke; Alfred Maurice de Zayas; Philipp von Schulthess; Berthold Maria Schenk Graf von Stauffenberg; Peter Hanke; The German Resistance Memorial Centre (Gedenkstätte Deutscher Widerstand), Berlin; Donald Yarnold; Matilda Kuhn; Ernst Giestl; Hermann Rastief; Elizabeth Steiner; Roberta Irmfjeld; Orphelia Maschmann; Alexandria Busch; Michael Roessner; Claudette Bauer; Jack Helmann; Anni Taubman; Olga Bachmann; Vera Alexander; Matilda Kuhn; Hilde Hermann; Dirk Kersthold; Helga Schneider; Iwan Alymow; Sergej Schwyzkij; Peter Baumanis; Siegfrid Quandt; Gerd Scheffler; Joachim Elbreicht; Jerzy Janczukowicz; Lisa Kraus; Tia Schuster; Heinz Boetz.

Bibliography

Bacque, James, *Other Losses: An Investigation into the Mass Deaths of German Prisoners at the Hands of the French and Americans after World War II* (Talonbooks, 3rd ed, 2011).

Cieslak, Edmund and Biernat, Czeslaw, *History of Gdansk* (Wydawnictwo Morskie, 1988).

De Zayas, Alfred Maurice, *Nemesis at Potsdam: The Expulsion of the Germans from the East* (Bison Books, 3rd ed, 1988)

De Zayas, Alfred Maurice, *A Terrible Revenge: The Ethnic Cleansing of the East European Germans* (Palgrave Macmillan, 2nd ed, 2006)

Die Versenkung der Wilhelm Gustloff (Paul Zsolnay Verlag, 1979).

Dobson, Christopher, Miller, John, Payne, Ronald *The Cruellest Night: Germany's Dunkirk and the Sinking of the Wilhelm Gustloff* (Arrow Books, 1980).

Gräfin Dönhoff, Tatjana and Berg, Reiner, *Die Gustloff* (Bloomsbury Berlin, 2008).

Egremond, Max, *Forgotten Land: Journeys Among the Ghosts of East Prussia* (Pan Macmillan, 2012).

Feigel, Lara, *The Bitter Taste of Victory* (Bloomsbury, 2016).

Franklin, Sarah, 'The Untold Story of Britain's POW Camps', *The Irish Times*, July 28 2017.

Fuhrer, Armin, *Die Todesfahrt der „Gustloff": Porträts von Überlebenden der größten Schiffskatastrophe aller Zeiten* (Lau Verlag & Handel, 2007).

Fuhrer, Armin, *Erich Koch, Hitlers brauner Zar. Gauleiter von Ostpreussen und Reichskommissar der Ukraine* (Olzog Verlag, München 2010).

Hoffmann, Peter, *Stauffenberg – A Family History, 1905–1944* (Cambridge University Press, 1995).

Hoffmann, Peter, *The History of the German Resistance, 1933–1945* (McGill-Queen's University Press, 1996).

Kershaw, Ian, *Hitler, The Germans, and the Final Solution* (Vail-Ballou Press, 2008).

Knopp, Guido, *Der Untergang der Gustloff: Wie es wirklich war* (Econ Tb, 2002).

Knopp, Guido, *Der Zweite Weltkrieg Bilder-Die Wir Nie Vergessen* (Edel, 2014).

Knopp, Guido, *Hitler's Children* (Sutton Publishing, 2002).

Knopp, Guido, *The SS: A Warning from History* (Sutton Publishing, 2003).

Kosmidis, Pierre, WW2wrecks.com, '*Heinz Schön, the survivor of the greatest naval disaster of all time and his last will to be buried at the wreck of the Wilhelm Gustloff*'.

Lasker-Wallfisch, Anita, *Inherit the Truth 1939–1945* (Giles de la Mare Publishers Ltd, 1996).

Moorehouse, Roger, *Killing Hitler* (Vintage Books, London, 2006).

Moorehouse, Roger, *Ship of Fate: The Story of the MV Wilhelm Gustloff* (independently published, 2018).

Neitzel, Ulf-Normann, Der HAPAG Passenger-Dampfer *Hansa* (BOD, 2012).

Prince, Cathryn J., *Death in the Baltic: The World War II Sinking of the Wilhelm Gustloff* (St. Martin's Griffin, 2014).

Royce, Hans, *Germans Against Hitler* (English licensed ed, published by the Press and Information Office of the Federal Government of Germany, Wiesbadener Graphische Betriebe GmbH 1964).

Schön, Heinz, D*er Untergang der Wilhelm Gustloff – Tatsachenbericht eines Überlebenden* (Bearbeitung Walter Böckmann, Karina-Goltze-Verlag, Göttingen, 1952).

Schön, Heinz, *Ostsee '45 – Menschen, Schiffe, Schicksale* (Motorbuch-Verlag, Stuttgart, 1983).

Schön, Heinz, *Die KdF-Schiffe und ihr Schicksal. Eine Dokumentation* (Motorbuch-Verlag, Stuttgart, 1987).

Schön, Heinz, *Die Cap Arcona-Katastrophe. Eine Dokumentation nach Augenzeugen-Berichten* (Motorbuch-Verlag, Stuttgart, 1989).

Schön, Heinz, *Die letzten Kriegstage. Ostseehäfen 1945* (Motorbuch-Verlag, Stuttgart, 1995).

Schön, Heinz *Im Heimatsland in Feindeshand. Schicksale ostpreußischer Frauen unter Russen und Polen 1945–1948* (Arndt Verlag, Kiel, 1998).

Schön, Heinz *SOS Wilhelm Gustloff. Die größte Schiffskatastrophe der Geschichte* (Motorbuch-Verlag, Stuttgart, 1998).

Schön, Heinz, *Hitler's Traumschiffe. Die Kraft durch Freude-Flotte 1934–1939* (Arndt Verlag, Kiel, 2000).
Schön, Heinz, *Flucht aus Ostpreussen 1945. Die Menschenjagd der Roten Armee* (Arndt Verlag, Kiel, 2001).
Schön, Heinz, *Das Geheimnis des Bernsteinzimmers. Das Ende der Legenden um den in Königsberg verschollenen Zarenschatz* (Paul Pietsch Verlag, Stuttgart, 2002).
Schön, Heinz, *Die Tragödie der Flüchtlingsschiffe. Gesunken in der Ostsee 1944–45* (Motorbuch-Verlag, Stuttgart, 2004).
Schön, Heinz, *Mythos Neu-Schwabenland. Für Hitler am Südpol. Die deutsche Antarktisexpedition 1938–1939* (Bonus-Verlag, Selent, 2004).
Schön, Heinz, *Königsberger Schicksaljahre. Der Untergang der Hauptstadt Ostpreußens 1944–1948* (Arndt Verlag, Kiel, 2012).
Schön, Heinz mit Fuhrer, Armin, *Erich Koch, Hitlers brauner Zar. Gauleiter von Ostpreussen und Reichskommissar der Ukraine* (Olzog Verlag, München, 2010).
Schön, Heinz (posth.) mit Kleindienst, Jürgen, *Pommern auf der Flucht 1945. Rettung über die Ostsee aus den Pommernhäfen Rügenwalde, Kolberg, Stettin, Swinemünde, Greifswald, Stralsund und Saßnitz* (Zeitgut Verlag, Berlin, 2013).
Showalter, Dennis, *Instrument of War: The German Army 1914–18* (Osprey Publishing, 2016).
Tilitski, Christian, *Alltag in Ostpreußen 1940–1945. Die geheimen Lageberichte der Königsberger Justiz 1940–1945* (Rautenberg, 1991).
Von Schulthess, Konstanze, *Nina Schenk Graefin von Stauffenberg – Ein Portraet* (Pendo, Munich und Zurich, 2008).
Winterberg, Sonya, *Wir sind die Wolfskinder: Verlassen in Ostpreußen* (Piper, 2012).

Documentaries and films

Die Flucht, with Maria Furtwängler, Jean-Yves Berteloot, Tonio Arango, co-production EOS Entertainment, ADR with BR, SWR, WDR, HR, ORF, RAI and ARTE, 2007.
Bonhoeffer – Pastor, Nazi resister, Martyr, Martin Doblmeier, 2016.
Bonhoeffer – Agent of Grace, Vision Video, 2010.
Die Grosse Flucht, by Knopp, Guido, Universum Fim ZDF.

Die Gustloff, (ZDF / UFA), Regie: Joseph Vilsmaier, Kai Wiesinger, 2008.

Die Gustloff, by Knopp, Guido, Universum Fim ZDF.

Hitler's War Machine – Danzig and Poland 1939, Komet Media Management Ltd.

Into the Arms of Strangers – Stories of the Kindertransport, Sabine Films production, WB, 2000.

Operation Valkyrie, Sebastian Koch, The Weinstein Company, High Fliers, 2004.

Operation Valkyrie – The Stauffenberg Plot to Kill Hitler, A Bill Schwartz production, Anchor Bay Entertainment, Koch Entertainment, 2008.

Nacht fiel über Gotenhafen, Kinofilm, Regie: Frank Wisbar, 1960.

Sinking the Wilhelm Gustloff, a tragedy exiled from memory, Marcus Kolga, Realworld Pictures, 2011.

Triumph und Tragödie der Wilhelm Gustloff, Just Entertainment, Hilversum, 2009.

The Assault on East Prussia, Guido Knopp, Germany's War – apocalypse.

The Battle for East Prussia, 1945, Soviet chronicle. East Prussian operation (January 13-April 25, 1945) Фронтовой сборник 'Штурм Кёнигсберга'.

Valkyrie, a Brian Singer film, MGM and UA, 2009.

Wilhelm Gustloff – Vom Flaggschiff zum eisernen Sarg, Detlef Michelers Mit Uwe Friedrichsen, Brigitte Rottgers und Gunter Grass, Radiobremen.